Rt Hon. Dr David Owen, MP

A United Kingdom

Penguin Books

Penguin Books Ltd, Harmondsworth, Middlesex, England
Viking Penguin Inc., 40 West 23rd Street, New York, New York 10010, U.S.A.
Penguin Books Australia Ltd, Ringwood, Victoria, Australia
Penguin Books Canada Limited, 2801 John Street, Markham, Ontario, Canada L3R 1B4
Penguin Books (N.Z.) Ltd, 182–190 Wairau Road, Auckland 10, New Zealand

First published 1986

Made and printed in Great Britain by
Cox & Wyman Ltd, Reading
Photoset in 9/12pt Linotron Plantin by
Rowland Phototypesetting Ltd, Bury St Edmunds, Suffolk

For D.S.O.

Contents

Acknowledgements

This book, for which I alone bear responsibility, could never have been written without the help of many people in the SDP, too numerous to mention. To some I owe a particularly heavy debt – first and foremost, Alex de Mont, for help over writing and researching speeches and articles on which the book draws extensively, and Maggie Smart. Thanks are also due to Tom Burke, Annette France, John Roper, Sandra Jantuah, Vernon Bogdanor, Sarah Smillie, Nicholas Bosanquet, Ann Sofer, Roger Carroll, Wendy Buckley, Tom McNally, Sue Robertson, Christopher Smallwood, Augusta Southern, Roland Rudd and Sarah Horack.

Introduction

A United Kingdom advances an argument and poses a challenge. It explains why we in Britain are so disunited and challenges the British people to do what is necessary to recreate the country's essential unity. Britain's economic decline has been accompanied and compounded by a political decline in which our capacity to respond to problems has become progressively weakened. Not only are we worse off; we are also less capable of doing anything about it.

The pattern of our predicament, with its intertwined economic and political dimensions, is now clear. Economic decline impoverishes the nation and destroys our ability to solve the problems of deprivation in our society. Deprivation deepens the divisions between us, exaggerates political differences and thus cripples our capacity to sustain policies for economic and industrial regeneration and recovery. Our decline is accelerated by the constant chopping and changing of policies introduced by Governments that are not sustained by majority support.

Our political structures at every level – from the composition of the House of Commons to the class-based nature of the Conservative and Labour Parties – encourage dissension and division and work against compromise and negotiation. Under the pressure of decline our politics has become increasingly unstable and polarized. The remedies produced in our divided society are partial and increasingly ideological. Our greatest weakness is the absence of a constitutional structure that creates and fosters the necessary consensus.

To halt our economic decline we must halt our political decline. Proportional representation can provide the key to building a new consensus. As a constitutional mechanism it ensures majority government, generally through coalition government.

The facts of our economic decline are becoming familiar. Our slide from leader to laggard in relative standards of living is visible across a wide range of economic indicators. Disfiguring fissures creep across the face of the United Kingdom as the true depth of our political decline becomes apparent. Far from rethinking their attitudes and policies, we see the old parties resorting to more dogma and more extremism. Instead of a natural synthesis of ideas and attitudes – combining what have often been seen, wrongly, as opposites – we are constantly faced with artificial choices.

Creating more wealth takes time; meanwhile we have to grapple with our present poverty. Combining the two tasks is possible, provided we are prepared to experiment with new techniques in social policy and to adopt new attitudes towards efficiency. Proportional representation can create new attitudes and put new heart into our democracy; its implementation could remake the bonds that should unite us as one country.

This argument is developed in detail throughout the book. The first three chapters describe our decline, identify the roots of bad government and explain why proportional representation will give us better government. Chapter 4 goes to the core of the nuclear debate and demonstrates that we have lost our unity even over national security. Chapters 5, 6 and 7 deal with industrial regeneration, incomes strategy and industrial partnership, which together could form a triangle of lasting economic recovery, giving us growth without inflation. Chapters 8, 9, 10 and 11 show how we can create a public and private partnership for urban regeneration, improve efficiency in education and in health and, with changes in attitudes, encourage a greater sense of social responsibility. Between them these qualities provide a foundation for social compassion combined with economic competitiveness. Finally, Chapter 12 argues a fundamental democratic point – that the people should be trusted, in a referendum, to choose whether they want proportional representation.

The chapters on industrial regeneration, health and education suggest how central government can help to increase economic efficiency by producing greater output without incurring extra expenditure. Economists now try to distinguish between 'allocative efficiency', whereby changes normally involve consuming more of one thing and less of another, and what the US economist Professor Leibenstein has called 'X-efficiency', where more output relative to input can be produced without a reduction in input.'[1] To provide 'allocative efficiency' consumers have to be well informed about the choices, whether they are parents, patients or just purchasers. To provide 'X-efficiency', incentives must be well judged and the institutional framework geared to encouraging competition.

In the United States this analysis is at the heart of the 'service redesign' strategy that attempts to change the way the public sector is organized, and operates so as to 'do more with less'.[2] Government determines the services to be provided, which are then 'designed' in partnership with the private sector through a contract, franchise, voucher or other flexible arrangement.

British politics from now until the next general election is likely to be dominated by argument over whether there should be cuts in the standard rate of tax or whether those resources should be devoted to industrial growth and reducing unemployment. This argument goes to the heart of the problem that divides Britain. Achieving greater value for money has considerable public support, but there is also a growing awareness of the dangers for the cohesion and unity of the nation in the widening gap between private affluence and public squalor.

The remaining years of this century pose an immense challenge to this country. We need new leaders – political, industrial, trade-union, intellectual and military – with the courage and vision to face the facts and find the solutions to our national decline. We need the radicalism to challenge the failed record of our political institutions. We must have the patience to change attitudes to improve our long-term economic performance. We need to develop the ingenuity to adopt new techniques of profit-sharing and partnership to transform our industrial relations. We must acquire the sensitivity needed to listen and the desire to bind the United Kingdom together in a new spirit of cohesion and unity. We must foster the generosity of spirit to tackle the deprivation, racial discrimination and inequalities in our midst. We need to find the wisdom to choose, select and concentrate on essential priorities. We must encourage the readiness to work with people in other parties in order to fashion a programme of recovery that will carry with it the support of at least the majority of our citizens. And we must have the will to reform the voting system.

We can be certain of one thing: we will not be able to reverse our decline until our country becomes less divided – until it becomes, once again, a united kingdom.

1 National Decline

Our citizens are encouraged to believe in the myth that the United Kingdom is economically sound and growing stronger. Our self-esteem is boosted by our international status. We are one of the five permanent members of the United Nations Security Council, with the USA, the USSR, China and France. The UK has the world's sixth largest Gross Domestic Product (GDP) and is one of the seven Western industrial nations that meet for the Economic Summit with the USA, Japan, Canada, West Germany, France and Italy. We are one of the five countries that meet to co-ordinate the major world currencies – the dollar, the yen, the franc, the Deutschmark and the pound.

This is all very comforting. It is easy to assume that we are still a strong, prosperous nation until one remembers that, sadly, judged by our standard of living, we are now the nineteenth industrial country in the world.[1] Our slide to this position has been largely unnoticed because our decline has been relative. Most people's standard of living within the UK still increases year by year, but our national standard of living in relation to other countries' is increasing at a much slower pace. The slide is also masked by the comparative affluence of those who live in the southern part of the UK. Unemployment north of a line drawn from Bristol to the Wash has persistently been higher than in the south; it is now 60 per cent higher than it is south of that line. As a nation we are complacently living on our past. There is a risk that in the late 1990s we could face absolute decline and a fall in people's standard of living. It is easier to go on pretending that we enjoy a relative standard of living and a degree of global influence that we no longer have than to face reality. Yet that reality must be faced, for North Sea oil revenues mask our true position, and those revenues will soon start to fall.

The UK has become a low-growth, low-skill, low-wage economy by comparison with our principal competitors in the Organization for Economic Co-operation and Development (OECD). As a result, we have been unable, rather than unwilling, to invest sufficiently in our National Health Service (NHS), our educational system, our stock of housing or our inner cities. We have allowed the very seed-corn of our future – the brains and skills of our young – to stultify and to fall short of their full potential. If we continue to ignore the need to invest in our future, we will hasten our decline. We are consuming more than we should. The present pre-election consumer boomlet is designed to feed complacency. Consumption and imports are expected to rise, while investment and exports are projected to fall. These predictions are exactly the opposite of what a country facing an imminent loss of oil revenues should be anticipating.

Anger is an inadequate response to these trends. Although there has been some improvement in the UK's competitiveness and growth in the 1980s, compared with our performance in the 1960s and 1970s, only effort will reverse the relative deterioration in our standard of living and will make good the gaping trade deficit that appears when oil revenues are removed from the positive side of the balance of payments. We have, over the last few years, had to tolerate very high unemployment, but there has been no action, no fundamental reversal of our underlying economic decline, despite the golden opportunity of North Sea oil revenues. We must now face up to the reality that economic decline is inseparable from bad government.

In 1950 the UK's standard of living in terms of real GDP per head was not far behind that of the USA.[2] In the world as a whole the UK was in the first division of nations, with a standard of living behind those of only Switzerland and the USA. In 1960 we were still the richest country in Europe, easily outstripping Japan but clearly behind the USA. Twenty-five years later the UK's real income per head is between half and two-thirds of France's and West Germany's.[3] We have become the poor relation of Europe and now lag behind Japan.

Worse still, in the world as a whole the UK is in the third division of nations in 1986. The first division includes the United Arab Emirates, Kuwait, Qatar, Switzerland, West Germany, the USA, Canada and Sweden.[4] Next comes a second group, made up of France, Austria, Japan, the Netherlands, Australia and Denmark. In the third group comes the UK, rubbing shoulders with Hong Kong, Puerto Rico, the USSR, Yugoslavia and Taiwan. Thirty-five years ago the UK's standard of living was nearly five times higher than that of newly industrializing countries like Puerto Rico and Taiwan. Today theirs are almost on a par with ours. Prince Charles's warning that we are in danger of becoming a fourth-rate country is too true for comfort. Why has this happened?

The UK's rapid relative decline is rooted in low economic growth. In 1950 our real growth rate was ahead of the USA, Japan and France and, in the OECD, only slightly behind West Germany's. But in the three and a half decades since then we have consistently notched up the slowest growth rates of all the OECD countries, with the lowest productivity and investment per head.

While the gap between the UK and our principal European competitors has narrowed in the 1980s by comparison with earlier decades, the UK's performance is still poor – a fact highlighted by Italy overtaking the UK in 1985, for the first time ever, in the average standard of living of its citizens.

The result of our low growth has been a steady deterioration in the UK's international trade position. In 1950 the UK's share of world trade was the highest in the OECD. By 1984 our share had been halved. This deterioration is the more alarming because we in Britain, being the second largest exporter in the OECD (after Japan), have to export nearly a third of our national product to earn a living in the world. Unlike the domestic markets of the USA, France and Italy, our own cannot support itself. The cause of low growth has been a steady decline in the UK's competitiveness. Measured by relative unit labour costs, our industrial competitiveness has continuously deteriorated at differing rates since the 1960s. Measurements of cost competitiveness are always influenced by exchange rates. If the exchange-rate factor were taken out of the calculation and the measurement limited to unit labour costs in the local currency, the UK's rate of deterioration would be considerably worse. The maintenance of a high and uncompetitive exchange rate in 1985 was Mrs Thatcher's recipe for curbing domestic inflation. It was that very policy that ravaged much of our industrial capacity in 1980–81.

In 1986 it looks as if the Government will allow the exchange rate to fall as oil prices move down, and this will help industry to compete. The danger is that the sudden depreciation of sterling may cause an increase in inflation, which the Government has threatened to choke off by a further increase in interest rates. But the key to our competitiveness lies in changes of attitude, in greater skills and in productive investment rather than in short-term financial decisions.

Our relative decline is not inevitable. Optimism can still be justified if only we would read the writing on the wall. Hope that we can reverse this decline lies in the oil, gas and coal under our territorial seas. The production fall-off in North Sea oil has started, but it will still provide us with substantial revenues into the mid-1990s, according to most projections. Hope lies also in the continuing gas discoveries, in reserves that are far in excess of previous estimates sufficient for our needs well into the twenty-first century. Coal reserves on land and under the sea will make us self-sufficient for a further three hundred years. The UK will therefore be, for some decades, an energy-rich country.

There have been signs in recent years of an emerging realism, and for that credit needs to be given, in part, to Mrs Thatcher. Although her style of leadership is abrasive and autocratic, there has been less of the fudging and deliberate muddying of the waters that was the hallmark of the 1960s and 1970s, when the corporatist state seemed to engulf individual effort, energy and enterprise. But her style has also revealed a strange and perhaps fatal weakness: insensitivity to other people's views and circumstances. This has too often produced a degree of governmental incompetence that one would not expect from such an obviously well informed leader. Indeed, it is the combination of insensitivity and incompetence that has been the distinguishing feature of this Government. We are not being well governed, but that is more a reflection on our system of government than a criticism of Mrs Thatcher and Mr Tebbit, or Mr Kinnock and Mr Foot, as individuals. It is the system of government, even more than the politicians, that is at fault.

For a fleeting moment, after the Falklands had been recaptured in 1982, there was evident in the nation a mood of buoyancy and a sense of revitalization. The disillusion with the system of government that was so obvious in 1981, at the zenith of the SDP's success, was quickly forgotten. The 1983 election campaign was deliberately called a year early and was dominated by the single issue of the Falklands success. The country had experienced a collective uplift such as had not been felt since the end of the Second World War. Perhaps not unreasonably, despite the bad domestic record, the electorate was ready to give the Government another term, but the size of the majority was a distortion of the electorate's mood; fewer people voted for Mrs Thatcher's return in 1983 than had voted her Prime Minister in 1979, but in 1983 she had a larger parliamentary majority.

The next election will take place in a more sober atmosphere, even if it is temporarily relieved by the confetti of consumer spending. That election must focus on whether our nation can start the long process of reversing its relative industrial and economic decline. Consciously breaking out of the cycle of decline will mean first admitting to its depth and seriousness. It will also mean learning from the past and being wary of a strange rewriting of history.

In 1985 Harold Macmillan, the Earl of Stockton, was being depicted as the apostle of financial rectitude and sound finance because of his criticism of the Government's privatization programme. As a leader Harold Macmillan was an unscrupulous practitioner of the profligate handling of the nation's economy; this was the characteristic of the stewardship of the Conservative Party when it was in government for thirteen years in the 1950s and early 1960s. The Conservatives reduced income tax by sixpence in the pound in April 1955; not even the most charitably disposed could fail to note that this move was followed by a general election in May. In July, after Sir Anthony Eden had been re-elected, the boom was promptly reversed by tougher hire-purchase controls, a credit squeeze, cuts in public investment and increases in taxation, which continued for the next two years.

The 1958 Budget was only slightly expansionary, but by July credit controls and public expenditure had been relaxed. The April 1959 Budget was a real bonanza: the standard rate of income tax was reduced by ninepence in the pound, purchase tax was cut and tuppence a pint was taken off the price of beer. By the autumn of 1959 consumption was soaring and unemployment was falling. Macmillan won the October election with an increased majority, but victory was rapidly succeeded by the days of reckoning when imports soared and the balance of payments plunged into the red.

By the spring of 1960 Macmillan's Government was squeezing credit and cutting consumers' expenditure, and in July 1961 it introduced its fiercest deflationary package. By 1962–3, under Chancellor of the Exchequer Reginald Maudling, a pre-election boom was under way again. Harold Macmillan had gone; now it was Sir Alec Douglas-Home who held off until the last possible moment before calling an election. But it was too late. The electorate's memory of the Conservative 'stop–go' or 'go–stop' economic management – all go before an election and all stop after – had not been blurred by consumer satisfaction.

Harold Wilson just squeezed in as Prime Minister in October 1964. The Labour Party in government proved little better: between 1964 and 1966 everything was subordinated to electoral advantage. A sweeping victory came in March 1966, only to be followed by the June 1966 deflation. This 'stop' was not sufficient, and in 1967 the much-delayed devaluation came, followed by further retrenchment. By now 'go–stop' had become associated with Labour as well as Conservative Governments,[5] in the process inflicting serious damage on the strength and competitiveness of the economy.

Economic decline was accompanied, and intensified, by damaging institutional instability. Major reforms were introduced, only to be restructured or reversed with a rapidity that made it virtually impossible to achieve good administration. This was particularly true of local government, the NHS and industry.

It was a Conservative Government in 1963 that introduced the Greater London Council, only to abolish it twenty-two years later without any consultation or serious study. It was a Conservative Government in 1971, when Mr Peter Walker was Secretary of State for the Environment, that overthrew the recommendations of the Maud Royal Commission for unitary local authorities and chose instead a two-tier system that led to extra costs and massive rate rises in 1974. It was a Labour Government that set up the Layfield Committee to look into local government finance; one of the Committee's recommendations, the introduction of a local income tax, was subsequently rejected by both Labour and Conservative Governments. Now a Conservative Government, without any independent study or consultation, wants to reintroduce a poll tax, last seen in this country in 1660.

The same problem has plagued the efficient running of the NHS. It was a Conservative Government in 1973, when Sir Keith Joseph was Secretary of State for Health and Social Security, that reorganized the NHS and created the three-tier Regional, Area and District Health Authorities. Nine years later it was another Conservative Government, with Patrick Jenkin as the Secretary of State that took away the Area tier. It was Sir Keith Joseph who introduced consensus management, involving administrators, doctors and nurses in 1974, and yet it was Norman Fowler in 1985 who abandoned this structure, implemented a single executive manager and abolished District Management Teams. This has reduced the input of nurses in particular, but also that of doctors, into health administration. The change was made across the board without any pilot scheme to assess its worth, and it is causing justified resentment at the Royal College of Nursing.

Industry and commerce have suffered particularly badly as a result of constant institutional change, not least in the areas of incomes strategy and industrial policy. A Conservative Government created a National Incomes Commission in 1962. Labour replaced it in 1964 with the Prices and Incomes Board (PIB). The Heath Government abolished the PIB in 1970, yet set up a Price Commission in 1973; it was expanded by Labour in 1974, only to be abolished by Mrs Thatcher in 1979.

This institutional reshuffling has been mirrored within Whitehall. It was a Conservative Government that set up the new Ministry for Trade and Consumer Affairs, to which Sir Geoffrey Howe was appointed in 1972. It was then expanded by the Labour Government in 1974, when Shirley Williams was appointed as the new Secretary of State for Prices and Consumer Affairs. Mrs Thatcher's Conservative Government abolished the whole department in 1979.

It was a Labour Government that set up the Industrial Reorganization Corporation in 1966 and the Commission for Industrial Relations in 1969; both were abolished by the new Conservative Government in 1970. Prime Minister Edward Heath established two new bodies, the Pay Board in 1970 and the National Industrial Relations Court in 1971, both of which were disbanded by the Wilson Government in 1974. The National Enterprise Board was instituted in 1975, only to be severely restructured by the Conservative Government in 1979. The new British Technology Group came into being; the National Enterprise Board became a subsidiary after being effectively merged with the National Research and Development Corporation. This institutional instability is clearly a product of political instability. The two combined have made a considerable contribution to the record of bad government.

How should the Social Democratic Party react to this past pattern of political manipulation and institutional instability? Our politics necessitates a different approach: a readiness to face the truth of our decline and to learn from past errors; a reluctance to look back in nostalgia to past failures and instead a willingness to fashion a new political approach. That does not mean peddling false optimism or pretending that there is a silver lining to every black cloud. It means talking frankly to the voters, even at the risk of being depicted as a doomster. It means championing the altruistic side of people's nature, even at the risk of being labelled naïve.

There is some opinion-poll evidence that the public is becoming more sceptical of false optimism, less ready to be lulled by pre-election talk of an economic miracle. The response to Band Aid's fund-raising for famine relief shows there is an untapped reservoir of altruism. There is a greater readiness to forgo reductions in the standard rate of tax if people are convinced that something constructive will be done about reducing unemployment, raising health and educational standards and investing in the future as a consequence.

At the next election the SDP/Liberal Alliance will not be promising instant prosperity. The Alliance will fight the election with open scepticism about the consumer boom; we will be censorious of the candy-floss economy flagrantly designed to whip up votes to win the election. It will be argued that the US Democrats' last presidential candidate, Walter Mondale, found it hard to win support when he criticized President Reagan for running an irresponsibly large deficit and warned of the need for tax increases or expenditure cuts to reduce it. But voters will recognize that the weak UK economy in 1987–8 is very different from the far stronger US economy of 1984. It will be a strange and revealing epitaph to Mrs Thatcher's period in government if she is electorally exposed for practising the same old mixture of cynicism and opportunism that she once so effectively criticized and that has contributed so significantly to this country's present decline.

Mrs Thatcher still cannot make up her mind whether to make a virtue of the Government's failure to reduce public expenditure or to draw attention to her unremitting determination to attempt further retrenchment. Despite the rhetoric of spending reductions and financial rectitude, the fact is that on current plans public expenditure will be 12 per cent higher in real terms in 1988–9 than it was a decade earlier. A Government that intended to cut back has failed to do so but has sought to disguise this with a variety of accountancy devices. Asset sales, for example, have the appearance of budgetary prudence but in reality are helping to finance the pre-election boomlet and significant increases in consumer demand.

The problem of public-expenditure control is a serious one for all political parties to recognize and grapple with. The momentum of public spending is strong and cannot be sustained in every area, however desirable the demands for more spending. The problem is one of choosing priorities. What is needed is a set of new expenditure priorities – to put capital before consumption, to increase the quality of public-service output through more internal and external competition, and to target resources more selectively to those most in need.

The experience of the last twenty years suggests that higher public expenditure across the board – rising from 35 per cent of national income in 1960 to nearly 46 per cent in 1985 – resulted only in sluggish growth, persistent inflation and rising unemployment. This is why this book will explore different ways in which greater efficiency and social justice can be achieved without major increases in public spending.

It is time that we as a nation faced up to our true economic and strategic position. The choices are not simple ones. The choice between Atlanticism or Europeanism was always too simplistic. Continental or blue-water diplomacy? One is as unrealistically confining as the other was romantically overstretching. Britain is, by referendum decision, now committed to acting as a European power. The British have strategic interests to protect on the continent of Europe, but to do this we have to build up our national economy on a European scale. Our skills, brains and technological strength hold the key to reinvigorating and regenerating our country.

We have in the past been forced to reassess our future with regard to Europe. In 1945 we chose, in the wake of victory, to dismantle the Empire, the pre-requisite to closer links with the Continent. But then in 1955 we deliberately ignored at the Messina Conference a chance to help shape the European Community. In 1965, after successfully confronting Indonesia, we grudgingly but correctly started to withdraw from east of Suez. But despite the massive majority in our first-ever national referendum, which endorsed membership of the European Community in 1975, we still do not act as Europeans. We are hesitant and sometimes still hostile members of that Common Market. We give the impression of being reluctant competitors, disliking the harsh disciplines of the market-place where, like it or not, our standard of living will be set.

To revive our scientific, technical, industrial and commercial base as a nation, we need to be part of a European strategy, a strategy that ensures that our twelve democratic Community states stretch out commercially and politically, to both the east and west. We cannot take for granted either NATO's future success, or the prolongation of the current US level of commitment to the defence of Europe. The remaining years of this century pose an immense challenge to this country. Are we yet ready to face the need to change the structure and style of the way in which we govern ourselves?

2 Bad Government

The United Kingdom has been badly governed for at least three decades. Admitting the dismal failure of our political institutions is the first step along the path of recovery.

Perhaps that record of bad government extends over a longer period: certainly the inter-war years were not distinguished by vision or vigour. The handling of the 1956 Suez Crisis was probably the best example of bad government this century. Characterized by the deception of our allies, deviousness, duplicity in Parliament and sheer incompetence, it seems to have marked a turning-point in our national fortunes. Only two junior Ministers, Anthony Nutting and Edward Boyle, resigned. Anthony Eden ceased to be Prime Minister because of ill health, rather than being forced out by a party revolt. Although the Conservative Party escaped paying the political price for Suez and recovered enough to win the 1959 election, British public life suffered enormously. Rab Butler and Walter Monckton clung to office, thus endorsing a style of government in which, despite semi-public agonizing, loyalty to one's party seemed to come higher than loyalty to one's country. Selwyn Lloyd, who had lied to Parliament, not only stayed on as Foreign Secretary but became later its Speaker.

Prior to the Suez Crisis, the resignation, on principle, of Cabinet Ministers who disagreed with the Government or who bore responsibility for failure was expected. Tony Benn stayed on as a Cabinet Minister from 1974 to 1979 despite being in fundamental disagreement with the Labour Government. At a lesser level of disagreement, Peter Walker has remained in Mrs Thatcher's Government since 1979.

In earlier days the usual consequence of disagreements of principle within parties was the realignment of those parties or, more precisely, sections of those parties. In 1846 Sir Robert Peel split the Conservative Party over the repeal of the Corn Laws. 'His allegiance,' as his biographer tells us, 'was to an older concept than party loyalty; it was to the service of the state.'[1] In 1886 the revolt of the Liberal Unionists led to the defeat of Gladstone's plans for Irish Home Rule. A tragedy, in my opinion, but nevertheless it cannot be denied that the Liberal dissenters were brave men, willing to put their conception of the national good above that of mere party conformity. In 1916 a large number of Liberals were willing to split their party to make Lloyd George Prime Minister – and many would argue that without Lloyd George's leadership we would not have been on the winning side in the First World War. In 1931 leading members of the Labour and Liberal parties joined the National Government, putting what they conceived to be their duty to the nation above their party commitments. In 1940 forty-three Conservatives voted with the Labour Party and another seventy abstained. The Conservative Government, which normally had a majority of about 250, carried the day by 281 to 200, but Neville Chamberlain was finished; the vote paved the way for Churchill and the wartime coalition Government.

Party realignment has always been a feature of British politics, but in the post-war period its nature has changed. Party has come to dominate principle, and British politics has become artificial and rigid. The two main parties have realigned themselves by moving, as bodies, to the extremes. The two-party system has become ossified, frozen in its attitudes, as the dominance of the party machine has grown. Only the SDP can break the stranglehold on British politics of the old parties. The decline in the standards of political morality has been the most striking development in political life during the last few decades.

As the Labour and Conservative parliamentary parties narrowed their ideological base, 'Butskellism' – the idea that there was initially much common ground between the policies of the two Chancellors of the Exchequer, Gaitskell and Butler – failed. It started to die with Butler's 1955 pre-election Budget, which put the economy at risk in order so obviously to buy votes. By 1979 Mrs Thatcher was rejoicing in abandoning any attempt to seek common ground. Divisions over economic, social and defence policy have ever since grown deeper.

Labour's switch from applying to join the European Community when in government in 1967 to hostility to entry when in opposition in 1971, was a turning-point. Then, sixty-nine Labour MPs (including many who are now Social Democrats), decided that they could not oppose membership of the European Community and voted to accede to the Treaty of Rome. Without that decision the United Kingdom might never have entered the European Economic Community. Three hundred and sixty-five MPs voted to join, while 244 voted against joining, including thirty-nine Conservative and Ulster Unionist MPs. That was the time when a new centre-left realignment should have emerged. Instead the Labour Party did not split. Unwisely, none of those who later joined the SDP resigned either from the Party Whip or from the Shadow Office. However, as the Party's hostility to the European Community grew, Roy Jenkins, Harold Lever, George Thomson, Robert Maclennan, Dick Mabon and I resigned as Labour spokesmen on 10 April 1972.

The Shadow Cabinet, having first rejected Tony Benn's proposed referendum on the European Community, had suddenly switched to supporting a referendum. I resigned, however, not over the principle of a referendum but over the growing hostility to the European Community. Privately I had argued that we would have been wiser to accept the referendum and then, if it ever came, to fight openly to win the endorsement of our membership.

After the two general elections in 1974 a referendum on the European Community was held on 5 June 1975: 17,378,581 people (67.2 per cent) voted to stay in the Community, and 8,470,073 people (32.8 per cent) voted to come out. It was reasonable to hope that the vote would have settled the issue, but the Labour Party's hostility to the Community led it, in the 1983 election, to campaign for withdrawing, without a referendum. Voters sensed that Labour did not trust them; the Party's anti-European Community stance contributed to its defeat. Next time hostility to the European Community is more likely to be modified by talk of renegotiation and promises of another referendum if a Labour government wants to withdraw. In whatever form the Labour Party's hostility is expressed, the continued questioning of our membership of the Community is a recipe for debility.

Views on foreign policy, which had polarized on party lines over Suez, had by 1962 split fundamentally over the European Community. Defence looked as if it might suffer a similar division over the December 1962 Nassau agreement to purchase Polaris, but Harold Wilson, to his credit, sidestepped that division, going ahead with the Polaris-building programme in 1964. It was not until 1980 that defence fell victim to the post-war political polarization. Labour espoused first unilateralism in 1980 and then semi-neutralism in 1983.

Only history will show whether the political realignment that followed the foundation of the SDP in 1981 will lead to greater stability, better government and the reverse of our relative economic decline. Despite the serious problems now facing the UK, it is not unreasonable to hope that our country will pull back from the edge of the precipice and restore its fortunes. The question is, when? The sooner we start, the easier it will be.

We should begin by challenging the power of the Prime Minister. There are insufficient checks and balances on prime ministerial power in the British system; both the power of patronage and the power to call an election at will need to be curbed.

Lord Hailsham's comment, made from the safety of the Opposition benches in 1978 (and, sadly, not reiterated during his service in the Thatcher Government) that we have in the UK an 'elective dictatorship' was perceptive. There is abundant backing for this view in the circumstances surrounding the Westland Affair. The most damaging evidence suggested that Mrs Thatcher had misled the House of Commons, but the most worrying implied her systematic undermining of Cabinet government. All Prime Ministers have manipulated their Cabinets, but I believe Mrs Thatcher has developed this art to an extent rarely seen before. In the Westland Affair she was accused by a Cabinet colleague of ignoring official advice, obstructing collective Cabinet decision-making, manipulating the agenda and acquiescing in the partial reporting of Cabinet proceedings. Her private office staff accepted the selective leaking of the Solicitor-General's letter, and we are asked to believe that this was done without the staff knowing her view or seeking her authority. All the ingredients of Lord Acton's famous dictum, that 'Absolute power corrupts absolutely,' were on display in the Westland Affair.

As the whipping system throughout the post-war period has grown tighter, so the use and power of prime ministerial patronage (already tarnished by David Lloyd George) has increased. As Prime Ministers, Macmillan, Wilson and Thatcher have all understood that the use of patronage has become an important lever, as more MPs now regard Parliament as their only career and as money plays an increasing role in political parties' election campaigning. Mrs Thatcher has created fifty-nine knights from the ranks of Conservative MPs, though to prevent by-elections during this period (caused by newly created peers moving to the Lords), only Willie Whitelaw has been created a peer. All eleven private-sector industrialists who received peerages between 1979 and the middle of 1985 worked for companies that gave in total £1,856,393 to Tory Party funds; the same is true of forty-four of the sixty-four other people who worked in the private sector and were given knighthoods. Their companies contributed £4.3 million to Tory Party funds.[2]

Party leaders are allocated by the Prime Minister their own shorter Honours Lists for political appointees. To accept the existence of such a list is to accept that politics is an activity separate from public service, where honours are bestowed according to the criteria generally applied but in order to reinforce the power of the party leader. The SDP has not availed itself of this dubious privilege. Political honours ought to be part of the wider public-service honours system. A Prime Minister more conscious of the true dignity of the office than Mrs Thatcher is would not want to distort an independent allocation to politicians with purely party-political considerations. A ration system is applied to civil servants, diplomats and military figures; they dominate the list and are honoured purely for their position, irrespective of the quality of their work. The whole structure is now a sham, with its titles that still refer to the Empire, its names that bring dishonour and its party politics that distort. It needs a complete overhaul; until that is done the SDP will continue to keep its distance from the system.

Patronage is only a minor source of prime ministerial manipulative power. By far the greatest is the cynical pandering to consumer satisfaction that takes place before an election, as discussed in Chapter 1. This Government, in the best tradition of past Conservative Governments, has geared the present consumer boomlet to a 1987 election. Linked with manipulation of the economy is abuse of the power to call an election at will.

Mrs Thatcher retains the prerogative to call an election after less than four years, and this may well mean that she will go to the country before the election that is constitutionally due in June 1988, the excuse being to approve a Reagan–Gorbachev arms-control agreement. The country would then be told that the agreement needed its support. Defence would be used to obscure the failure of the Government to address Britain's economic decline. This is what happened in 1983, when the Falklands war crushed any doubts about domestic policies.

It would be worth while at this point to review the history of the two major parties individually in order to set the political developments discussed above in context. To start with the Labour Party, some events in its recent history stand out as particularly poignant and significant, partly because from them one can trace the development of the SDP. One was the death of Hugh Gaitskell, the leader of the Labour Party, on 18 January 1963. Gaitskell's death has increased in importance in terms of British political history. When he died he was still three months short of his fifty-seventh birthday. It had once seemed certain that he would become Prime Minister, yet after Harold Wilson won the 1964 election Gaitskell's former policy fights appeared to have little future relevance. The politics of circumnavigation was in the ascendant, and Gaitskell was depicted as an unnecessary confrontationalist. At Labour's Scarborough Conference in 1963 it seemed that Wilson's 'white-hot heat of the techno- logical revolution' speech had rendered future arguments about national- ization obsolete. Even in 1966 those of us who had come into Parliament at that election still believed that the 'stop–go' 'go–stop' economy was over and that our propaganda about thirteen years of Tory misrule was true. All looked set for good government, yet disillusionment was soon to follow. The deflation of summer 1966, the refusal to devalue, the absurd remarks about our frontiers being on the Himalayas and the reluctance to withdraw from east of Suez were painful learning experi- ences. Admittedly, the Wilson Government improved its performance in office, helped greatly by Roy Jenkins's period as a responsible and prudent Chancellor of the Exchequer. But from my vantage point on the back benches and then from the Ministry of Defence I could see that it was not a good government.

Where did Labour go so badly wrong after Attlee? Had Gaitskell lived, the Labour Party and British politics would have been very different. A Government with him as Prime Minister might well have succeeded; the politics of the 1960s and 1970s might not have debased the currency of centre-left thinking. It is sad that Gaitskell's political career is remem- bered primarily for battles fought within the Labour Party. His promise to 'fight and fight and fight again to save the party we love' is his most often quoted statement,[3] his campaign to reject unilateralism his most widely acknowledged victory, his fight to remove Clause IV from the Labour Party Constitution his most generally criticized and humiliating defeat. It is only in the 1980s that the nature of those battles and Gaitskell's role in them has been given a new political significance that stretches far beyond that of a purely party squabble.

Labour under Neil Kinnock is not just a firmly unilateralist party.

With its 1983 commitment to turn the United States out of all its UK nuclear bases the party has undertaken a massive shift of policy in which semi-neutralism is coming through slowly, in addition to unilateralism. No leading figure is yet prepared to fight within Labour for holding to NATO's defence policy of deterrence based on conventional and nuclear forces, or to set Labour's international defence policy in the mainstream of the Continental democratic left. Probably Labour can change back to a serious defence policy only under the pressure of an inter-party agreement, for even the trade-union block vote cannot be assumed to return to supporting multilateralism as part of any new realism that might slowly emerge.

But it is the lost battle over Clause IV that still haunts the Labour Party; it plays a larger part in explaining why Labour is no longer capable of governing well than many are prepared to recognize. Nostalgia and respect for the Attlee Government should not lead sensible Labour Party members into believing that recycling that same mix of state socialism can contribute to Britain's recovery in the 1990s. Such nostalgia explains why Labour still fails to grapple with the needs of a high-tech economy, appears incapable of fostering a climate of innovation, flair and enterprise, seems hostile to creating a climate in which profits engender new investment and new jobs. Clause IV has often been ignored and has frequently been the subject of reinterpretation, but it remains on the membership card of every Labour Party member, a symbol of the Party's constitutional commitment to nationalization and, perhaps more important, of the analysis that underlies the party's policies.

Originally introduced in 1918, and subject to some minor alterations before attaining its final form in 1929, Clause IV in Labour's Constitution declares its aim to be 'To secure for the workers by hand or by brain the full fruits of their industry, and the most equitable distribution thereof that may be possible, upon the basis of the common ownership of the means of production, distribution and exchange, and the best obtainable system of popular administration and control of each industry and service.' For a party that had previously been simply an alliance whose aim was to achieve greater representation for working people in Parliament, the importance of Clause IV is that it locks the Labour Party into Marxist economics and provides inspiration for the militants.

All post-war leaders of the Labour Party have attempted to evade the true meaning of the Clause; another attempt is under way, in 1986, to

bury it in a new statement of democratic socialist principles. Neil Kinnock
is trying to shift Labour's language towards efficiency, with increased
production coming before the redistribution of wealth. This change is to
be welcomed if it goes deeper than mere rhetoric. However, apart from
his ideological past which saw him fighting the leadership election on the
basis of endorsing the 1983 manifesto, there is more than a suspicion that
he is still talking to two audiences, the voters and his activists, in two
different languages. Whatever the outcome of the next election, there
will be as many as a hundred Labour MPs, as a result of early retirement,
reselection and the leftward lurch of the party, to whom Clause IV is an
article of faith. However, no amount of speeches by Neil Kinnock or Roy
Hattersley about Japan or Marks and Spencer will change the fact that
for party activists Clause IV is perfectly and painfully clear: it declares
a commitment to securing common ownership of the means of production,
distribution and exchange. The activists will not allow that commitment
to be translated, as some have suggested, into calling simply for 'social
ownership', 'more widely distributed ownership', 'more diverse ownership' or 'more responsive ownership'. Labour's leadership, from Harold
Wilson to the most recent, might want it to say this; but so long as
Labour's constitutional objective is to make all ownership common to all
people, there is an in-built self-destruct mechanism ticking away at the
heart of the party's economic policy. In government it would explode,
and the best that could come out of it all would be a rehash of Labour's
policies of the 1960s and 1970s.

Experience of over eleven years of Labour in government since 1964
reveals that the political and economic attitudes and analysis that underpin
Clause IV have bedevilled the actions of successive Labour Governments.
It is no accident that Labour was – and remains to this day – debilitatingly
split within its ranks over protectionism. Many reject the market principles that underpin the European Community. Mr Kinnock has always
been in the vanguard of opposition in principle to UK membership.
Although some still oppose the European Community on nationalist
grounds, a deep-seated antagonism comes from Marxist-inspired economists who rightly see that involvement in the Community threatens to
take away their opportunity to practise their economic theories.

To Labour's Marxist economic wing, protectionism is as necessary as
hostility to private enterprise. They distrust the profit motive. They
believe that the proper achievement of equality, co-operation and social

welfare can only be attained once the system of private enterprise is overturned. Public ownership, common to all, holds the key to their social objectives. Techniques for administering nationalized industries may need to be changed, but new administrative reforms are still envisaged in the context of common ownership.

This very fundamental divide between Marxists and socialists is difficult to contain within the Labour Party. It is a divide that is perpetuated and upheld across normal party divisions by the public-sector trade union leaders who want the safety net of state-run, centralized industries and services and yet, on other issues, have little in common with either Marxists or militants. In government, from 1964 to 1970 and from 1974 to 1979, that tension within the Labour Party constantly made for uneasy bedfellows. In the 1990s it is going to be hard enough to grapple in government with the relative decline of the British economy. It will be impossible for a Labour Government to halt the decline when it is deeply divided on whether it wants to promote the all-powerful state or to encourage the entrepreneur, accept the profit motive and believe in both individual initiative and local, decentralized decision-making.

As Prime Minister, Jim Callaghan tried, with some success, to bring common sense to the fore within the Labour Party. But since his and the party's defeat in 1979, Labour has drifted into being an ever more uneasy grouping, held together by habit more than common interest. A growing number of fundamentalists who support both the analysis and the commitment of Clause IV have exploited that rift with zeal. They have persuaded the mainstream Labour Party members, aided by the large trade-union block vote, into making numerous small policy decisions, of themselves not perhaps too damaging but cumulatively destructive of any understanding of what makes a market economy function successfully.

Since the 1983 defeat the small and diminishing democratic socialist wing of revisionists inside Labour count for less and less. They realize competition is essential, but their view remains muted. They distrust the extension of public ownership but acquiesce in its extension. They have abdicated from the nuclear debate and cling to nominal membership of NATO as a life-raft, though they know in their hearts that this must involve accepting nuclear deterrence.

Meanwhile, the privatization/nationalization switchback gathers momentum, with Labour offering a commitment to renationalize British Telecom and British Gas for the 1987 election (though Mr Kinnock is

trying to give it low legislative priority). Labour appears unable to
distinguish between the objectives of the public and the private sector.
The effect of most of its policies would be to constrain the driving force
of private enterprise without being able to engender a new offsetting
dynamism within the public service. Labour is devoid of new ideas,
isolated within the international spectrum of leftward thinking, suspicious
of new methods of participation, apprehensive about extensions of share
ownership. The political decline of the Labour Party mirrors the economic
decline of the nation.

It has been a strange feature of that decline that as Labour has become
more ideological, so an opposed ideological fervour has taken hold of the
Conservative Party. In the 1970s Labour and Conservative ideologues,
as represented by the activists around Tony Benn and Margaret Thatcher,
believed that only a complete break with the past would suffice. Consensus
became a dirty word, and the art of compromise a dubious political asset.
Both sets of activists still portray compromise as abandoning conviction
or forsaking commitment.

There is nothing wrong with either compromise or consensus. Compromise is entered into deliberately as a deal, a trade-off between interests.
It allows for clarity of intention, which persists even if the outcome
reflects a negotiated arrangement in which beliefs or principles are openly
tempered by circumstances. Compromise, part of the art of collective
bargaining as well as of coalition government, is perversely abused by
many in the Labour Party. Compromise is stupidly equated by Mrs
Thatcher with consensus, and both are despised. Compromise is not
always right, in which case the risk is confrontation; consensus may not
always be attainable. But to reject both compromise and consensus
without trying for either is to perpetuate division.

Where did the Conservative Party go so badly wrong in 1945? Throughout the long history of the Conservative Party, its wisest politicians have
sought reforms that can be sustained. Radical Conservatives understood
that injustice and prejudice must be rooted out if society is to be held
together. The present threat to the stability of our society stems not only
from revolutionary action but also from reactionary passivity over a long
period. The great Democratic American President, Franklin Roosevelt,
once said, 'Wise and prudent men – intelligent conservatives – have long
known that in a changing world worthy institutions can be conserved
only by adjusting them to the changing time.'[4] The shrewder Conserva-

tive leaders of the past, men such as Peel and Disraeli, would have agreed. They were ready to change institutions but understood that national leadership was something more than mere party leadership. To understand the decline of the present Conservative Party, one has to go back to the last century.

The attempt to construct a modern Conservative Party began with the Tamworth Manifesto, when Peel accepted the Great Reform Act of 1832 and ensured that the Conservatives adopted a moderate and liberal path. The Great Reform Act gave the vote to an extra 217,000 voters, in addition to the previous total of 435,000 voters, and was a crucial step in the building of Britain's constitutional democracy. It gave the country the unity and the cohesion that it needed to govern the Empire and to create wealth and stability in the nineteenth century. Peel promised to reform where he could find 'proven abuse' or 'real grievances'. Reform, he declared, meant just that; it did not mean following every popular whim, or providing instant redress for every alleged abuse, or abandoning respect for basic rights. Some Conservatives today claim Peel rather than Disraeli as the spiritual forefather of the modern Conservative Party. They have not, however, thought through exactly what the Peelite legacy to British politics really entails. It was Peel, rather than Disraeli, who was the originator of the 'Middle Way' philosophy, for Peel sought to steer a moderate and sensible path between the extremes of revolution on the left and reaction on the right. His success was demonstrated by the fact that Britain, alone of the great European states, avoided revolution in 1848, despite the existence of the Chartist movement.

Peel's prime ministership from 1841 to 1846 was successful because he did not hesitate to act on what he thought was right for the country. He had, at one time, been a strong defender of the Corn Laws, and it was deeply painful for him to repeal them. Peel was one of the greatest Prime Ministers of the nineteenth century, more truly a 'one nation' leader than Disraeli, with whom the term is associated. Only Gladstone can be compared with Peel; Gladstone himself referred to Peel as 'My great Master and generous friend'. Peel was a man of government; in that sense, there were similarities in his approach to that of Edward Heath, a man whose potential was never fulfilled.

In spite of constantly switching from party to party, Churchill was the greatest Conservative Prime Minister this century. Besides changing from Liberal to Conservative, he risked all in his 1930s opposition to appeasement and actively wanted in 1939 a coalition Government. He chose coalition; it was not forced on him by Labour, nor was he afraid to adjust his views to uncomfortable realities, as he did in 1951, when he reluctantly accepted the end of the Empire. Churchill, though one of the most decisive of politicians, appeared happier and more effective when working within the framework of coalition politics. Although Disraeli is credited with saying that 'England does not love coalitions',[5] there is no evidence that this sentiment is widely held.

Edward Heath can also claim, with Churchill, to have put the national interest before that of the Conservative Party, first by sacking Enoch Powell in 1968 for inciting racial tension with his 'rivers of blood' speech, then by forcing through membership of the European Community against a divided party in the House of Commons. At Sunningdale, when creating the new concept of power-sharing in Northern Ireland, he again risked splitting the party.

The Heath period of government has to be seen in two parts. Elected in 1970 on a manifesto that was conceived at the Selsdon Park Conference in 1968, its policies gave a foretaste of the economic and social policies to be pursued by Mrs Thatcher as Prime Minister from 1979. The 1970 Heath Government started the disease of 'repealitis', in which all the institutional and other innovations of one Government are scrapped by its successor because of commitments made in opposition. Yet two years later, in 1972, facing high unemployment, Heath responded both intellectually to the facts and emotionally to public concern. Policies were changed fundamentally. That shift, criticized on the right of the party, was the intellectual stimulus for the Conservative rethink started by Sir Keith Joseph and followed through by Mrs Thatcher.

If Heath had gone to the country over the miners' strike in the summer of 1974, not in January of that year, he would have won. The election would have been fought in a calmer mood and on a trade-union reform package thoughtfully designed to avert a repeat of the Government's humiliating defeat by the miners. Without a sense of crisis, the electorate would have been more likely to endorse the 1972 shift of position as a relevant adjustment designed to tackle the deep-seated problems of the nation's decline. That year might then have been a major turning point in the nation's fortunes. Our European commitment would have been strong, and the new Heath policies might have succeeded.

To revert to developments that occurred in our political system, the pendulum inherent in the present voting system swung to return Harold Wilson to government in 1974 with no outright majority. His Government from 1974 to 1976, until Jim Callaghan took over, was particularly bad. Its main achievement was to conduct the referendum over the European Community in a manner intended to keep the UK within the Community. On that historic issue Wilson at least made amends for his shameful tactical retreat over Community membership in 1971. But the Social Contract proved a disaster, with inflation reaching 27 per cent and the trade unions being given far too much power. Labour should never have been allowed to wield absolute power from a minority position.

The Liberals did spectacularly well in the February 1974 election, but they (and particularly their leader, Jeremy Thorpe) paid a huge price for appearing to let Labour into government. Immediately after the February 1974 election Edward Heath offered to come to an agreement with Thorpe. The electorate that had voted Liberal in February had been attracted by the cleverly reiterated and justified claim by Thorpe that neither the Heath Government nor the Wilson Government could unite the country. Thorpe should have stuck to this theme and let it be known publicly, before he saw Heath, that he had a specific agenda of changes of policy and attitudes for a government of national unity. Heath badly misjudged the public mood by calling the election. It was always going to be hard for the Liberals to be seen to be keeping him in power, particularly when, even with the support of all Liberal MPs, the Conservatives would still have been short of an overall majority.

The Liberal Party had appeared to be very divided over whether they even wanted to reach an agreement with the Heath Government. They appeared to have no agreed agenda to put forward, even though on the critical issue of European Community membership and the Sunningdale Agreement on Northern Ireland they shared common ground with the Conservatives. In February 1974 the Liberal Party undoubtedly missed an important opportunity to influence the future shape of UK politics. Not surprisingly, the electorate was not keen to give the Liberals another opportunity in October, and their votes fell from 6,063,470 to 5,346,800 in the second 1974 general election. One of the internal psychological difficulties that the Liberals probably faced in being seen to work with the Conservatives was that much of the rhetoric of realignment, as originally proposed by Jo Grimond, was designed to replace Labour as the new party of the left. There had been perhaps insufficient discussion of how, in the process of achieving electoral reform and creating a multi-party system, it would be necessary for the Liberal Party to act as a pivot and to be prepared to form coalitions or inter-party agreements with the Conservatives as well as with Labour.

There are important lessons for the SDP/Liberal Alliance in what happened in 1974, as there are from the 1977–8 Liberal–Labour pact. Then the Liberals, under David Steel, courageously exerted some influence on a Labour Government. It was an agreement made easier by the obvious moderation of Jim Callaghan's style and outlook as Prime Minister. The Liberals are never given sufficient credit for helping to achieve a far better period of government over the years of the pact in 1977 and 1978 than that of 1974 to 1976. Tony Benn, whose wings had already been clipped by Harold Wilson, had no power at all during the pact. It was amazing that he stayed a member of the Labour Cabinet, despite voting with five other Labour Ministers against forming the Lib.–Lab. pact. But by then over twenty years had passed since Butler's decision not to resign over Suez, and Cabinet Ministers had frequently stayed on in Governments with which they were clearly out of sympathy.

The weakness of the Lib.–Lab. pact, from the Liberal point of view, was that the Liberals were seen to achieve too little. The Cabinet had, prior to the loss of the Government's majority and any discussion of a pact, already accepted a version of the Finnish regional system of proportional representation, which I, as Foreign Secretary, had suggested for the elections to the European Parliament. It was very surprising that the Liberals did not privately make it clear to Jim Callaghan that their support could not possibly continue if the Cabinet's advocacy of proportional representation for elections to the European Parliament was not carried on to the statute book. In the event, the only concession Jim Callaghan made was to promise to use his own personal best endeavours to put proportional-representation legislation through. Michael Foot, who was also party to the negotiations, was vehemently opposed to direct elections for the European Parliament, let alone proportional representation. He eventually extracted from Callaghan the extraordinary concession of allowing the Cabinet, as well as the Government and the Parliamentary Labour Party, a free vote on the issue. The commitment to proportional representation was envisaged under the Treaty of Rome; it provides for a comparable system of voting across the Community. All the other countries in the EEC had already planned a proportional system for their elections. It would have been quite legitimate to put the Whip on for this legislation, which was in keeping with the country's 1975 referendum decision, and when Labour refused to commit itself to do this, perhaps the Liberal Party should have called Jim Callaghan's bluff and forced Michael Foot to decide whether he wanted Labour to continue in office.

The best achievement of the Lib.–Lab. pact was to allow time for the economic realism that followed the International Monetary Fund (IMF) crisis to take effect. Inflation dropped steadily throughout the period of the pact. In 1978 the Liberals also extracted a useful concession that encouraged wider share ownership.

The real importance of the pact may prove to be that the Labour Party crossed the threshold of realignment. It did not venture far across, but it will now always be harder for Labour to argue – following further election defeats – that an inter-party agreement remains out of the question. The ghost of Ramsay MacDonald has not yet died, but there are now in the House of Commons senior Labour figures who have experienced government on the basis of inter-party agreement. Forming a coalition with Labour will probably always be blocked by the hard left within the Parliamentary Labour Party, but the logic of working with the SDP/Liberal Alliance will not disappear because of political blindness.

There are among Conservative MPs senior figures who in 1974 were ready to contemplate an inter-party agreement or a coalition. It is those people whose influence will be stronger if the Conservatives lose their large majority. The Thatcher style of no compromise will have been rebuffed by the electorate, and a sensible voice will be raised demanding negotiations with the SDP/Liberal Alliance. The Alliance is an inclusive, not an exclusive, concept; if it can broaden its base beyond the Liberal and Social Democratic parties, it could increase its potential to govern well. Despite what either Margaret Thatcher or Neil Kinnock may say prior to the election, they may both find after the election that with neither party having an outright majority, politics will become very different. Parties that refuse to put the national interest first and refuse to seek a wider national unity will pay a heavy price at the subsequent election. People know they need to be better governed, even though some politicians will not recognize that need.

The formation in 1981 of the SDP, the first new UK-wide political party since the Labour Party was formed in 1909, was a reaction to the ideological polarization described earlier in this chapter. But it was also something much more – a response to the belief that the political system itself was part of Britain's decline, that the system had to be reformed before Britain could revive its fortunes. The creation of the SDP was inevitably criticized by both Labour and Conservative leaders, but what was interesting and revealing was that so much of their criticism was directed to challenging the legitimacy of realignment. The concept that loyalty to party came before loyalty to country was expressed very strongly. Mrs Thatcher, for instance, was still saying in November 1985: 'Why I criticize the SDP so much [is that] they ought to have stayed in and done the in-fighting and made the extreme left split off.'[6] She criticizes those who had previously been members of the Labour Party but who were not prepared to endorse the totally new 1983 manifesto commitment that would have pledged them to support unilateral disarmament. She criticizes those who were not prepared to advocate coming out of the European Community without even repeating the 1975 referendum. Were Mrs Thatcher's remarks to be taken seriously, one would have to ask? What price her patriotism or her principles? The fact that Mrs Thatcher and others in Parliament even talk in these terms makes one wonder whether the politicians who subscribe to our present political system have forgotten the traditional concept that the good of the country and its effective government should be put before party nostrums or ideology. What these politicians still do not understand, and what many commentators still ignore, is that 64 per cent of SDP members have never been members of the Labour, Conservative or Liberal parties. The SDP represents a new political force; it was never just a reshuffling of the old political pack of party allegiances.

The old political groupings, as represented by the class-based Labour and Conservative parties, fear above all the claim that they can no longer provide good government. Many of their supporters recognize that their parties have become the victims of political zealots. It is not just Labour, however, that is extreme. It is a revealing commentary on Mrs Thatcher's style of leadership that in December 1985, even before the Westland Affair, Gallup found that 52 per cent of the population described the Conservative Party as extreme, whereas only 39 per cent used that description of the Labour Party. Despite knowing that some of the changes introduced by this Government are necessary, many see the manner of the change as unnecessarily partisan and divisive. The same poll found that 69 per cent saw the Conservatives as good for one class, whereas 66 per cent saw the SDP/Liberal Alliance as good for all classes. It is possible to identify in the UK a large potential constituency for a reformed political system. The challenge is to mobilize that constituency and to convince it that such reforms are the starting-point for national recovery.

3 Better Government

Those who might agree that we have been badly governed may not find it so easy to reach agreement as to how we can be better governed. Although the interests of a powerful few may be served by polarized politics, the interests of the vast majority are not. The *status quo*, for all its faults, is at least familiar. Though the centre ground is where most people's interests lie, it has never previously been used as the platform for a political force; this means that the SDP/Liberal Alliance must be strong and determined. Moderation, common sense and stability are essential for lasting change. These are strong and positive characteristics, and we will only reverse our decline by building them into our system of government. The militant moderate is needed in centre politics as much as 'the Church militant here on earth'. It is a necessary way of thinking if moderation is to be seen to have passion, commitment and the inner toughness needed to override vested interests.

Since 1945 the polarization of choice rather than consensus has been the dominant feature of the British political system. The choice in the early part of the century was between home rule and tariff reform; then later between protectionism or socialism. A fundamental objective of the SDP when it was formed was not just to replace the Labour Party in a two-party system, as happened when Labour replaced the Liberals in the 1920s. It was to create a multi-party system in Britain where coalition Governments became the norm and single-party Governments the exception.

The SDP has brought new people and a wholly new political commitment to politics. The majority of our members had never before joined any other political party. This new political element finds it natural that the SDP should be open about its intention of acting as a pivot in the transition to multi-party politics. They see a readiness to form a coalition with either the Labour or Conservative parties as a natural development.

The SDP/Liberal Alliance, far from being, as Neil Kinnock claims, the politics of power without responsibility, is ready to share both power and responsibility. Coalition politics stems from the belief, backed by practical experience, that until Governments start to speak for more than 50 per cent of the electorate in the UK, we will continue to slide down the international league table of prosperous nations. The SDP's readiness to consider coalition government and to put into practice an alliance with the Liberal Party stems from its diagnosis that division is a cause of our national decline, and that unity will be part of national recovery.

It is in the nature of the social-democratic approach to be suspicious of dogmas or creeds. We believe in concentrating on the basic details of practical living. In spite of our advocacy of proportional representation, we do not try to depict the system as the single talisman or key that will alone quickly transform our future. Social Democrats see the capacity of government to influence attitudes as being more important than increasing government's statutory powers. Changes of attitude can only derive from a new constitutional settlement, not from the institutional juggling that we saw in the 1960s and 1970s. Proportional representation, partnership, participation, devolution and decentralization are powerful long-term political concepts that will, we believe, produce profound changes in attitudes. We are not ashamed of presenting them as central ingredients for providing our nation with better government. We predict no miracles but that constitutional reforms will produce a steady improvement in the quality of central and local government.

It is true that Social Democrat and Liberal activists have a vested interest in achieving proportional representation, but it is also true that Conservative and Labour activists have a vested interest in not having proportional representation. That is why this issue will in the end be determined by the people, not by politicians. The strongest argument for proportional representation is that the country has had sufficient experience of the present system with its unfair voting, adversarial politics and alternation of governments to know that it does not work. The system has failed us as a country, and has provided us with long periods of bad government.

The strongest political argument against proportional representation stems from examples of those systems that are the fairest and give the purest proportionality. These systems – such as that in Israel, where a Labour supporter simply votes for the Israeli Labour Party and candidates' names do not appear on the ballot paper at all – produce numerous small parties. The critics of proportional representation fasten on to the problems of these pure systems. In fact, most advocates of electoral reform are only too well aware of the need to find a balance between perfect proportionality for the parties and discretion for the voters among the candidates. In judging that balance, the SDP/Liberal Alliance has chosen a Single Transferable Vote system for the UK as likely to provide the best form of government. It does not give perfect proportionality and is more accurately described as a preferential voting system. There is, however, a political case for continuing to use the more widely understood term 'proportional representation'. Where there is not perfect proportionality a party with the most votes may not win the largest number of seats, but criticism of imperfect proportionality comes strangely from those who advocate retention of the British system, with its massive disproportion between votes cast and seats gained. It is a criticism that comes a little oddly too from Labour Party opponents of proportional representation in the UK, when in the last general election they gained only 27.6 per cent of the votes (as compared to the SDP/Liberal Alliance's 25.3 per cent) and nevertheless won 32 per cent of the seats as against the SDP/Liberal Alliance's 3.5 per cent of the seats.

The frequency of changes of Government under some proportional systems is often cited critically; Italy has had more than forty-four changes of Government since the war. In Italy the Communist Party has polled well over 30 per cent on a number of occasions. If the British electoral system had been used, Italy would have had majority Communist Governments, whereas the Communists in power in many regional authorities have as yet not even been members of a coalition Government. Despite the frequent changes of Government, the fact that Italy in 1985 surpassed the UK in its standard of living implies that the quality of Italian government is better than ours. It is possible, under different systems of proportional representation – as happens in Germany and the Netherlands – to provide for virtually a fixed-term parliament. This procedure makes it very difficult to hold a general election other than at a set point in the cycle, reducing the short-term manipulative power over consumer spending that has been so economically damaging in the UK.

Critics of proportional representation often cite the potential delay in forming a Government attributable to proportional representation as a cause of chaos. The 1981 Dutch general election voted on a national list in eighteen regional districts and produced ten parties with MPs in the

Dutch Lower House; only one party had as much as 30 per cent of the vote. It took 118 days, from 26 May to 11 September, to form a Government that only lasted until May 1982, when it was followed by another coalition Government, which took seventeen days to form. This Government faced a general election on 8 September 1982 and was re-elected.

Nevertheless, throughout this period the Dutch managed to patiently carry on despite considerable public dissent over the NATO decision to deploy Cruise missiles on Dutch territory. The Dutch faced difficult public expenditure constraints after the peaking of their gas revenues and were grappling sympathetically with high unemployment. I found in 1977, as President of the Council of Foreign Ministers in the European Community, that it was easier to get quick decisions from the interim Dutch Government in the Hague than from the Labour Cabinet in London. Despite criticisms of its system, the Netherlands is well governed.

The critics of proportional representation also complain that in the Federal Republic of Germany, the German Liberals (the FDP), who have not won a single constituency seat since 1957, are nevertheless always represented in Parliament through the national list, since they get over 5 per cent of the vote and have been in government for most of the post-war period. The FDP is criticized too for switching from support of the Social Democrats (SPD) to the Christian Democrats (CDU) between elections. This criticism goes to the root of the different approaches to coalition government. The German system is geared to creating only majority Governments; one party alone rarely achieves power. In 1980, when Helmut Schmidt began to lose his dominant influence as Federal Chancellor because of the leftward shift within the SPD, the FDP began to look towards the Christian Democrats and then coalesced with the CDU/CSU. This was their sanction and they could argue that they were safeguarding the electorate's wishes. If the SPD moves back away from the left towards the centre and distances itself from the Greens, the FDP may well coalesce with it again to form a Government. In the meantime, the CDU–FDP coalition means that Chancellor Kohl can use the Liberals to keep Franz Josef Strauss's right-wing Bavarian CSU party in check.

This is no more than accommodation on the part of the Government of a shift of position within the political spectrum. In somewhat similar circumstances, when Jim Callaghan had lost influence after ceasing to be Prime Minister, the Labour Party shifted its political stance. Under our system that shift went far further than in West Germany; it led to a split within the Labour Party and the creation of the SDP. But the 7.78 million voters for the SDP/Liberal Alliance, as distinct from Labour's 8.45 million, could under our system get only twenty-three MPs in 1983, whereas a proportional result would have given us around 160 MPs and a considerable check on the absolute power of a Conservative Government. In the German system, despite the growth of the Greens, government policies remained stable, moving around the centre of German politics. In the UK the swings of the political pendulum have, by contrast, had savage consequences for the steady application of industrial and social policies designed to produce a long-term return. We cannot go on brushing aside the case for reforming our UK system of government.

Parliament, both the House of Commons and House of Lords, is the only major structure in British public life that has remained virtually unchanged since the Representation of the People Act in February 1918. Then 8.4 million women over thirty were for the first time allowed to vote, and 5 million male voters were added to the existing 8 million. This was followed in 1928 by the decision to let women over twenty-one vote. The last real chance for reform of Parliament came with the 1916 Speaker's Conference presided over by the Speaker, Sir James Lowther, at the suggestion of Asquith. The Conference recommended proportional representation in rural areas unanimously and the Alternative vote in the boroughs by eleven votes to eight. The Commons rejected proportional representation five times, but did support the Alternative vote – whereby one votes 1, 2, 3, 4 and so on in order of preference in single constituencies – by a majority of only one. The Lords rejected the Alternative vote and reinstated proportional representation in the Bill. Lloyd George was reluctant to deal with the question of electoral reform for two reasons. He was worried about the Conservative reaction to the Conference's suggestions, and not without reason; the Chairman of the Unionist Party, Sir Arthur Steel-Maitland, had circulated a note stating that the Speaker's proposals would be 'absolutely disastrous' to his party,[1] while Carson had circulated a petition that condemned the proposed changes. But the second reason was to do with Lloyd George himself.

Lloyd George disliked the idea of proportional representation because he feared it would bring into Parliament a new group of people better left outside, and would act as a catalyst in breaking up the established two-party system. So the Liberal Party helped to secure its defeat in the House of Commons; in the words of the historian Robert Blake, 'The party has been kicking its collective self ever since. And Britain has bumbled along to this day with what is virtually a unicameral sovereign legislature elected on the first-past-the-post system – the least fair, most arbitrary and least democratic of all methods of election in the democratic world.'[2]

Parliament, unlike the other two-chamber systems of democratic government found elsewhere in the West, also suffers from a toothless upper chamber; the power of the House of Lords is largely illusory. Based on heredity and patronage, it is not defensible on democratic grounds, yet it is dangerous to ignore the pledge of abolition to which the Labour Party is fully committed. There is a strong case for a second legislative chamber with the power to revise draft legislation. House of Lords reform as suggested by the SDP/Liberal Alliance, with 50 per cent of the membership of the second chamber elected on the basis of proportional representation from the nations and regions of the UK, would be a worthwhile reform. This would be particularly true if prime ministerial patronage for the other half of its members was replaced by an independent commission charged with reflecting the varied interests and experience found within the UK. Such reforms would enhance its credibility as a genuine revising chamber, that checks rather than challenges the authority of the House of Commons.

It is also important that the UK should start the process of devolution with the early establishment of a legislative Parliament in Scotland and should make progress towards devolved government in Northern Ireland, Wales and the English regions. The SDP/Liberal Alliance is committed to incorporating the rights and freedoms of the European Convention of Human Rights into the laws of England and Wales, Scotland and Northern Ireland, as well as introducing a Freedom of Information Act.

Coalition government is sometimes criticized in the UK for being an undemocratic bargaining process. Following an election in West Germany, even when the two parties that have been governing in coalition meet to form another coalition, a period of negotiation is normal. Although the meetings are held in private, no reader of the newspapers or watcher of television is unaware of the controversial issues in the negotiated programme. There are none of the normal connotations of 'smoke-filled-room' negotiations about these pre-coalition meetings; they meet within a structured negotiating framework.

The original six countries that formed the European Community at the Messina Conference in 1955 have a long history of negotiating programmes and policies. The British found the openness of the European Community in 1973, when we eventually joined, rather unsettling. In Brussels, where the day-to-day negotiating takes place, the positions of the Governments are all known. The shape of the compromise, as it emerges from Council of Ministers meetings, is disseminated quite deliberately; leaking information is not an accurate description for this process. There is rarely any attempt to hold on to information tightly, and when there is, Ministers either meet alone or with only one or two official advisers. There is nothing in Europe approaching the 'lobby' system, whereby journalists in Westminster are continuously briefed on an 'off-the-record' (unattributable) basis. This system is a source of endless confusion. In West Germany, as in the US White House, there is a named Government spokesman who attends Cabinet meetings and gives a press conference afterwards. Since the Government is a coalition, the Liberal FDP and CSU coalition partners are represented by one spokesman as are government departments. The openness of politics in continental Europe is a marked contrast to the closed, secretive nature of British politics and is one of the attractive features of coalition politics.

To compare such systems with the British system is difficult because the attitudes behind the two systems are so different. To advocate introducing proportional representation in the UK as a marginal change, taken on grounds of fairness alone, is to cheapen a great and far-reaching constitutional change. As there are dangers of claiming too much for proportional representation, so there are also dangers in underplaying the profound nature of the changes in attitudes that will follow. Once introduced, it will in time transform British politics. Since this is exactly what most of those who advocate it want, there are no advantages in underselling its potential.

Public opinion appears to be growing more critical of our political system. Comparing 1973 with 1985, the Constitutional Reform Centre has published findings showing that whereas there is growing public confidence in the instruments of the state – the courts, the armed services, even the police and the Civil Service – confidence in the political parties has declined. The critics of proportional representation sometimes claim that extremism manifests itself under proportional systems and that Hitler rose to power under this system. In fact Hitler never did win a majority of seats under proportional representation. A truer criticism of the system that operated in pre-war Germany is that it tended to reinforce existing divisions within society and to keep them rigid. The Nazis gained 5.5 million more votes in 1930 than in 1928. If Germany, however, had had the British system, the Nazis would have won a huge majority, perhaps taking every seat in July 1932, when they were the biggest party. They had then a 16 per cent lead over their nearest rivals, twice as much as any British party has had since the war. The critics of proportional representation make less headway with generalized criticism than with specific criticisms of particular systems. Their success perhaps owes much to a tendency by some advocates of proportional representation to play down the virtues of the system.

The SDP/Liberal Alliance, in its selection of the Single Transferable Vote as the system that, we believe, should be adopted in the UK, has had as its leading criterion the desire for a system which would give better government. Public disenchantment with political parties and the way in which the party machines have become the preserve of the activists in recent times for both the Labour and Conservative Parties, contributed to our rejecting arguments for any form of party list. We came down against even a topping-up list element, as in West Germany, which does assure total proportionality.

Proportional representation has to be seen in the context of changing attitudes in our country and as a means of providing us with a framework for a better standard of government. The experience of other countries indicates that it does not inhibit radical decisions, nor is it a recipe for paralysis. The most radical post-war foreign policy initiative was *Ostpolitik*, first taken by the Grand Coalition of Christian Democrats and Social Democrats in the Federal Republic of Germany when Willy Brandt was Foreign Minister. It was carried on through thirteen years of the Social Democrat/Liberal coalition, and now continues under the Christian Democrat/Liberal coalition. It was a difficult and dangerous policy initiative, on which there was no public consensus in the early stages. The public consensus that now sustains the policy was built up patiently by courageous political leadership. The economic consensus that came after the SPD Bad Godesberg Conference in 1959 around the principles, though not the execution of the 'social-market' economy, was built up equally patiently.

The 1979 NATO theatre nuclear-weapons modernization programme has presented difficult moral as well as strategic choices for all the participants. Though the British Government had no parliamentary difficulty with the decision, there is no evidence that our system has been more successful in convincing the public than those of the West German, Dutch, Belgian and Italian Governments. In Italy agreement has been easiest, but all four Governments have had to make a constant effort to inform, sway public opinion and negotiate within their coalitions in a way that the British Government has not had to do. It is not surprising that the British Government's attitude to defence is far closer to that of the Reagan administration than that of any other European Government.

Some of the harsh economic readjustments necessary in all Western European countries have been made with surprisingly high levels of consent in Holland and Belgium. Wherever one looks it is hard to find evidence to support the caricature of the centrist, coalition-minded European politician as a dithering, indecisive, broken-backed figure. What Michael Foot depicts as 'sitting in the muddled middle, playing on the fuddled fiddle' is far more likely to emerge from Labour's present coalition of incompatibles.

Both Labour and Conservative politicians quite obviously now have deep divisions within their parties, yet both feel bound to pretend to publicly agree while frequently disagreeing. Coalition politicians do not have to pretend to always agree, nor do Liberals and Social Democrats within our Alliance. The strength of the SDP/Liberal Alliance is that we have common objectives but do not have to pretend to be one party in total unanimity on every issue. What we in the Alliance have to negotiate are open and honest compromises to fulfil an agreed programme for government. Coalition politics represents a completely different style of politics; not only is it far less ideological, but it also puts a higher premium on facts and research.

An absolute essential for better government in the UK is a better information base for wiser decision-making. The true radical who wants to make changes has to act on well researched evidence. Much continental European success stems from the high quality of the countries' civil servants, who give continuity to the political process. Too much of the

British Civil Service effort has gone into outwitting the ideological nature of the political masters.

The SDP/Liberal Alliance has developed a system which we call Community Proportional Representation.[3] This involves preferential voting in constituencies that correspond to natural communities in order to produce a reasonable degree of proportionality between the competing parties' share of the votes and share of seats. This system avoids grouping constituencies on a purely arithmetical basis, which would ensure very close to perfect proportionality but would make little sense to people on the ground. There is merit in representing in Parliament a definable geographical entity, an area that sees itself as a community, but the existing constituencies are by no means always reflective of a community. Take my own experience.

I was elected in 1966 to represent the Sutton constituency of Plymouth, when the city only had one other constituency, Devonport. The city boundary was then expanded to include Plympton, where I was born, and Plymstock, which had previously been in Devon. For the 1974 election Plymouth was back to having the three constituencies – Sutton, Drake and Devonport – that it had last had at the 1945 election, though the boundaries were now different. After the City of Plymouth lost its status as a local authority with responsibility for Education and Social Services in 1973 and was absorbed into Devon, new ward boundaries had to be drawn up and by the 1983 election, the boundaries of the constituencies had been changed again to reflect these new wards. Confusingly, however, the traditional names of the constituencies were retained. In the space of twenty years, therefore, from 1966 to 1986, representing the City of Plymouth as an MP, I have represented all those parts of the city which originally made up the two constituencies Sutton and Devonport from 1951 to 1970, and some voters have been covered by three separate constituency boundaries. If that account has confused you as the reader, just imagine how confusing it has been for the average Plymothian. Constituency boundaries on occasions have crossed one long street only to cross back again near the end of the street. People in the same house have lived in the space of ten years in three different constituencies by boundary and by name.

Plymouth is currently represented by one Social Democrat and two Conservatives. Under a system of Community Proportional Representation the City of Plymouth would have its three constituencies grouped.

Taking the same voting pattern and candidates as in 1983, as a result of people voting 1, 2, 3, 4, 5 and so on down the list of fourteen names Plymouth would probably have been represented by one Social Democrat, one Conservative and one Labour MP. In Cornwall, where there are five constituencies, the consultations that the SDP/Liberal Alliance has had so far indicate that people would prefer to group across the whole county, for there is a strong sense of community and a feeling that Cornwall is one unit. At the last election Cornwall sent back to the House of Commons four Conservative MPs and one Liberal MP. Taking the same voting pattern and candidates voting 1, 2, 3, 4, 5, etc., down a list of twenty-two names, Cornwall under Community Proportional Representation would probably be represented by two Conservative MPs, one Liberal, one Social Democrat and one Labour. So Labour, instead of having no MP west of Bristol, as under the present system, would under Community Proportional Representation have some MPs in the far South-West, and rightly so. There would also be some Conservative MPs in Glasgow, whereas at present there are none. No longer would we have the absurd situation where electors in cities and large rural areas can be disenfranchised and have within reasonable travelling distance no MP who is a member of their party.

Bristol, where there are four existing constituencies, under our community grouping system would be taken as a single unit, as would, for example, Edinburgh with its six constituencies. Bigger cities would have to be split into groups, bearing as close a community interest as possible. By having these larger groupings of existing constituencies in the urban areas, one is able to keep proportionality overall in the UK, with somewhat smaller groupings in the rural areas where travelling distances are long. The critics argue that this is anomalous, but in striking a balance as to what is a genuine community, one cannot reasonably ignore geography. The tradition of having a smaller number of electors in rural, as compared with urban, seats has been long accepted when fixing existing boundaries, for example. Caithness and Sutherland, at the uppermost tip of Scotland, had 23,288 electors, whereas Gloucester had 74,268 electors.

There are a few constituencies where it is very difficult to group. The three island constituencies – Orkney and Shetlands, the Western Isles, and the Isle of Wight – do not group naturally with the mainland. In these three cases there is a strong case for accepting the Alternative vote and keeping the existing constituency as the electoral unit. There is too a case for exceptional treatment where the grouping of two constituencies creates a unit that is so large that there is little community interest by virtue of distance. Such may be the case with the Highlands, where if Caithness and Sutherland were grouped with Ross and Cromarty, the combined area would be more than twice the size of Skipton and Ripon, and with Richmond (Yorks), which would, under Community Proportional Representation, be grouped into two units. Grouping in the way described would not destroy the existing intimacy of the conscientious MP with his constituents.

One advantage of choosing the Single Transferable Vote is that it is a preferential system; the quality and views of the candidates are of considerable importance, and the voter can discriminate between candidates of a particular party or between parties. For example, traditional Labour supporters could drop a militant Labour candidate from their selection, and a traditional Conservative voter could drop a Monday Club right-wing Conservative candidate. SDP/Liberal Alliance voters could discriminate in their pattern of choice giving their preference within the Alliance to SDP or Liberal candidates. The critics of preference voting see it as undermining the authority of the party, encouraging individualism and reducing the power of the party whip. For many people this will be an advantage rather than a disadvantage. Again a balance has to be struck – politics is a group activity; there has to be a sensible degree of compromise between individuals. Some collective discipline is necessary, and few would deny that total freedom would lead to anarchy and ineffective decision-making in government. Experience with preference voting does not indicate that these potential problems are severe, and for many the alternative of strengthening the influence of party discipline and patronage (as happens within a list system) is undesirable.

If a system of Community Proportional Representation were introduced for the UK as a whole, it would increase the voice of minorities within the House of Commons. It would ensure that more constitutional nationalists represented Northern Ireland. With it might come more Sinn Fein MPs, but would that be wrong if we want to encourage the IRA to come in off the streets? The Welsh and Scottish Nationalists would continue to be represented, perhaps in slightly higher numbers than has been the post-war average. It would be very unlikely that the National Front or Communist Party would ever be strong enough to achieve representation but the remote possibility exists.

Representation of women would increase and would make the House of Commons a more credible institution. That 51.3 per cent of the UK population is represented by only 3.8 per cent of the House of Commons is a democratic travesty; it also contributes to bad government. Britain would have better policies for education and health if there were more women decision-makers, if for no other reason than that, through their children, they are more actively involved as consumers of public services than are men. Policies in every other area, from economics to defence, would also benefit from more women decision-makers. The record of proportional representation speaks for itself on this issue of involving more women. In the Netherlands women hold 14.6 per cent of the seats, and in Denmark women hold 25.7 per cent of the seats.

Ethnic minorities could also expect to be better represented in a House of Commons elected on the basis of Community Proportional Representation. Until there are black MPs, no amount of rhetoric about integration and eradicating discrimination will carry conviction. Of the 523 English parliamentary constituencies, fifty-two have New Commonwealth and Pakistan populations of 15 per cent or more. Brent South has 46 per cent, Ealing South 43.7 per cent, Birmingham Ladywood 42 per cent. In London, fourteen out of the thirty-two London Boroughs have New Commonwealth and Pakistan populations of 15 per cent or more. The number of black voters in the electorate as a whole is thought to be below 3 per cent. In at least thirty-three constituencies, however, it is the black vote that holds the balance and, with that, possibly the key to the overall election result. As the pressure mounts for the creation of black sections within the Labour Party, if there is no change, we may see pressure for a new political party devoted entirely to representing black interests. Perhaps one of the most constructive ways of channelling this frustration would be an all-party campaign for electoral reform to benefit our black citizens.

Electoral reform cannot, however, be limited to voting for the national Government; it is urgently needed in local government as well. It is in this area that extremism is currently most rampant, and because of this government is bad. It is also in local government that the change to proportional representation would be the easiest to achieve, for local councils operate on the basis not of an executive decision-making body overseen by a legislature but of a corporate decision-making body, and votes at either full council or committee level are taken as the authority for executive decision-making.

The evidence of electoral distortion in local government is overwhelming.[4] In the 1982 council elections in Islington Labour won 51.9 per cent of the vote and took fifty-one out of the fifty-two seats; the 49 per cent of people who voted for other parties were represented by a single seat. The turnout had only been 40 per cent, and the council had therefore been elected by only 20 per cent of the people. The single seat was won by an SDP candidate, who was then denied the normal rights of an opposition member in local government. In the 1982 council elections in Kingston the Conservatives won 52.4 per cent of the votes, but took forty out of the fifty seats. The turnout had been 46.5 per cent and so the council was elected by only 25 per cent of the electorate. In Lambeth the result was even more dramatic. The Conservatives won 39.4 per cent of the vote and won twenty-seven seats. The Labour Party, with 33.2 per cent of the vote, won thirty-two seats. The SDP/Liberal Alliance, which received 26.9 per cent of the vote, won only five seats. The GLC provides another example of misrepresentation. In the 1981 election Labour won 41.8 per cent of the vote and took fifty seats. The Conservatives took 39.8 per cent of the vote and won forty-one seats. The Liberals, with 17 per cent of the vote, only won one seat. Under a system of proportional representation the result would have been: Labour forty-five seats, Conservative forty-three seats, Liberal four seats, resulting in a balanced council in which Ken Livingstone would never have been able to immediately displace the Labour leader.

The critics of proportional representation in local government attack the concept because it leads to what they term 'hung' councils. They should remember that since the 1985 council elections twenty-six out of thirty-nine shire counties have had councils without an overall majority under the present system; these councils have successfully governed their shires since the election. The largest party cannot always guarantee a majority in these councils, but that is no bad thing. There is more independent voting, which is irritating for the leaders, but it does allow local councillors to exercise their judgement.

Proportional representation would immediately end the polarization that is so marked in some of the most extreme areas of local government. Had it existed in Liverpool, Labour would have been denied its overall majority, for by winning 46 per cent of the votes cast it would not have won 60 per cent of the seats. The sorry problem of urban decay has been exacerbated by party dogmatism. More important, had we experienced good local government, the trend towards ever increasing central government interference would never have begun.

The steady acceleration of central government power has been fuelled by two factors. First and foremost is the unwillingness of central government to change the financial arrangements for local government and to replace it with the single most viable and self-sufficient form of local financing – local income tax. This unwillingness to change the system has been fed by the centralizing tendencies of national politics, irrespective of whether they have been Labour or Conservative. It has also been powerfully sustained by the Civil Service, which wants to retain and build up its own power base. Some have argued for keeping the present rating system by pointing at extremist, badly governed councils. Local income tax will probably come only with proportionally elected councils, which people can trust with the power to tax personal incomes.

Bad decisions will still be made under the best designed proportional-representation systems, whether covering local or national government. Genuine political differences will still exist, and rows, ill feeling and abuse will still surface. But better government is far more likely to emerge from the introduction of proportional representation locally and centrally than from sticking with the failed existing system. The link between majority government and better government is real, and it is vital that this link should be fully developed if we are to unify as well as to revive the fortunes of the United Kingdom.

4 National Security

A country seeking greater unity cannot hope to do this while it is divided on the all-important questions raised by national security. Defence policy, on which there was broad all-party agreement from 1939 until 1979, is the latest casualty of our political divisions. Neither the Conservative Government nor the Labour Opposition speaks for the majority of this nation about the critical areas of nuclear deterrence, nuclear arms control and how the UK should respond to the attitudes and initiatives of President Reagan and General Secretary Gorbachev. Public opinion is not static on these issues, but people do not like Mrs Thatcher's perceived subservience, or Mr Kinnock's antagonism, to the United States. Most people are more European-minded when it comes to defence than over other areas of policy. The opinion polls show majority support for Britain's remaining a nuclear-weapon state – retaining Polaris but cancelling Trident – and for accepting Cruise missiles if they cannot be negotiated away, provided British control is assured through a dual-key mechanism.

Britain's defence budget faces a serious crisis requiring difficult and painful decisions, which Michael Heseltine, when in office, continually postponed. The 1985 target of 'level funding', or a real-terms 'stand-still', for defence expenditure over the next three years had been abandoned in January 1986 with his agreement. In 1986 the Government is making sizeable cuts, amounting to a total of £1.2 billion in real terms by the end of 1988–9, the equivalent of a 7 per cent cut. This poses a major threat to existing conventional defence projects if the Trident commitment remains unchanged, and if we continue to refuse to negotiate with the Argentinians over a possible sharing of sovereignty of the Falkland Islands or transfer of sovereignty to the UN. The cost of maintaining the present 'Fortress Falklands' was £552 million in 1985–6; although this sum is forecast to fall, it will still be £192 million in 1988–9.

The impending crisis over the defence budget will probably be even more serious. The Government's inflation assumptions are very optimistic – 4 per cent for 1986–7, 3.5 per cent for 1987–8 and only 3 per cent for 1988–9. If a 5 per cent Forces pay rise were agreed rather than the assumed 4 per cent, then roughly £200 million would have to be diverted from other parts of the defence budget. Similarly, a 10 per cent sterling depreciation against the dollar in 1986–7 would add about £300 million to the real-terms cost of Trident. Like the cuckoo in the nest, it promises to take more and more from other parts of the defence effort.

The Ministry of Defence will have to undertake a major reassessment of existing spending priorities. Against such a background it will be hard to contain the bitter party political wrangle that lies ahead over defence strategy. National security looks certain to be a live issue for the next few years. The next general election in 1987 or 1988 will determine whether Britain remains a nuclear power. The decision will have profound implications. It must be taken not in the narrow context of domestic politics but in the context of how the UK sees its own role in Europe and Europe's role in relation to the United States and the Soviet Union.

Ever since the May 1980 Labour Special Conference it has been clear that Labour is intent on unilaterally abandoning nuclear weapons. That commitment, put to the electorate for the first time by Michael Foot in 1983, will be stated again by Neil Kinnock but this time in an even more extreme form, as Labour is now also committed to the removal of all American nuclear bases from the UK.

Try as some will to evade or avoid the matter at the next election, the question of whether the UK should retain the capacity to remain a nuclear power will have to be faced. The argument over the cancellation of Trident is a secondary issue. The prior question is, quite simply, should the United Kingdom give up all its nuclear weapons – for that is what Labour intends to do by cancelling Trident and dismantling Polaris. It is also what is implied by refusal to contemplate replacing Polaris when the last of the four submarines becomes too old to continue in service, on present plans in 1997.

The UK Government decided to develop an atomic-energy programme in 1945. This became a nuclear-weapons programme in October 1946, after the US Congress passed the McMahon Act, which called for strict American control of atomic energy. Despite the pooling of knowledge during the war years and certain specific agreements reached at Quebec and at Hyde Park by Roosevelt and Churchill, the British sensed that they were being excluded from the development of atomic weapons. Prime Minister Attlee called a small meeting of Ministers to discuss the building of a gaseous diffusion plant for the enrichment of uranium. For reasons of cost it looked as if the plant was not going to be authorized. The Foreign Secretary, Ernie Bevin, arrived late at the meeting and, with a graphic turn of phrase that expresses so well all the psychological and political feelings that made Britain develop nuclear weapons, changed the mood of the meeting. 'PM,' he said, 'I don't care a damn about these arguments. No other Foreign Secretary should have to sit in front of the US Foreign Secretary and be talked to as I have been talked to by Byrnes. It shouldn't happen, and the only way to stop it is to have the plants in this country [and not in Canada, as the USA would have wished] with the Union Jack on the top.'[1]

It is easy to scoff at those sentiments, but those around that Cabinet Room table had lived through the perils and dangers of 1939–41, when the United Kingdom stood alone waiting for the USA to enter the Second World War. They remembered only too vividly that it was not until the US fleet had been attacked in Pearl Harbor on 7 December 1941 that President Roosevelt was able to persuade a reluctant Congress to declare war against Japan. It was only after Germany declared war on the United States on 11 December that Roosevelt obtained congressional approval to declare war on Germany later on that day. Some, like Major Attlee, who had fought in the First World War and would also have remembered that the US came into that war only in 1916, may even have recalled that the USA did not make its first attack on German positions until 28 May 1917. They believed that the UK should not rely on the US.

It is also worth remembering that the first nuclear arms race was not between the Soviet Union and the USA but between Nazi Germany on the one hand and Britain, the United States and Canada on the other. For those few people who knew of Hitler's atomic weapons programme, its existence was an ever-present menace throughout the war. So long as the Soviet Union has nuclear weapons, those who now challenge NATO's nuclear capacity should be wary of assuming that no country will ever again use them. They should ask themselves what would have happened if German scientists had been able to test a nuclear bomb before Hitler had taken his life on 30 April 1945.

It is easy to argue now that the atomic bomb should never have been used. But we should put ourselves in the position of the Allied leaders who had lived through the war against Germany and still faced the casualties and horror associated with the war against Japan. When President Truman told Prime Minister Attlee about his intention to drop an atomic bomb on Japan at the Potsdam Conference in mid-July 1945, there is no evidence that Attlee demurred.[2] Neither man knew much about the nuclear weapons programme, for the circle of those needing to know had been kept very small. Truman, as Vice-President, had not been told, until he took over after Roosevelt's death in April 1945, that the Manhattan project was to make a nuclear bomb. Prime Minister Attlee, until he won the July 1945 election, and despite having been Churchill's deputy, knew nothing about the purpose behind Tube Alloys, the code name for the Allies' Atomic Weapons Project.

In seeking to create a world without nuclear weapons after the war, those putting forward the 1946 Baruch Plan were never able to ignore one irredeemable consequence of the Hiroshima explosion: that even if the USA destroyed its atomic weapons, it would still know how to construct a bomb. The 1986 Gorbachev proposal to eliminate all nuclear weapons by the year 2000 will face that same problem. In discussions about the Baruch proposals the Soviet Union, not unreasonably, feared that the USA could quickly reconstruct a bomb if political or military relations deteriorated.

By 1946 mistrust between the two was already building up, and the USSR would not accept an American monopoly of nuclear knowledge. The Soviet atomic weapons development programme started in 1942, and the country's first atomic explosion was in 1949. A British bomb was first tested in October 1952, at Monte Bello in Australia. The first thermonuclear, or hydrogen, bomb was exploded by the USA in November 1952, the Soviet Union following in August 1953. France first tested a nuclear device in 1960 and China in 1964. India has exploded one nuclear device, claiming it was for peaceful purposes. Israel, South Africa and Pakistan have probably not yet tested, but all have the capacity to assemble a nuclear weapon, with the near certainty of its being effective. There are other countries that could, over the next five years, develop a similar capacity.

A decision about British nuclear policy cannot be sensibly taken without reference to French nuclear policy. France's desire to become a nuclear-weapon state, with an inevitable time lag because of its limited involvement in nuclear issues during the war, was motivated by exactly the same factors as those that determined the British decision. The initial French decision to carry out a nuclear test explosion was taken by a socialist Prime Minister, Felix Gaillard, in the Fourth Republic in April 1958, not, as often believed, by General de Gaulle, at the start of the Fifth Republic. The political, social and economic factors that combined to make Britain and France decide to become, and then to remain, nuclear-weapon states were very similar. Both countries' political leaders have never believed that it is prudent to rely in perpetuity on the readiness of the USA to risk itself for Europe. Successive Prime Ministers and Foreign Secretaries have believed it essential for Britain to retain nuclear weapons as part of NATO's nuclear deterrent strategy. In France, while the position of independence set out by de Gaulle will not change, each President since Pòmpidou has been content to associate increasingly with NATO. European political leaders have all felt that we are more likely to bind the USA into the defence of Europe if there is a European contribution to nuclear deterrence. Nothing is stranger than to see some of those most hostile to the USA, those concerned that Britain should not become the fifty-first state of the Union, being prepared to put all their trust in the American nuclear guarantee.

The proverbial man from Mars, looking down on the 22 miles that separate Dover from Cap Gris Nez (now to be linked by a tunnel), would be amazed that Britain and France do not have an integrated defence policy. They are both nuclear-weapon states, both members of the European Community, both obligated by the Western European Union Treaty to come to each other's defence, yet they have no relationship, formal or informal, over nuclear weapons or nuclear strategy.

It was Prime Minister Mauroy who in 1981 urged Europeans to reflect on 'the perspective of [Western Europe as] a political whole mounting an autonomous defence'.[3] That concept of autonomous defence stems from persistent French anxiety about the American commitment to Europe. The anxiety is shared in Britain, though not felt with the same intensity and less often publicly voiced. Whatever weight one gives to concern over whether the USA really would commit itself to Europe in a crisis that did not directly threaten it, it cannot be denied that the stronger NATO is in both its conventional-deterrent and its nuclear-deterrent strategy, the less likely is it that the US commitment will ever be put to the test. We are now readier to co-operate in Europe over conventional defence equipment, but no such European effort is undertaken over nuclear defence equipment. France and the UK have gone their own way over nuclear deterrence.

There are, sadly, few signs that Western Europe is reflecting seriously on the implications of developing a greater autonomous defence capacity, particularly in relation to nuclear policy. Whereas Britain and the United States have a close relationship on nuclear matters, both countries appear to want it to remain bilateral. In recent years a slow and tentative dialogue about some aspects of nuclear strategy has developed between France and the Federal Republic of Germany. This is welcome, but it is insufficient without the UK and can never encompass nuclear weapons themselves, since the Federal Republic of Germany is, and wisely wishes to remain, a non-nuclear-weapon state.

France has had a private, varied and edgy relationship with the United States over nuclear matters; this can, and should, be improved. The fact that there is almost no nuclear co-operation between Britain and France cannot be blamed on US–British agreements restricting the exchange of information to other countries. If Franco–British nuclear co-operation became close, the USA would not prevent the sensible exchange of nuclear information. It is therefore essential that the nuclear issue, and bilateral co-operation and collaboration on nuclear matters, should become a major agenda item every time a French President and British Prime Minister meet to discuss political issues.

Edward Heath tried first to put these topics formally on the agenda in the early 1970s but met with tremendous institutional resistance in London. At Guadeloupe in January 1979 Carter, Schmidt, Callaghan and Giscard D'Estaing discussed nuclear questions more fully than ever before. Ironically, it is the Soviet Union that is now forcing the UK and France to devote time to discussing their shared interests by giving our nuclear forces prominence in Soviet–American arms-control negotiations in Geneva. As a result, there have been spasmodic discussions between France and Britain about how to influence, or keep a distance from, the primarily US–Soviet negotiations – INF, START or Strategic Defence. There has been a particular emphasis on how to thwart Soviet attempts to count French and British deterrents in with those of the USA. But these discussions are tactical and are no substitute for a sustained attempt to understand each other's strategic philosophy.

There is considerable scope for sharing knowledge and equipment manufacture between France and Britain and for avoiding the duplication of research and development costs. There would be advantages in some informal linkage over targeting and the timing of patrols and refits. The British defence budget will fall in real terms, at 1984–5 prices, from a £17.4 billion out-turn in 1985–6 to a planned £16.2 billion in 1988–9, a sizeable reduction that acknowledges our reduced economic status. Within that budget the scope for spending on nuclear armaments will be much reduced. A more modest nuclear role should be part of such economic realism. Yet with the Trident programme we are embarking on a substantial increase, by comparison with Polaris, in warhead numbers, megatonnage and cost.

Those who believe in NATO's nuclear deterrent but argue that we should give up our own nuclear weapons, concentrate on conventional defence, and rely solely on the US guarantee, have an economic case. This is a view held by some military commanders to whom the political ramifications matter less and who want to get on with their job of improving NATO's and our own conventional forces, on which they spend most of their time and effort. The military, while expecting politicians to grapple imaginatively and constructively with nuclear matters, accept that these are matters of political judgement, traditionally an area where the views of the Heads of Government dominate. The quality of the nuclear deterrent, the degree of certainty of penetration that is acceptable, its destructive capacity and its targeting and control are political, not military, issues. If the politicians decide that our system must be able to hit Moscow, that dictates the choice of Trident. If politicians are prepared to settle, as they now should, for other Soviet targets, that will allow for a less costly and smaller nuclear investment by Britain as part of NATO's overall deterrent strategy.

It is an indictment of the way in which we still see our European destiny that there was so little Anglo–French discussion before Britain bound itself to the USA over Trident. For the next thirty years, unless it is cancelled, the US procurement link will again dominate UK military thinking. There was little discussion about Britain's sharing in the development of, and possibly acquiring, the French submarine ballistic missile and virtually no Anglo–French discussion about a European Cruise missile, whether with a conventional or a nuclear warhead, sea-, air- or ground-launched. There has been some Franco–German discussion about possible Cruise development, but as yet neither Britain nor France has made the key decision, dictated by our common European destiny, to co-operate on nuclear defence matters. It is high time that we did.

It was likely that there would be little Anglo–French nuclear co-operation until France had caught up with, and probably even surpassed, the British nuclear capability. The moment for co-operation came in the early 1970s, but even then no discussions followed on an equal footing, when there was no need for any French sense of inferiority. The 1974 NATO Ottawa Communiqué acknowledged for the first time that both France and Britain possessed 'nuclear forces capable of playing a deterrent role of their own, contributing to the overall strengthening of the deterrence of the Alliance'. Four French nuclear-powered ballistic missile submarines (SSBNs) had entered service in 1978, matching the four British Polaris boats; the number increased to six French SSBNs. Since 1983 three of these have been on patrol at all times, giving France, with its additional land-based missiles, a greater capacity than the UK in terms of megatonnage and warheads.

French and British strategic thinking has, however, been moving closer together on a number of matters. In 1978, as the shape of the SALT negotiations began to unfold, as the NATO theatre-modernization options started to become clearer, considerable common ground emerged between France and Britain. Neither of our countries believed in a US–Soviet Eurostrategic nuclear balance, being content to compare US and Soviet nuclear arsenals worldwide. Also, parity in nuclear weapons, in contrast to conventional defence forces, is an irrelevance. Sufficiency is a more appropriate concept, which is why we in Europe can think and talk in terms of a minimum deterrent. Both France and Britain were critical of Helmut Schmidt's speech to the International Institute for Strategic Studies in 1977, in which, without warning, he suddenly made the Eurostrategic nuclear balance respectable in some parts of NATO thinking. Louis de Guiringaud, the French Foreign Minister, spoke out in March 1978, in terms that exactly matched my own sentiments as British Foreign Secretary, saying that to endorse the Eurostrategic nuclear-balance concept would be 'equivalent to recognizing that the central strategic forces of the US do not protect Western Europe'.[4]

In 1978, in the context of SALT, France, Britain and West Germany made representations to the USA to keep open the Cruise missile option for NATO's European theatre-modernization decision, due in 1979. At that time there was no decision, not even among the technicians, about whether it should be sea-, air- or ground-launched, though the military had a predisposition to agree to land-basing. In the UK in 1978 the politicians noted the potential political problems in off-the-base deployment – a realistic assessment in the light of the protests staged around Greenham Common. From 1977–9 the UK Labour Government recognized that US–European theatre nuclear weapons would have to be modernized, not primarily in order to match Soviet SS20 deployment but to couple the US deterrent with Europe by having a new generation of US land-based missiles in Europe. Giscard D'Estaing, as French President, never had any doubt that US deployment would be necessary and made that clear at Guadeloupe. President Mitterrand has always been openly supportive of the NATO decision to deploy Cruise and the Pershing II missiles. The plans for modernization of NATO theatre nuclear weapons proceeded without controversy under the Labour Government from 1977 to 1979.

The replacement of Pershing I was seen as mainly a decision for West Germany, though it was becoming clear that in addition that country wanted its European allies to share the political burden of deployment and to accept Cruise or a new medium-range missile. While it is likely that Labour Ministers would have wanted to deploy Cruise missiles at sea, on submarines or on aircraft rather than on land, Denis Healey and other colleagues were well aware that these issues would have to be determined one way or the other by NATO late in 1979 and did not demur.

Although France had pursued under de Gaulle a wholly independent line on nuclear weapons, French policy began to change in the 1970s and to take account of the US–Soviet arms-control negotiations; in July 1976, for the first time, France accepted an admittedly very limited Franco–Soviet nuclear agreement to prevent accidental or unauthorized release of nuclear weapons. I signed a somewhat similar Anglo–Soviet agreement in September 1977 in Moscow. Both Britain and France were clear, throughout SALT II, that their nuclear forces should not be formally counted in with the US total. Giscard D'Estaing, though lukewarm in his support for SALT II, ensured that by the time the agreement was signed in 1979, he was able to assert, 'The independence of France's nuclear force is not affected in any way.'[5]

Both countries rightly resisted the Soviet Union's cynical shift in position when in 1982 it demanded that British and French forces should be counted in the INF negotiations. Both will now find it harder, particularly after the successful Reagan–Gorbachev meeting in Geneva, to escape the more logical Soviet demand that our nuclear weapons should be taken into account against the background of both the INF and the START negotiations. It is reasonable for Britain and France to stress that before they can give any consideration to cutting their warhead numbers, the two superpowers must have agreed deep cuts in their warhead numbers, since our forces are already near the minimum level required for a second-strike deterrent.

France and Britain both choose deliberately to operate their deterrents at levels lower than those of the superpowers. France espouses a policy of identifying the minimum punitive response necessary to deter an aggressor from launching an attack. This is in contrast to the maximum level of credibility thought necessary by the superpowers. The UK cannot deny the Soviet Union's interest in counting our nuclear weapons in with the total of US strategic forces because of their assignment to NATO, but nor can the Soviets deny that the UK's four Polaris submarines are different in kind, aiming only for minimum deterrence. Yet for all the differences in nuclear philosophy, it is increasingly hard to justify Britain's and France's detachment from the bilateral US–Soviet arms-control dialogue and their refusal to consider either the implications of their warhead numbers or the overall level of their nuclear megatonnage. This stance will become impossible if the USA and the Soviet Union make progress towards the political goal set by both Gorbachev and Reagan, that of a 50 per cent cut in strategic warheads.

In Britain, for all the stress of the Conservative Party on the independence of the British deterrent, the fact is that it is primarily a contribution to NATO's deterrent strategy. The illusion about its primary role stems from the somewhat artificial political requirement to have one Polaris boat constantly poised to fire. As long as the USA has submarines with that capability and NATO is in good shape politically, there is no need for the UK to maintain such a high state of readiness at all times. That condition would be necessary only at moments of tension or if NATO's political cohesion were frayed and it looked as if the Soviet Union might be tempted to exploit US–European divisions.

The key area now for Anglo–French nuclear discussions is not the party political debate in the UK about whether or not it should remain a nuclear-weapon state. That has little or no echo in France among socialist or communist politicians. The real issue for those in the UK who are prepared to consider replacing Polaris is what nuclear-weapon system would make most sense, both as a contribution to NATO and, *in extremis*, as a credible deterrent with French nuclear forces, were the USA to pull back from its nuclear guarantee to defend European territory.

Nuclear co-operation between the UK and France will not lead to a centralized command and control structure – the ultimate decision will reside with the French President and the British Prime Minister. But what needs discussing is Europe's strategy, both when the US guarantee is operating and if it is ever called into question. To what extent should Europe attempt to influence the USA's strategic thinking and command and control procedures in Europe?

There is already a dual-key system controlling the US Lance battlefield nuclear weapon deployed with British forces in West Germany. UK public opinion believes strongly and rightly, with the SDP, that we should have a dual-key arrangement for US Cruise missiles deployed in the UK. Since France has no US nuclear weapons on its territory, the situation does not arise. West Germany, which formerly had dual-key on Pershing I as well as Lance, decided in 1979 against having dual-key on Pershing II because both it and Cruise have the range to reach Soviet territory, and Helmut Schmidt's Government did not welcome such involvement for political reasons.

As a nuclear-weapon state the UK is in a different category from West Germany, Italy, Belgium or the Netherlands, which have Cruise missiles on their territory. An accidental firing from the territory of a nuclear-weapon state would risk certain nuclear retaliation against that state, whereas an accidental firing from the territory of a non-nuclear-weapon state would be more likely to invite retaliation against US territory. For that reason among others, past UK Governments have insisted on being involved in the control mechanism for all US missiles based on UK territory: in the early 1960s, for example, RAF personnel were involved in the firing mechanism for Thor missiles stationed in the UK, in association with USAF officers. The UK, having wisely refused to follow de Gaulle's nationalistic stance in relation to US bases, must be wary of ignoring the overwhelming wish of the British people to have their Prime Minister visibly in control of US missiles based in the UK. The same anxiety does not apply as much to US aeroplanes, since they can be recalled after take-off. It is the irreversibility of an accidental firing of a nuclear missile that causes understandable anxiety. Underlying this rather technical issue is the powerful force of nationalism. One of the reasons why nuclear weapons are more acceptable in France is that they are seen to be French in every possible way. The USA is the UK's strongest friend and ally, but Britain is not, and must never become, a mere appendage to US policy.

It is a central task of national political leadership to strike the right balance between independence and interdependence. The SDP is currently more in tune with public sentiment on the correct national posture for Britain than is Mrs Thatcher's brand of Conservatism, with its combination of animosity towards Europe and dependence on the USA. The Westland helicopter saga reinforced this impression for, from the start, the Prime Minister obviously preferred the American Sikorsky–Fiat deal to the European proposal. Labour's new commitment to remove US nuclear bases from the United Kingdom demonstrates its hostility to the US, but this is matched by its antagonism to Europe. It is hard to understand how Neil Kinnock can advocate such a move towards neutrality and the weakening of NATO. He cannot have forgotten the Soviet Union's invasion of Hungary in 1956, its incursion into Czechoslovakia in 1968, its masterminding of the suppression of the Polish Solidarity movement in 1980. The scant respect for freedom that the Soviet Union displays within its own sphere of influence should be a warning. It is a supreme optimist who believes that, given the opportunity, the Soviet Union would be any more respectful of freedom in countries at present outside its sphere of influence. President Mitterrand understands this, as does every other socialist Prime Minister in Western Europe, with the possible exception of the Greek Prime Minister, Andreas Papandreou. The fact that Neil Kinnock, like Michael Foot before him, does not wish to understand it raises a very grave question mark over his capacity to be Prime Minister.

A principled rejection of Labour's new defence policy was, for some of us, a critical factor in our breaking away to help found the Social Democratic Party in 1981. The SDP, since its foundation, has been committed to cancelling Trident. That decision stemmed from the fact that we never saw Trident as the natural replacement for Polaris – the Trident missiles are much larger, the megatonnage far higher and the number of warheads greater. In addition, the cost of Trident, much of it in US dollars, is a massive burden on the defence capital-equipment programme. It is already biting into the conventional defence budget, particularly that of the Royal Navy and the Royal Marines, and is also affecting the Army and RAF budgets. It was those predictable factors, in addition to the arms-control implications, that made me oppose the purchase of Trident throughout my period as Foreign Secretary from 1977 to 1979. I argued then, as I do now, that Cruise missiles, which had been first successfully fired from a US submarine in February 1978, were in the circumstances, the correct replacement for Polaris.

The SDP in Government is committed to cancelling Trident and to initiating open discussions with the French on all matters concerning nuclear weapons.[6] In particular we would want to talk to France before deciding what should replace Polaris. The belief that Trident should be cancelled, held by those committed to NATO's conventional and nuclear-deterrent strategy, is not confined to Social Democrats and Liberals. There is considerable unease over Trident costs within the Conservative Party. Yet Mrs Thatcher, not unlike Britannia, clutches Trident even tighter to her bosom, seemingly unaware of the damage that this commitment is starting to have on our conventional defence programme.

After the next election, should no one party have an overall majority, attitudes to Trident among Conservatives and to Polaris among Labour MPs would become subjects for discussion with the SDP/Liberal Alliance. The whole question of the deterrent strategy of the West Europeans within NATO could then beneficially be rethought and Anglo–French nuclear co-operation placed much higher on the political agenda. This could also be a unique opportunity to reopen some of the key issues raised in General de Gaulle's perceptive 1958 memorandum to President Eisenhower and Prime Minister Macmillan, proposing a three-power directorate and a relationship covering global nuclear planning. That memorandum was never given the consideration its contents deserved on either side of the Atlantic, but nor was it probably ever intended by its author to be taken seriously. Thirty years on, there should be fewer inhibitions, though it would be even more necessary to keep other European countries closely involved, in particular West Germany.

After a 1987–8 election the situation over the USA's Strategic Defence Initiative (SDI) research programme will also perhaps be a little clearer, and either we will have seen a strategic-arms agreement between General Secretary Gorbachev and President Reagan or we could be asking in Europe whether any USA–USSR strategic-arms accommodation is possible. We may know too whether the 1972 ABM Treaty is likely to be strengthened through a US–Soviet agreement to accept the continuation of research on space defence and whether the warning period for abrogation will be extended from six months to five years. This would mean that neither side could rapidly develop strategic defence systems in space following a breakthrough in the research programme. An increase in Soviet ballistic-missile defence capabilities in response to a US increase is not in the interests of either the UK or the French Government. It *is* in our interests that the ABM Treaty should be maintained and its interpretation clarified, so that the minimum deterrent force, which is all the French and British should aim for, can retain its credibility.

SDI is itself a reason for rethinking the case for purchasing Trident because if American research and deployment were matched by Soviet research and deployment, then the strategic viability of Trident during its thirty-year service period from the mid-1990s could change dramatically. After President Reagan's advocacy of 'Star Wars' in 1983–4 the strategic situation has become far more unsettled than when the initial decision was taken to purchase Trident C4 missiles in July 1980. That decision was itself modified in March 1982, when Mrs Thatcher's Government thought it right to purchase the longer-range D5 missile for the four British SSBNs, each capable of carrying sixteen missiles, with a theoretical total of 846 warheads. Since the British Government has said that it will place only eight warheads on each missile, there will be 512 warheads, still a significant increase over Polaris. There was, however, little reason to believe even in 1982 that the D5 missile might have to overcome defences in space rather than just to cope with improved Soviet ballistic-missile defence around Moscow, which it is well able to do.

Similarly, the situation has changed for France since July 1981, when President Mitterrand decided to construct a seventh SSBN during the period 1985–9, to be equipped with the advanced M5 missile and to be in service around 1994.

It was, therefore, understandable and correct for President Mitterrand, and initially Mrs Thatcher, to be deeply sceptical about President Reagan's advocacy of SDI research in order to create an impermeable defence shield. It was not, and is never likely to be, a specifically European ambition to embrace the SDI concept and abandon the more traditional arms-control strategy of trying to agree deep cuts in warhead numbers. President Mitterrand has wisely maintained that position and has been more robust than Mrs Thatcher in refusing to be forced into supporting the SDI concept by the lure of US dollars in exchange for SDI research. At the same time he has been more realistic than Mrs Thatcher about the likelihood of longer-term changes in the strategic environment and the need to rethink nuclear strategy in Europe.

Research under the SDI programme, despite the sceptics, may well come up with proposals for 'defences' against long-range inter-continental submarine-launched ballistic missiles that could affect the viability of Polaris or Trident. Although it would not provide an impermeable defence, it could have a disproportionate effect on a small ballistic-missile system's credibility. Research into defences in space is allowed under the 1972 ABM Treaty, though testing and deployment are not. (The Soviet Union has for some years proceeded with such legitimate research.) It becomes ever clearer, however, that if developed and deployed, such defences in space would not, as Mr Reagan has argued, make nuclear weapons 'impotent' or 'obsolete'. Most experts are dismissive about creating an impenetrable defensive shield but quite confident that 80 per cent or so of any incoming missiles could be destroyed.

Whatever the outcome of SDI research, it is unlikely to create strategic stability – rather the reverse. Fears will arise that a first strike will be more likely if missile defences are deployed and the risks of a devastating second-strike retaliatory action recede. Technological competition between West and East will increase. More important, there is no evidence that SDI will serve the interests, military, political or economic, of the European members of NATO, and there promises to be a growing sense of 'decoupling' from the United States. SDI may also weaken the credibility of the French and British nuclear-weapons systems.

It is inevitable too that a well endowed SDI research programme will develop technologies that could be as useful to offence as to defence; it would also accelerate the requirements, within NATO as elsewhere, for ever greater investment in the defence industries of resources of all kinds – financial, human and organizational. The initial SDI research budget of $26 billion over five years is, however, being cut back by the US Congress in 1986 to a total of nearer $14 billion, and the more ambitious space experiments are being postponed, as less money is available. Perhaps the only good thing that can be said for limited SDI research is that if a research breakthrough occurred the knowledge that a non-nuclear defence system could be deployed might make it possible for leaders to consider the dismantling of all nuclear weapons. But this theory is rather far-fetched. With luck SDI may be the bargaining counter that unlocks the US–Soviet stalemate and reverts to being a modest laboratory research programme.

Against this background Europe needs to establish very carefully, before being drawn into SDI programmes, the precise conditions of involvement. An unacceptable price for participation would be to become party to breaking the ABM Treaty or acquiescence in its circumvention or erosion. Six weeks before the November 1985 Geneva Summit Robert McFarlane, who was then President Reagan's National Security adviser, let it be known that the administration no longer considered that the ABM Treaty prevented the testing of devices, such as lasers and particle beams, that were not in existence when the treaty was drafted. Amid strong protest from the USA's European Allies, the Secretary of State, George Schultz, sought a compromise of sorts; it was declared that the United States did indeed believe that some testing was allowed but would in the meantime implement the treaty according to a strict interpretation of its terms. European allies are still left with the uncomfortable thought that the USA might breach the treaty at any time. Europeans should commit themselves publicly, as part of any SDI research they undertake, to act only in ways that will strengthen the ABM Treaty. They should openly affirm their wish for an amendment to extend to five years the period for warning of the deployment of any defensive systems. This is a reasonable price for our involvement in – and, by implication, political support for – the SDI research programme. Without such reservations Europe will aid those in the USA who want to scrap the ABM Treaty and go for the widespread deployment of ABM defences.

As a European response the Eureka programme is better than nothing, but it needs much more thought and the clarification of its intentions. It is, however, a response not so much to SDI as to Europe's progressive technological inferiority to Japan and the USA. If Europe is to redress the balance, it has to co-operate over aerospace, which is so closely linked with defence procurement. Here there is stronger motivation for

European co-operation than in some other industrial areas. Also it is an area of proven technological success for Concorde and commercial success for Airbus. Europe is hesitantly combining over helicopters, despite the Westland saga. The British have agreed with the West Germans and the Italians to combine over the new fighter aircraft. But we are not working closely enough on medium-range missiles, ever more important as the long-term future of the manned fighter aircraft is increasingly questioned.

In arms-control negotiations Cruise-missile verification has been a problem for some time. Cruise is not inherently more difficult to verify than multiple warheads, which are capable of destroying several targets with independent re-entry vehicles, each carrying up to ten warheads. The problem arises because of the existence of conventionally armed as well as nuclear-armed Cruise missiles, but it should not inhibit France and Britain from developing their own Cruise missile programme, for this is an issue that has also to be faced by the US and Soviet Governments, which have both now deployed substantial numbers of Cruise missiles, armed conventionally and with nuclear warheads.

The January 1986 call by Mr Gorbachev for a three-stage process of general or complete disarmament raises important and fundamental questions, which the British as well as the other three nuclear-weapon states should consider carefully and seriously. This is the first proposal for general and comprehensive disarmament since the McCloy–Zorin joint statement in 1960 and the subsequent Soviet and American drafts that were exchanged in 1961. The Soviet Union now accepts, for the first time, that both Britain and France could have intermediate forces until all nuclear weapons are eliminated. There is, therefore, a much stronger case than hitherto for reconsidering the question of whether Britain and France should build Cruise missiles themselves or purchase the technology from the USA. The Cruise missile offers a far better way forward, if Britain is to retain a minimum deterrent, than crippling our conventional defence effort with the Trident costs. If deployed forward in submarines, the missiles could threaten the Soviet Union from all points of the compass. Mobile Cruise missiles would be far more effective than France's existing fixed, land-based missiles, which will probably be phased out, and would be a modernization acceptable to the Soviet Union, since they need not increase the overall capacity of French nuclear force.

In the USA by the early 1990s over 140 ships and submarines armed with more than 2,500 launchers will be able to carry the nuclear-armed Tomahawk Cruise missile. Some 83 attack submarines will carry around 1,255 missiles, able to fire the missiles from standard 21-inch torpedo tubes or from 12 vertical-launch tubes, which will not reduce the torpedo load. Cruise missiles are seen by the US Navy as part of its strategic reserve – that is, those weapons that would survive massive nuclear exchanges. The Soviet Navy is also extensively deploying its equivalent of the Tomahawk Cruise missile. It is not essential for the Royal Navy to follow Polaris with a ballistic-missile system. Cruise missiles offer a sufficient capability for political realists to accept it as an adequate replacement for Polaris.

Neither France nor Britain can separate decisions about their military missile programmes entirely from the European civilian space programme. If they were to develop their own Cruise missile, it would be prudent for its ground-hugging TERCOM guidance to be independent of US mapping information. This means that the digital maps will need to be updated by information from European satellites. The alternative is to buy into American technology and build or purchase US Tomahawk missiles. The Royal Navy could fit them into existing attack submarines, to be fired from torpedo tubes, and could build in a vertical-launch capability in the attack submarines still to be built. Also, if the Trident missile were cancelled after the first hull had been built, or even if the second hull had gone beyond the point when it made no economic sense to scrap it, then Cruise missiles could be put into the section of the submarine designed to hold Trident missiles, which would be fitted out for vertical Cruise missile launch.

The need to think afresh, with the emphasis on Anglo–French and European co-operation, has been highlighted dramatically by Mr Gorbachev's 1986 three-stage proposals to eliminate all nuclear weapons. The Stage One and Stage Two proposals, besides representing a massive shift in the Soviet position, are ingenious and logical. Stage Three, the elimination of all nuclear weapons by the year 2000, has more than a tinge of propaganda to it. There is no hope that it will be reached unless there is trust – a commodity in short supply between nuclear-weapon states. It is, however, crystal-clear that if US and Soviet nuclear arms are to be subject to deep cuts, what Britain and France do is no longer marginal and cannot be ignored. The Soviet Union's proposals envisage that agreement on the first stage, lasting over the next five to eight years, would require the USSR and the USA to reduce by half the nuclear arms that can reach each other's territory. They would retain no more than 6,000 warheads on these delivery vehicles. The Soviet Union has further proposed that there should be complete elimination of American and Soviet intermediate-range missiles in the European zone, both ballistic and Cruise missiles, during this time. This means, in effect, that the USSR is now adopting the European part of the 1981 US offer of a 'zero option', but has rejected the US call for the elimination of all Soviet SS20 missiles not only in Europe but also in Asia. The Soviet Union appears to be prepared to accept British and French missiles on the European front in exchange for keeping its missiles on the Asian front. It is also requesting that, in exchange for accepting French and British nuclear weapons, the USA should undertake not to transfer its strategic and medium-range missiles to these countries, while Britain and France should pledge simply to maintain, and not to increase, their respective nuclear arsenals.

The Soviet Union has been most ingenious in turning the zero option to its own advantage in a way that it might have chosen when NATO first endorsed it. The European members of NATO, in accepting the 1981 zero option, took the risk that the USA might be seen to be decoupling from Europe. That risk remains in the modified Soviet proposals, for in exchange for the withdrawal of all Soviet SS20s and other Soviet theatre weapons from an area stretching from beyond the Urals to the East German/Czechoslovak frontier with Western Europe, European Governments would be forgoing the original motivation for requesting the USA to modernize its theatre weapons, which was to demonstrate the coupling of the US to NATO's deterrent by having American nuclear as well as conventional forces deployed on European territory.

The Soviet proposals on British and French weapons are logical, in that it would be absurd to pursue a US–Soviet agreement that the USA circumvented by simply selling either Pershing II or Cruise missiles to Britain or France.

NATO can certainly claim, with justice, that had it not responded to the Soviet SS20 build up with its own theatre-weapon modernization decision, and held to that decision steadily from 1979 to 1986 despite internal domestic protest, these 1986 Soviet proposals would never have been put forward. But now we who believe in multilateral disarmament have to be able to respond constructively to the Soviet Union or we will not be able to hold off the persistent attacks of the unilateralists, who declare that we are not serious about disarmament. There is too much in it for which NATO has long argued to portray it all as mere propaganda.

The Soviets are being realistic in asking France and Britain neither to give up being nuclear-weapon states nor to forgo our own theatre or strategic nuclear weapons. Britain should respond positively and start talking direct to the Soviet Union on those matters that are purely bilateral and not primarily for collective decision in NATO. We should be ready to declare a moratorium on future British nuclear tests in Nevada and express our readiness to restart the Comprehensive Test Ban negotiations with the USA and the Soviet Union. The fact that President Reagan is not yet ready to do this should not deter Britain. It is an independent decision for us to take and would provide a very useful lead for those Republican and Democratic Senators and Congressmen who are hoping to press the President to go along with an agreement to halt nuclear testing. The US and British Governments are dissembling when they claim there are still technical obstacles to verifying a test ban. The obstacles are political – President Reagan wants to go on testing and, sadly, so does Mrs Thatcher.

Were Britain to announce a readiness to forgo the Trident missile and start discussions with the French to explore the joint development of a Cruise missile, the UK would have to consider carefully whether to challenge the Soviet position that we should not be able to purchase the US Cruise. Under the Soviet proposal both Britain and France would be able to retain nuclear weapons with a range of more than 1,000 kilometres during Stage Two. There is nothing in the Non-Proliferation Treaty against such joint Franco–British development. But it would be a bad precedent for Britain to accept that there can be, in principle, no purchase of US missiles or technological exchange with us as a nuclear-weapon state. It is a legitimate Soviet interest to put the numbers of Cruise missiles into the overall bargain in Europe, but how we replace Polaris, whether by Anglo–French or Anglo–US co-operation, is not a legitimate Soviet interest. If Britain wanted to purchase the US Cruise missiles at Greenham Common prior to putting Cruise missiles on ships or on aircraft as the Polaris boats come out of service, that again is a British decision and not one for the Soviet Union. The USSR should confine its intervention to putting French and British nuclear forces under the same constraints governing overall numbers and megatonnage as would affect it and the US.

It is envisaged in the Soviet second stage from 1990 that all nuclear powers would eliminate their tactical nuclear weapons with a range or radius of action of up to 1,000 kilometres. The SDP has long advocated a battlefield nuclear-weapon-free corridor 150 kilometres wide on either side of the border and has nothing against this proposal for the elimination of all tactical nuclear weapons. Deployed forward, such nuclear weapons present us with a dangerous 'use or lose' dilemma. Once used, even if only overrun because of a border incident, they would unleash a devastating chain of events. Agreement on the proposed second stage would mean Britain's withdrawal of Lance and nuclear artillery from the British Army on the Rhine. France has decided to introduce Hades in 1992 as a Pluton replacement; it has a range of 350 kilometres as opposed to Pluton's 150 kilometres. This development, important for relations with West Germany since it can hit East German targets from French territory, also has implications for the British Army on the Rhine. The French would, under the Soviet proposal, have to forgo Hades. But it would still mean that Western Europe could have French and British theatre nuclear weapons after 1990, when US theatre nuclear forces had been withdrawn with Soviet forces. This would be an important European compensation for the perceived asymmetry, since the Soviet Union, which is a continental European and Asian power, would retain theatre weapons beyond the Urals and on the Chinese front, whereas the US could not base any intermediate missiles in Europe. In effect, it would make for a more realistic political bargain than the original zero option.

The proposed Soviet third stage, when all five nuclear states would give up all their nuclear weapons, has the obvious propaganda advantage of being able to talk of a nuclear-free world by the year 2000. Sadly, but realistically, it is an unlikely achievement. China, as much as the USA, would refuse to believe that the Soviet Union had dismantled its nuclear weapons, certainly until their relationship of deep mutual suspicion had dramatically improved. But if such a third stage could be agreed, Britain would have every interest in conforming, particularly if there had been progress in conventional disarmament. It looks likely that agreement will be reached in the Mutual and Balanced Force Reduction (MBFR) talks in Vienna, and there will be some success in Stockholm with respect to the framing of confidence-building measures. A more modest but achievable third-stage agreement would be to move towards a 'no first use' pledge, no longer an inconceivable dream. Such a pledge, to be worth anything, would have to be accompanied by the opening up of the respective military establishments, so that it could be seen that the armed forces of the countries concerned were no longer being trained on the assumption of the first use of nuclear weapons. If there is confidence in the conventional balance, and if tactical nuclear weapons had gone, it would be folly for either NATO or the Warsaw Pact to continue to plan, as they both currently do, on using nuclear weapons within days of facing a strong conventional attack.

It is essential, in responding to the Gorbachev initiative, that nuclear issues should be frankly discussed between Britain and France. It is not intended to create a forum in which to argue that France should rejoin NATO's integrated command structure. That decision will not be reversed. Within the political framework of the Western European Union, however, the seven countries that are committed by treaty to come to each other's military defence have a growing interest in discussing all topics, including the nuclear dimension of their commitment, and should not await the outcome of the US–Soviet negotiations. To stress Anglo–French collaboration on nuclear weapons is not to jeopardize relations with other European countries like West Germany, Italy, Belgium or the Netherlands. Nor is it to distance Britain from the USA or to split up or weaken the all-important Franco–German relationship. Above all it is not to minimize the vital importance of improving the Franco–British–German contribution to conventional defence in the Central Front in Europe. That co-operation has been strengthened by the German decision to stick with Britain and Italy over the next generation of fighter aircraft and not to be seduced by the French. If the French drop their own national fighter project and decide to combine instead on a European fighter, so much the better, but it would be hard to justify running both in harness.

The two nuclear-weapon states in Europe owe it to themselves, Europe, the US and the Soviet Union to work together a good deal more closely on both nuclear and conventional deterrent strategy than has been attempted hitherto. For the UK to opt out of the nuclear-deterrent debate and leave France as the only nuclear-weapon state in Western Europe would be to tilt the balance of European politics not just against UK interests but in a way that would make it harder for Europe to build an assured unity. Enlightened opinion in the USA and in West Germany would welcome stronger Anglo–French nuclear co-operation. Only the nationalistic dreamers of the unilateral disarmers in our two countries will continue to resist a direction dictated by both logic and history.

5 Industrial Regeneration

The United Kingdom has to create the conditions for economic growth without inflation. Lasting economic recovery, based on industrial regeneration, an incomes strategy and industrial partnership, will require a well-judged blend of innovation and stability. The privatization/renationalization debate, however, has emphasized political divisions over industrial policy even more than did the return of the Attlee Government in 1945. The folly of our present debate is that it does not address itself to the central question – how to improve the ability of British industry to compete. The U K's place in the international economy depends critically on the competitiveness of our trading performance in overseas markets.

The increasing deterioration in Britain's international trade position is the fundamental cause of Britain's relative economic decline over the last thirty-five years. The House of Lords Select Committee's Report on Overseas Trade made it clear that this decline is very serious and all the evidence suggests that it has gathered momentum in recent years. The Lords Report argued clearly that our decline can only be reversed by the introduction of a long-term strategy. It proposed a timescale of twenty-five years for a strategy whose objective would be nothing less than the 'comprehensive regeneration and reconstruction' of the industrial, commercial, and technological base of the British economy.[1] Such a long-term strategy will not happen without fundamentally changing the political structure of our country.

The lessons of West Germany's recovery after 1948 are fairly well known, but the post-war lessons to be drawn from the experiences of France, Italy and Japan also demonstrate the effectiveness of a sustained industrial strategy, uninterrupted by major shifts of political direction. In all four countries, there has been broad political agreement about the proper scope for and extent of state intervention in the market-place.

In France, Jean Monnet started the post-war planning strategy that has continued through and beyond the Fourth Republic despite all the changes in Government. The success of 'indicative planning' where government and industry set a flexible framework for building a modern infrastructure and reconstructing many traditional industries was helped by the political stability of the Gaullist Fifth Republic. A consensus as to the correct economic strategy crossed from the Fourth to the Fifth Republic; this was challenged in the early years of the Mitterrand administration, with its considerable programme of state intervention, but this programme was, however, quickly disowned and is no longer advocated by most French socialists.

In Italy, the 'Einaudi Line', inaugurated by the liberal economist, Luigi Einaudi, when he became Minister of the Budget in 1947, established the fundamentals of an economic strategy which was pursued, with few variations, for the next two decades despite constant changes of Government. The result was an annual growth rate of almost 6 per cent during the period 1951–71 and the development of a large manufacturing capacity virtually from scratch.

In Japan, nearly 40 per cent of the capital stock was destroyed during the Second World War. The role of the Ministry of International Trade and Industry (MITI) in guiding industrial recovery and concentrating resources on strategic companies was in a large part responsible for rebuilding the capital stock to its 1940 level by 1970.

In the UK, by contrast, as described in Chapter 1, the overall effectiveness of policies for industrial recovery after 1945 has been reduced by institutional instability and the lack of a broad political consensus on the general shape of industrial policies. Conservative Governments in the 1950s relied primarily on market co-ordination, seeking to encourage the independence of companies and to create a favourable environment for the free market. Under Labour Governments in the 1960s the emphasis shifted towards large-scale organization of and intervention in market processes. As the Confederation of British Industry (CBI) recently pointed out in *Change to Succeed*, to dispute which had been the superior approach was irrelevant 'since either would have been better than a policy which vacillated between them, as governments changed'.[2] British industry has been bewildered to see both 'bigness' and 'smallness' in fashion at different times in the 1960s and 1970s. Institutions like the Industrial Reorganization Corporation and National Enterprise Board came and went, and there have been frequent changes in the value and types of financial assistance on offer.

Greater continuity of policy towards economic regeneration is essential if there is to be a more stable context for industry and commerce to plan their investment and longer-term development. It is an alarming fact that this Government no longer regards manufacturing industry as a critical part of the economy. Since 1979 our factories have shed 1.5m jobs, as many as in the previous twenty years. Mrs Thatcher repeatedly now describes her record as one of strong economic recovery. Yet manufacturing investment by the start of 1986 was still 25 per cent and manufacturing output nearly 9 per cent below pre-recession levels. The balance of trade in manufactures had swung from a surplus of £2.7 billion in 1979 to a deficit in 1984 of £3.7 billion, after going into the red for the first time in Britain's industrial history in 1983. The deficit had risen to over £4 billion in the fourth quarter of 1985, and 1986 started with evidence of continuing decline in the capacity and competitiveness of British industry.

These developments do not apparently trouble the Government. In his evidence to the Lords Committee in May 1985, Nigel Lawson, the Chancellor of the Exchequer, stated bluntly that the relative decline of manufacturing was 'neither new nor unhealthy'. Furthermore, he declared that he was at a loss to understand the 'selective importance' attached by the opposition parties and some Tories to the manufacturing sector. The Government's indifference could not have been stated more plainly or clearly. The absence of any coherent industrial strategy was visible in the Westland and Leyland cases. In the former the Government was not even-handed between the European consortium and Sikorsky–Fiat, as it claimed to be. It wanted the Americans to succeed. The Government did want Ford to take over Austin–Rover and changed its mind only because of a backbenchers' revolt. The minimum importance they attach to the demise of manufacturing industry, least of all in dependent sectors such as machine tools and mechanical engineering, was evident in the Government's review of regional policy. The importance of the regions is that just under half of the Department of Trade and Industry's budget is devoted to regional support. It is also in the regions where unemployment is highest and our social and economic divisions are at their deepest.

Government spending on regional aid reached a peak of £1.5 billion (at 1982–3 prices) in 1975–6. Since then, however, regional assistance has declined under successive governments and in 1983–4 it stood at £617 million, a fall of £883 million in six years. Under the 1985 review, this trend will continue and it has been estimated that total regional aid will be reduced from £401 million in 1985–6 to £320 million in 1988–9 in cash terms. This Government, in 1980 and 1982, cut down the size of the eligible Assisted Areas, and reduced the scope of those remaining. In 1985, the regional-aid map was significantly redrawn to include new areas such as the West Midlands, but also to exclude some of the depressed parts of other regions. The result is a sharp reduction in many regions' overall eligibility for grants from the European Regional Development Fund (ERDF). This was particularly damaging as a growing proportion of regional support is being financed by loans and grants from the ERDF. In the spring of 1985, the Government announced with some fanfare that the British regions were to receive £100 million of additional development aid, with £89 million from the ERDF and the British Government contributing another £11 million. Despite Government assertions to the contrary, it is clear that the new European-based aid package was designed to compensate for reductions in the UK regional-aid budget. Those regions left with a smaller number of Assisted Areas, such as the North-East and the South-West, now suffer the double blow of reduced support from the British Government and from Europe.

Under the 1985 review, a large percentage of regional aid will in future be switched to Selected Financial Assistance (SFA) and proportionately less will be spent on universal Regional Development Grants (RDGs). A new and restrictive ceiling of £10,000 on the cost per job created under the RDG system has been introduced. In practice this means that companies will receive severely reduced automatic aid and will have to press for additional support, which will now be at the discretion of the Government. The CBI has argued that this shift will discourage firms from moving to depressed areas since many, especially new and small businesses, need the certainty of an automatic grant system to make the move worthwhile; if every penny of regional aid has now to be meticulously argued for, many companies will just give up trying and stay where they are.

The Government is right to argue that the cost to the taxpayer of job creation under the RDG system at £35–40,000 per job had become too high. The system had to be made more discriminating and selective. But instead of switching resources to relatively expensive Selected Financial

Assistance projects, the Government could have used the money to strengthen the more effective Office and Service Industry Grant Scheme. During 1982–3, £8 million was spent on forty-five projects under the Scheme involving an estimated 3,000 jobs in the Assisted Areas. The grants currently rise to a maximum of £8,000 per job created, and the nature of the Scheme means that most of them are net additional jobs to the Assisted Areas. It has been estimated that a partial switch in resources of £100 million in RDGs could create over 20,000 new jobs in four years. The service industries have received little regional backing – under £10 million per annum in the last three years – despite being one of the best sources of new employment in the recession; an expansion of the Office and Service Industry Grant Scheme could redress this omission in the Government's conduct of regional policy.

Exercises in housekeeping economics are no substitute for a considered regional strategy designed to encourage industrial recovery. Successive Governments have been forced to make further reductions in the real level of regional assistance because of immense difficulties in controlling the growth of total public expenditure. If we are to put the needs of industry first, as we should, then we have to face the implications of this decision for other areas of public expenditure.

Most people believe that this Government has, since 1979, been cutting public spending. The fact is that it has done nothing of the kind. Between the financial years 1979–80 and 1985–6, public spending rose in real terms – by just over 8 per cent if one takes the published planning totals at their face value;[3] these, however, give an incomplete picture. Purely by convention, asset sales are counted as negative public spending. Also adjustments must be made for reductions in the national insurance surcharge as well as for accounting changes in the treatment of housing and sickness benefits. When these factors are taken into account, the evidence suggests that public spending has grown by 15 per cent in real terms since 1979, or annually by nearly 2.5 per cent; or, another way of putting it, 50 per cent faster than the overall increase in national output since the Conservatives came to office.[4]

The fastest rate of growth in spending was from financial years 1979–80 to 1982–3 – principally caused by the escalating costs of unemployment, the impact of the 'Clegg' comparability awards and the boost the incoming Government gave to spending on its priority programmes – defence and law and order. But in the three most recent financial years since 1982–3, public spending has continued to grow on an adjusted annual basis by 1.5 per cent in real terms – a £5.9 billion increase since 1982–3 at current prices. Of this £1 billion is attributable to the half a million increase in the number of unemployed since 1982 and just over £1 billion to the continuing costs of the miners' strike.

Public spending has maintained a momentum which even a Government strongly against public spending has been unable to curb. Every year planned reductions have been published. Every year these plans have not been achieved. The best illustration of this is that, despite the common perception of 'cuts', local authority current spending has grown by between 1 and 2 per cent in real terms every year since 1979. Health and personal social services expenditure has grown by 19.5 per cent – £2.5 billion – in real terms between financial years 1978–9 and 1985–6. Education and science expenditure has suffered reduction in real terms of 5.6 per cent since 1979.

Far from industry being put first, it is industry, energy, trade, transport, housing and employment budgets that, taken together, have fallen by nearly 36 per cent in real terms over the last seven years. These are the biggest losers and they reflect an ominous development: because total public spending has consistently overshot its targets since 1979–80, the Government has been mainly obliged to squeeze capital programmes, in some cases quite drastically, to get back on course and stay in line with inflation. The harsh reality is that in future, if extra resources for industrial recovery and higher employment are to be found, on present trends this must mean not promising considerable increases in the rates of growth in big spending programmes such as health, social services and local-authority services. Industrial competitiveness depends critically on reversing the decline in capital spending and improving the quality of our capital infrastructure. But to achieve this we must recognize there will be a price to pay elsewhere.

More fundamentally, we need to restructure the predominant role of central government in economic decision-making. The success of economic federalism in both the European Community and the United States offers a proven way forward for us in the UK. It would be a practical way of evolving towards a system of regional government and as in the case of the European Community, the initial building blocks would be economic, industrial and commercial. Political development follows rather than leads. The Development Agencies in Scotland and

Wales may prove to be the first step in this process. Decentralizing a large measure of micro-economic power to the regions will be resisted by Whitehall, but the experience of Scotland, Wales and Northern Ireland – where there is already considerable economic independence – is encouraging. An important lesson from the US is that despite the free-market economics of the Reagan Administration at the federal level, a large number of state governments have actively pursued an interventionist strategy to develop their local economies and create employment.

In Europe, where distances are more similar to those in the UK, the diversity of the German *Länder* and other countries' regions has allowed for experiment and innovation. In England, the mechanism for achieving similar results, in the light of successful experience with the Scottish Development Agency (SDA) and the Welsh Development Agency (WDS), already exists. All that is needed is to establish more Regional Development Agencies, starting in the regions facing severe economic difficulty and with an already definable regional identity. In Scotland, 'Silicon Glen' at Greenock is an outstanding example of what has been created by the effective co-ordination of different policies under the auspices of the SDA. The SDA was able to build up, virtually from scratch, a coherent micro-electronic industry by securing overseas investment from Japanese and US companies, encouraging higher education to focus research on key areas and on collaborative projects with industry, and providing the factories, infrastructure, and grants that were required. The Welsh Development Agency has also achieved a significant level of new industrial development, especially in high technology. Both are helped by the existing sense of nationhood and, particularly in Scotland, a tradition of national banking and financial institutions. The efforts of the Mid-Wales Development Board and the Highlands and Islands Development Board, initially in the agricultural sectors, have also been effective in reversing rural depopulation, encouraging inward investment and stimulating a rapid rate of new-business formation. With their proven record of success, they provide further lessons as to the appropriate structure for the different regions in England to build.

A major effort by the new agencies to focus on regional growth points is essential, stimulating new initiatives already underway within the regions. The role of central government should be to enable, not to inhibit, these developments. For instance, the Government could give a boost to current attempts to set up a Northern Regional Executive by establishing a Northern Development Agency with overall responsibility for co-ordinating the work of the local authorities, the Departments of Industry and the Environment, English Estates and the Northern Development Council.

A Far-South-West Development Agency in Devon, Plymouth and Cornwall could provide comprehensive single-source assistance and integrated financial packages to companies interested in moving to the region. It would broaden the remit and functions of the Devon and Cornwall Development Bureau. In the absence of government assistance, Devon and Cornwall – together with private banks and trusts – could combine to provide at least part of the capital and skilled labour needed. If such a scheme were based on self-provision and self-sufficiency, it would be easier to persuade central government to help with extra capital.

Public finance is limited, but the Government could do more to encourage private finance for regional development through the conversion of small-scale licensed deposit takers and lenders into larger and better capitalized regional merchant banks. The impact of the new East Anglia Securities Trust (EAST) in financing new and existing businesses in the Eastern region is a vivid example of the latent potential which could be fostered in other parts of the country.

The sense of nationhood in the UK and of regionalism in England would be buttressed by a legislative assembly in Scotland and by the pulling together of many existing institutions in Wales and in London. The SDP/Liberal Alliance's proposed reform of the House of Lords, with half of the membership to be elected from the nations and regions of England, would provide a democratic voice and a focus for the furthering of economic and political devolution and decentralization.

In the UK, the decline of industrial capacity has gone further and faster than in virtually any other member of the OECD in the last fifteen years. Our manufacturing sector now represents a smaller proportion of national output than in any other western industrial country, except the United States. Apart from Norway, Britain is the only OECD country whose factories are producing less now than they were a decade ago.

Apologists for this situation claim that the advent of North Sea oil meant that there was bound to be some deterioration in the non-oil trade balance, but this can be expected to go into reverse as oil output gradually declines and the premium on sterling's international value disappears. The acceleration of manufacturing decline was influenced by sterling being a petro-currency. But they are wrong to argue that the decline in manufacturing does not matter because, once North Sea oil revenues fade, so exports of services and the income from oil-financed overseas assets will help to plug the gap in the balance of payments. Over the next four years, government figures in the 1985 Energy Brown Book forecast a decline of up to £5 billion in oil-export revenues. That prediction was made on the basis of a higher oil price than looks likely in 1986. The Saudi decision to increase output, which in 1985 dropped below the UK output levels, is bound to lead to a far lower price for oil during the rest of the 1980s. The decline in oil prices, even if offset by a decline of the pound against the dollar, will undoubtedly leave a large hole in the trade balance that manufactured exports and services will have to fill. Since only a quarter of services are tradeable, the services sector will remain highly dependent on the manufacturing sector. The key question is: in a climate of faster world economic growth, stimulated by lower oil prices, will the UK's manufacturing industry respond or grow as fast as its competitors?

Even if one takes a more optimistic view of UK oil production in the short term, it is becoming more likely that Britain will have to come to some informal agreement with OPEC on output levels. In the medium term, however, the UK gas-supply position is very encouraging. Estimates of the total benefit of the North Sea to the UK economy will fluctuate with oil-price forecasts. One authoritative estimate is that the decline will be from £14.2 billion in 1986 to £9.8 billion in 1993, a fall-off in the total value of gas and oil volumes of £4.4 billion over the next seven years.[5] The task of substantially improving our trading performance in overseas markets therefore remains urgent. According to the Lords Report, for every 1 per cent fall in exports of goods, service exports have to rise by more than 2 per cent. Whilst some service industries are growing rapidly, not all of traded services face expanding markets – so the burden will have to fall on a few very successful sectors like the City of London. But it would require a jump in City earnings of more than 30 per cent to compensate for a 1 per cent fall in other service exports. That is an impossible task at the moment and competition – most notably from the Far East – is getting tougher all the time.

In the long term Britain will need a higher volume of manufactured exports to help replace oil revenues in the trade balance. We cannot have a prosperous service industry unless we also have a strong manufacturing sector behind it. That is the vital message which Lord Weinstock of GEC told the Lords Committee, in his evidence, when he said, 'What will the service industries be servicing when there is no hardware, when no industrial wealth is being produced?'

It was the unrealistically high exchange rate in the early 1960s which did much to prevent the emergence of export-led growth. It was the wholly unrealistic exchange rate in the early 1980s which laid waste so much of manufacturing industry. Then Mrs Thatcher deliberately held up the exchange rate by tight monetary policies and high interest rates. These were more important factors than oil and the Government wanted to use the exchange rate to offset the inflationary impact of their decision to double VAT on taking office in 1979. The exchange-rate mismanagement in 1980–81 was an industrial disaster which left a permanent legacy, but it was not unreasonable to hope that Mrs Thatcher might have learnt from the experience. The nightmare is that in 1986, history is repeating itself. The Government's return to tight money and high real interest rates is squeezing British industry once again in the painful vice in which it had been trapped before 1981. Much of the gain in competitiveness achieved in 1983–4 was wiped out by sterling's sharp rise in the second half of 1985. In 1986 with oil prices moving down, the uncertainties over sterling remain because the government cannot decide whether it should give priority to exchange-rate stability at a competitive level.

Far from sharpening British industry's competitive edge, the Government's policies produced a warning from the CBI at the start of 1986 that manufacturers expected to shed jobs at a rate of 5,000 a month for as long as the squeeze continued. Unemployment, on a seasonally adjusted basis, had in January 1986 risen to an all-time high of 3.4 million, 14.1 per cent of the labour force, and the underlying trend is showing no sign of rapid improvement. With world markets in 1986 likely to respond to lower oil prices, United States growth projected to slow to an annual 2½ per cent in the first half of 1986 may hold up better than expected. The British economic outlook, however, has been made worse by a deterioration in the relative competitiveness of manufacturing exporters through rising costs and shrinking margins as a direct result of the Government's previous high interest-and-exchange-rate policy.

While it may be sensible in the middle 1980s for any UK Government to run a deficit on non-oil trade to balance a large surplus on oil – otherwise even more capital would have to flow abroad if the sterling exchange rate was not to rise even higher – there is nothing in economic logic or sense that says that non-oil output has to fall as well. With a more competitive manufacturing industry, the same deficit could be achieved at much higher levels of output and employment, exports and imports.

It would be absurd to pretend that there have been no gains from some of this Government's attitudes. The recession's survivors are more efficient and cost-conscious than they were. Manufacturers' quality control has improved. Britain now makes some of the most reliable domestic appliances in Europe and that is heartening news.[6] But it would be unwise to build false hopes upon it. The harsh reality is that British industry faces an uphill task in trying to gain a larger share of world trade, and markets once lost are hard to recapture. The chairman of ICI, one of Britain's most successful companies, John Harvey Jones, told the Lords Committee, in his evidence, that not only did ICI sell 11 per cent less of their products in the UK in 1984 than they sold in 1979, but the principal reason for this decline was that 30 per cent of their home-based customers had ceased to exist since 1979.

Nor is the immediate future any brighter. According to estimates by the London Business School, as much as 17 per cent of the pre-1980 manufacturing capacity has been scrapped and not replaced, whilst the boom in new business formation has scarcely touched the manufacturing sector. Forecasts for the growth of manufacturing output are being revised downwards. The underlying trend suggests that the annual growth rate in manufacturing production has slowed to under 2¼ per cent at the start of 1986, compared with 3 per cent in the year before. The level of manufacturing investment fell overall by some 5 per cent in 1985.

Restoring the strength of manufacturing industry should be an overwhelming priority. The present burden of high interest and exchange rates adds to business costs by a bigger margin than wage rises. The Government's strategy of trying to price British products back into lost markets, by lowering both selling prices and real wages, is the wrong way to tackle the problem of poor competitiveness. The future lies in higher-value-added products with an international market, where the accent is on design and quality and on a company's ability to respond rapidly to market requirements. The UK cannot rely on cheap labour and low skills to reduce industrial costs. The emphasis instead should be on achieving higher productivity from a better-paid and better-skilled labour force through the introduction of new technology and innovative production methods designed to develop a stream of new and more competitive products. Yet far too many people in the UK believe that encouraging technological change and innovation in manufacturing industry means there will be a smaller number of jobs in the future and that, as a result, for social reasons, this shrinking supply of jobs should be shared out as fairly as possible.

This pessimistic argument is mistaken. First, it ignores the economic implications of technological change. At its simplest, if ten people who previously could make only twenty television sets a week can suddenly make forty a week because of some advance in technology, then this will lead to an increased income for their company. That income can then be reinvested, used to reward the workforce, improve shareholders' dividends, or encourage more customers by reducing prices. Any or all of these actions can follow, but whatever action is taken, it will lead to an increase in spending in the economy, which will create new jobs.

Second, it is mistaken because it ignores what one can do with extra wealth to create more jobs. The tragedy of our present situation is that it combines a massive number of people without jobs with a large range of unmet needs. Smaller classes in schools, more nurses in geriatric hospitals, improved maintenance of country roads – all are very labour-intensive. We need to employ more people in these areas, but we cannot afford to without creating the wealth to finance these desirable objectives.

There are those who argue that the new micro-electronic technologies have created an entirely new situation, although it is not clear why the impact of micro-electronic technology will be qualitatively different from other kinds of technological change. In terms of its economic effects, the introduction of laser technology will not be very different from the introduction of welding robots in car factories or the introduction of the tractor or the arrival of new ploughing techniques. While it is not possible to predict all future work-patterns by extrapolating from past trends, it is possible to try to forecast the sort of jobs for which more employees will be needed in the years ahead.

In the post-war period there has been a steady decline of employment in the 'primary' sectors such as mining and agriculture. Simultaneously, however, agricultural output has gone up, so that 'jobless growth' has taken place. In the next decade, it is very likely that 'jobless growth' will also become firmly established in the 'secondary' sectors, such as manufacturing and commerce. Traditional large-scale manufacturing industry should no longer be expected to create major employment. The industry's capital-intensive character gives it high gearing ratios of output to employment, and progressive automation will increase these still further. Small manufacturing and commercial companies will generate some employment, particularly during their start-up phase, although the total number of jobs created may not be large. Much depends on overall economic activity, both nationally and internationally. A typical 'small firm' employs about ten people. So, to create 3 million jobs, 300,000 new firms would be needed – equal to the number of enterprises that already exist in Britain. The US small-business growth rate has, however, been far greater than predicted during the last decade. Already, the distribution of UK enterprise is heavily biased towards small firms – an indication of which is that 90 per cent of all British companies have only one telephone line.

All this means we must not be afraid of creating new jobs in the service sector. To some, this expansion of service jobs may seem undesirable, service jobs being thought of as inferior to manufacturing jobs, but this is no more than a reflection of past prejudices as many service jobs create wealth. Also it is logical to use the wealth created from greater productivity in manufacturing industry, partly through slimmed labour forces, to expand the service sector. An examination of change in the distribution of employment in the United States and in the UK between 1961 and 1983 reveals that in both countries, when the figures have been adjusted for population expansion, the only area in which the number of jobs has grown has been in the service sector.

The significant contrast between the two is that in the US, services' employment has increased by far more than the decline in manufacturing. For every job lost in manufacturing, there have been three created in services against one in the UK. Today McDonald's hamburger franchises employ more people than General Motors, albeit at lower wage levels.

The top ten job-creating service industries in the United States from 1969 to 1983 were listed, in the order of their percentage growth as: miscellaneous business services, miscellaneous professional services, medical services, eating and drinking places, banking, hotels, education (private), insurance, wholesaling and retail trade.[7]

What is especially interesting is the increase in miscellaneous business and professional services including, for instance, personnel supply, business services and computer and data-processing services. The top nine job creators in the United States service sectors forecast for the next five years show both a shift in growth as between sectors and some newly emerging growth sectors listed in order of their percentage growth: retail trade, health-care services, miscellaneous business services, eating and drinking places, miscellaneous professional services, credit agencies, non-profit organizations, real estate and banking.

Employment and technological changes are going to be substantial in the future and this must mean that education and training will be a critical factor in Britain's economic performance. This is particularly true in those parts of the manufacturing and service sectors which are exposed to international competition. The increasing impact of automation and competition from newly industrialized countries (NICS) with low wages will mean fewer unskilled jobs.

We need to alter the in-built bias in British education against applied science and technology. At lower levels skill shortages are now acute, and may well explain why in many of our industries there is lower productivity per man-hour even in factories using the same capital equipment as that used in other European countries. We need to move forward to a system of skill-training which is based on standards achieved rather than time served, which can be built up bit by bit on a modular basis, and which is open to adults as well as school leavers. A remissable tax system is required under which each company spending more than the standard percentage for its industry on training would have all its extra expenditure rebated from public funds, while any company which spent less than that percentage would have to pay a tax equal to its underspending. As a result, the system would be self-financing in the long term.

Not all new jobs in the service sector will be highly skilled, high value-added, highly paid jobs. Along with professional and information-technology jobs there will also be a lot of traditionally lower-wage jobs in areas such as fast foods, retailing and health care. This has two critical policy implications. It is imperative not to let minimum wage legislation prevent these jobs emerging; and sufficient wealth must also be generated in the tradeable manufacturing and service sectors to allow the country to afford improved public services and a better social security system that will guarantee everyone a decent standard of living.

It requires leadership of a far higher quality than we have yet seen to convince this country that technology does not destroy jobs and that there will be enough jobs in the future. Admitting our decline does not mean accepting the mood of defeatism. The reality is that the faster British industry adapts to the skills and opportunities of technological change, the more likely we are to achieve a higher level of employment in the future.

If there is to be a sustained recovery in the manufacturing sector however, the other engines of growth on the supply side of the economy, apart from technical innovation, need to be running smoothly and strongly. We need more private investment, better exchange-rate management, focused and relevant research and development, and effective export promotion; together these would form the type of coherent industrial strategy called for in the Lords Report, which recognized above all the length of time which such a recovery will take. The specific measures are nowhere near as important as the underlying analysis. If we could only obtain a greater consensus on the need for more private investment, how this can be achieved would become a more technical than political question.

The SDP has new ideas for employers' national insurance contributions to be cut and an industrial credit scheme introduced to help companies reduce costs and increase investment. For we believe that the burden of business costs is too severe and will worsen from the autumn of 1986 when industry will have to take over £250 million of the cost of redundancy payments at present borne by the Government. A 1 per cent cut in national insurance contributions would be worth £500 million to industry, while an industrial credit scheme (see pp. 107–8) – operating through the market and the existing banking and venture-capital system – would reduce the burden of interest rates on new investments. For instance, at a cost of £100 million per annum over five years, it would be possible to release £1 billion for loans at 10 per cent below market rates. That would be of real benefit to companies currently paying about 12½ per cent – an all-time high – on such loans.

Achieving a consensus on exchange-rate management should not be beyond the capability of UK politicians. The exchange-rate mechanism of the European Monetary System (EMS) offers us a way of reducing exchange-rate volatility and uncertainty, essential if industry is to plan long-term. The critical sterling/Deutschmark rate has to be maintained at a competitive level if export-led growth is to be achieved. The EMS provides a disciplined framework to maintain that competitive position.

Continuous depreciation simply adds to inflation. The EMS is not a soft option but would provide an important external means of imposing a greater degree of internal consistency on the way successive UK governments approach monetary policy.

Despite all that is said about the importance of industrial research and development, the size of intramural research and development expenditure in manufacturing – financed by government and private industry – at current prices has fallen slightly from £1.56 billion in 1978 to £1.48 billion in 1985. The priority must be both to increase the funds allocated to industrial research and development, and to aim them more specifically at the commercial exploitation of new technology and the development of prototypes. A measure of tax relief on increases in industry-financed research and development should be introduced; as a target, such expenditure should aim to reach 10 per cent of the OECD total by 1990 as opposed to 7.5 per cent in 1975. To achieve all this, we have to establish a far greater continuity of approach across successive Governments. Research and development has a time-scale of return which means that the benefits or disadvantages of a decision taken by Harold Wilson's first government are only now being felt in Mrs Thatcher's second term of office.

If greater priority is to be given to export support and promotion, then again British exporters must be reasonably assured that their efforts in trying to obtain orders in difficult markets and in fierce competition with foreign companies will receive continuing support from successive governments. The 1985 Annual Report of GEC, for instance, claimed that British companies have to overcome a 'sizeable handicap' in competing internationally, particularly in Third World markets, because they received 'insufficient government backing in overseas sales promotion and marketing'. The Overseas Projects Board, set up by this Government and consisting of senior industrialists and financiers from England and Scotland, in its Fourth Report in May 1985, expressed alarm 'at the Government's apparent ambivalence as reflected in delays in handling Aid and Trade Provision cases, some curtailment of ECGD's [Export Credit Guarantee Department] facilities, and pressure on ECGD and the BOTB [British Overseas Trade Board] to adopt a more cautious attitude to "country risk" than that taken by many of the UK's competitors'. Government must more aggressively back British firms competing for key projects throughout the world. Otherwise, the loss to the heavily subsidized Japanese competition of the £1 billion Bosphorus bridge contract, in which a number of leading British firms had an interest, will be repeated.

A sustained and successful export drive is essential to increase Britain's market share of world trade. Time is not on our side. Bluntly the Department of Trade and Industry allocation of £42 million for the year 1986–7 – the same in money terms as the allocation in 1985–6 – to be spent on export services and overseas trade promotion is insufficient and extra resources are needed.

A significant improvement in Britain's competitive position cannot be divorced from the urgent need to reverse the relative decline of Western Europe as an industrial and trading power. Much has rightly been written and spoken about Europe's current technological inferiority in relation to Japan and the United States. Not so much attention has been given to another, critical area of European concern, its maritime decline, where Britain has a vital interest.

During the last decade, the European Community's merchant fleet declined by 10 per cent whilst the number of flags of convenience grew by 26 per cent, the Comecon merchant fleet grew by 42 per cent, the Far Eastern countries' fleet grew by 312 per cent, and the rest of the world's fleet grew by 132 per cent. Europe's maritime decline is, therefore, recent. Within the European Community, Belgium, Denmark, France, Greece and Italy had larger fleets in 1980 than in 1975. The decline in the enlarged Community fleet of the twelve (including Spain and Portugal) over the last decade has mirrored that of the decline of the Community fleet of ten.

It is in Britain that the Merchant Navy's decline has been dramatic. The House of Commons Defence Committee reported last May that 'in 1975 the British merchant fleet was the largest ever in terms of deadweight tonnage (dwt). Thereafter the decline was spectacular. Between 30 December 1975 and 30 September 1984 the UK merchant fleet shrank from a total dwt of 49,985 million to 18,642 million, a reduction of 63 per cent. Measured in terms of total gross registered tonnage, the reduction was one of 59 per cent. The total number of ships fell from 1,614 to 711.'

The serious consequences for British industry of this continuing decline cannot be ignored indefinitely. We have been warned not just about the reduction in the size of our fishing fleet; but more ominously, that over the next seven years the forecast decline of British product carriers, break-bulk ships, trawlers, and tugs will result in a significant reduction in our market share of world shipping and the volume of commercial tonnage carried on British vessels.[8] This could have disastrous implications for the future health of the balance of trade as shipping payments, in the past, have usually made a positive contribution to an overall surplus on invisible earnings, which has been essential to offset a persistent deficit on visible earnings.

The decline of Europe's and Britain's maritime power is not inevitable, provided the European Community accepts that within its member states there must be a great degree of specialization and selectivity in assigning roles. The correction of Europe's maritime decline cannot be done by every nation spending just a little bit more or giving just a little higher priority to maritime efforts. We have suffered already from the universalists' dream whereby each nation state within the European Community strives for self-sufficiency and resists specialization so that we never benefit from the economies of scale and the advantages of specialization.

To selectively reassert a maritime role, a British Government should protect British commercial interests in offshore development in the North Sea as the Norwegians have done. We are not doing enough and the signs are that we are starting to lose vital market share. We need to determine a strictly minimum level for our shipbuilding and repairing industries on strategic grounds and maintain it. We cannot expect to build ship numbers up to previous levels; rather, it is a matter of setting and then holding to a chosen minimum level. We should also reverse the present expenditure cutbacks in marine sciences in our universities, polytechnics and colleges of technology. This is a natural area of specialization for British science where we already have an excellent reputation worldwide. Developing our extensive commercial shipping expertise in banking, brokering and insurance, which is an existing area of profitability and success, needs to be nourished or it too will wither.

There are many ingredients – attitudinal and mechanistic – to industrial regeneration at both political and economic levels. Choosing to designate 1986 as Industry Year has offered us a new opportunity to demonstrate our recognition of the importance of manufacturing industry to our economy, but this recognition should be sustained as a national priority for two decades. It has been said that for the Japanese and West Germans, every year is industry year. Changing our political structure and introducing proportional representation is supported by many in industry because they see other countries' political systems and voting arrangements and they know from their own practical experience on the ground that in those countries, industrial success and wealth creation are helped, not hindered, by the broad approach of their Governments. The motivation for both wealth creation and creating employment can exist side by side. Without a readiness to adapt and regenerate, we will fall even further behind, and our relative economic decline could easily become absolute decline.

6   Incomes Strategy

At 10.45 a.m. on 13 December 1978 a meeting took place in the Cabinet Room to discuss nuclear strategy. Chancellor of the Exchequer Denis Healey, the Defence Secretary, Fred Mulley, and I myself as Foreign Secretary were with the Prime Minister, Jim Callaghan, when he received a note from Michael Foot, the Leader of the House of Commons, and Michael Cocks, the Chief Whip, who wanted to see him urgently. They came into the room and announced the breakdown of their negotiations with the Tribune Group of Labour MPs, which had threatened to vote that night against the imposition of any government sanctions on Ford if the company broke the informal pay guidelines and gave its workforce a 17 per cent rise. Nuclear strategy was set aside and the future of the Government itself came under intense discussion.

Could Labour MPs in Europe be brought back in time for the division? I was asked if I could get Cledwyn Hughes back from Nigeria in time to vote. Should we declare that the vote that night would be taken as one of confidence in the Government as a whole? Would that measure ensure that all the Tribune MPs came into line? How critical were the sanctions for holding the line on pay generally? If we lost the vote, could we call a general election immediately and suspend campaigning over Christmas? We listened with incredulity as the Whips disputed whether a group of Labour MPs was in Brussels or Luxembourg! That did not exactly inspire confidence in our capacity to mobilize our full potential vote that night.

That same group of Ministers met again in the Prime Minister's room during the afternoon before the debate. We were joined by Roy Hattersley, who was due to open the debate and would have to announce at the start if the vote was to be taken as a vote of confidence. Cledwyn Hughes could not get a plane back in time. Various opinions were given as to whether the sanction power was vital. Both Denis Healey and Roy Hattersley thought it was. Eventually, Jim Callaghan followed Michael

Foot's advice and decided not to risk all on winning the vote. Our decision not to make it a vote of confidence ensured that we lost.

In retrospect, those economic ministers most closely involved were correct to argue that the sanction against Ford was vital. Pay restraint was swept away by the loss of the vote that night, despite a vote of confidence being carried next day. It was as if a finger in the dyke had been removed. Suddenly the whole fragile edifice of the Government's anti-inflation strategy, which had taken inflation from 27 per cent in August 1975 down to 8.4 per cent, collapsed. The 'winter of discontent' followed, fed by the growing feeling of unfairness between the public and private sectors. The credibility of the pay policy was destroyed because it was designed to be dependent on constraints being applied universally. If the Ford sanction vote had been declared a vote of confidence and had been won, the 1978–9 pay round guidelines probably would have held, though at the more realistic figure of 8 per cent rather than 5 per cent. If the vote had been lost and an election called soon after Christmas, Labour might well have won. 'Who dares wins' – and the Social Democratic Party might never have been formed.

So much for a vignette of history. Anyone tempted to feel that under Mrs Thatcher this is all old hat and that things are different now should reflect on past and present facts. While public-sector pay rises were below inflation in 1985, private-sector pay rises rose ahead of prices. The evidence suggests that the Government's strategy of keeping public pay down to encourage private employers to restrain pay has failed. It has caused disruption and lowered morale in the public sector, and the evidence suggests that it will be private-sector pay pressure in 1986–7 that will present the Government with one of its major problems, particularly if pay rises continue to outstrip productivity gains. The Government, though frustrated by the private sector's performance, disowns any mechanism to deal with the inflation threat that the private sector is generating. It continually bleats that real wages are too high but has no policies whatsoever to deal with this problem in the private sector. In 1986 the Government will attempt to hold the line in the area of the public sector that it controls and, given the likelihood of lower inflation – give or take some disruption and a faster drop in morale – it can probably achieve this. It cannot, however, prevent the independent pay-review bodies for nurses, doctors and dentists, the armed forces and those with top salaries from again making recommendations higher than

those for other public-sector employees, reflecting in part the likely
inflationary movement of wages and salaries in the private sector.

The Government was driven in 1985 to resort to the short-term expedient of 'staging' the award to nurses. This had the effect of diminishing
the impact of the 8.6 per cent increase on the bills for 1985–6 but raising
the 1986–7 baseline by 3 per cent – before any pay increase is discussed
for 1986–7. The teachers' pay dispute rumbled on through 1985 and
persists in 1986. The Government hopes that the 7.5 per cent rise in the
underlying growth in average earnings in 1985 was temporary and that
the 5½ per cent inflation rate – 1 per cent over the 4½ per cent target for
the last quarter of 1985 – will prove to be only an awkward bump in the
figuring.[1]

Yet a further widening of the gap between public- and private-sector
pay in 1986–7 – which will be the run-up year to the next general election
– will unleash political pressures that may be hard to resist. We are likely
to see in 1986 a good deal of ad hocery wrapped up in the rhetoric of
realism, and there is no doubt that the politics of managing public-sector
pay will become a major issue both before and during the next general
election.

Improvements in the private-sector pay-bargaining environment are
essential. Removing labour-market rigidities, increasing genuine competition, and breaking down monopoly pricing arrangements are all critical
ingredients. So too is the need to retain collective bargaining in the private
sector and in the commercial public sector. Whatever the failings of
existing collective-bargaining procedures, they alone have some hope of
reflecting, at a decentralized level, market realities. Companies that are
doing well and are in profit can pay their workers more generously so
that they share in the success. Companies that are doing badly, with low
or non-existent profits, cannot and should not pay their workers above
the inflation rate and, at times, will have to ask for sacrifices – involving,
in extremis, an absolute cut in pay. To succumb to the pressures for some
sort of overall, centralized statutory pay policy with fixed payments or
percentage increases, or a combination of both, is to follow once again
the path of unreality, to create distortions and to increase inefficiency.

The damage that polarized politics has done to economic welfare is
clearly shown in the history of post-war incomes policy. Governments
have stumbled from emergency policy to emergency policy without
winning support for such policies in any election. The incomes policies

of the 1970s were introduced by Governments that had firmly opposed incomes policy when in opposition. It is hardly surprising that the policies that they subsequently introduced lacked the flexibility or support to last. A temporary pay freeze covering the public and private sectors may be a necessary short-term expedient to check inflationary expectations, but that is as far as a Government can go in centralized interference without triggering adverse economic consequences.

The challenge is to work with the grain of the market and to retain collective bargaining but also to ensure that the overall outcome is non-inflationary, thus allowing more room for real growth and higher employment. To achieve this we need more widespread arbitration procedures – particularly 'pendular' or 'final-offer' arbitration – wider employee share ownership, more generally agreed consultative procedures and open information. But it will be some time before all of those factors, in combination, can promote in the British economy sufficient market realism to ensure that the collective-bargaining process does not fuel inflation. We have not reached that situation yet, and there is a temptation to relinquish that objective and advocate again the rigid and formalized statutory incomes policies or to believe that we can continue to use the discipline of high unemployment.

The lessons from overseas point in a different direction. The experience of European Governments like those in West Germany, Austria and Sweden, with their 'concertation' process and social-market approach, is familiar. It is less well known that Governments of the centre-left in Australia, New Zealand, Spain and Italy are all experimenting with different types of incomes policies, which they have deliberately chosen to place within a framework of greater market liberalism and reforms in order to enhance incentives and encourage more flexible labour markets.

On taking office in March 1983, Bob Hawke's Labor Government in Australia decided to expand the economy to reduce unemployment – so far, at least, with good results. The economy grew by 6½ per cent in 1985 and is expected to grow by around 4 per cent in 1986, according to the OECD. Inflation had halved to 6½ per cent and unemployment fallen to 8 per cent from 10.3 per cent by 1985, a fall of half a million over two years.

However, the Hawke Government chose to fight inflation and unemployment at the same time. The chief weapon against inflation has been an incomes policy under which the unions have been persuaded to regard wage levels indexed to consumer price rises as maxima rather than minima. The Government has also been phasing out a number of regulations in the labour market and has helped to reduce wage pressure through more competition. This growth will make it easier for the Government to restrain inflation by containing consumer price rises through cuts in indirect taxation. Tax cuts will stimulate demand and help to lower unemployment as well. The Hawke Government has not followed the conventional path, whereby a public-expenditure boost is the primary method of expanding the economy. Indeed Hawke's current aim is to reduce the budget deficit, and thus curb the rising cost of servicing the government debt.

Since the Labour Government of David Lange came to office in New Zealand in July 1984, it has scrapped exchange controls; virtually abolished most subsidies to industry, farmers and exporters; removed all tax concessions on new mortgages, life assurance contracts and pension schemes; and pursued a number of other supply-side measures to improve efficiency. This strategy seems to be having some success. The economy grew by around 4 per cent in 1985 and registered unemployment fell from a post-war peak of nearly 80,000 (5.4 per cent) to 49,000 (3.7 per cent) by September 1985. The Government recently announced its intention of cutting income tax by an average 25 per cent, to be paid for by an across-the-board imposition of a Goods and Services Tax (GST) starting in April 1986. Perhaps the most interesting result is that the Lange Government's wage-determination measures ended a price and wage freeze which had been instituted in June 1982; greater flexibility in wage settlements and bargaining attitudes has also been encouraged. Less rigidity in the labour market together with wage moderation will produce a better output-inflation trade-off. So far, the reforms have been effective. Inflation had risen from 8.5 per cent in 1985 to nearly 12 per cent at the start of 1986 but the OECD forecasts a fall to 9.5 per cent in 1986-7, providing the Government's anti-inflationary medium-term monetary- and fiscal-policy framework is firmly maintained.

The Spanish socialist Government under Felipe Gonzalez has pursued a number of market-oriented policies since October 1982. A more flexible and mobile labour-market is being created by reforms to Spain's rigid job-security and redundancy provisions; the public-sector deficit has been cut by 1 per cent as a proportion of GDP; jobs in the country's notoriously inefficient public-sector industries are being rationalized, whilst legislation to overhaul the chaotic and profligate social-security system seems imminent.

At the same time, the Government has pursued a modestly expansionary economic policy which has resulted in a steady 2½ per cent output growth and a reduction in inflation to 10 per cent from 12.5 per cent. Unemployment rose to nearly three million (19 per cent) but it has levelled off in 1985, and in the last quarter of 1985 fell by 8,000, the first fall in three years. The Gonzalez pay strategy is distinctive. Wage norms, between 7 per cent and 10 per cent for the principal public-sector industries and enterprises, have for the most part been strictly adhered to. Pay increases have also been held in check by linking them to improvements in both unit-labour costs and productivity. Wage rises in the private sector will have to slow down substantially if the official target of reducing inflation to 7 per cent in 1986 is to be attained. The Government has taken a number of steps – including easing the regulations governing the dismissal of workers, regularizing part-time employment and introducing fixed-term contracts – to liberalize the labour market and establish a closer relationship between wages and productivity trends, skills and the financial position of private companies.

In Italy, the coalition Government under the socialist Prime Minister, Bettino Craxi, has also pursued deregulation measures, not least in the financial markets. Artificial curbs on bank deposits have been lifted; the social security budget pruned and a range of anomalies ended; and the Government has committed itself to a programme of tax reform designed to improve incentives by broadening the tax base and increasing the emphasis on indirect taxes. Despite a strategy of budgetary austerity, the economy is growing by nearly 3 per cent, whilst inflation has been cut to 6 per cent from 8½ per cent last year, although the seasonally adjusted unemployment rate has fallen only slightly, from 10.2 per cent in the third quarter of 1984 to 9.8 per cent (or 2.2 million) in the third quarter of 1985.

The Government's incomes strategy has consisted of reforms to the expensive sliding wage-scale (*scala mobile*) system. Between 1983 and 1985, while retaining the basic index-linked mechanism, the Government has reduced by 15 per cent the index-linked position of wages, lowering price rise per capita 'wage elasticity' from 0.60 per cent in 1983 to 0.51 per cent in 1985. For 1985–6 the Italians have set a target limit of 7 per cent on the increase in total wages; but for the private sector it has been left to the unions and management to establish a formula through arbitration which will reduce the rate of growth of nominal-wage costs.

The chief lesson to be learned from these countries is that incomes strategies can work effectively to restrain inflation when placed in a framework of incentives and market-oriented devices which are not normally associated with governments of the centre-left. Market-liberalism and incomes policies can, it seems, work together to promote greater competitiveness both in the labour market and in other parts of the economy.

In the U K a flexible and decentralized incomes strategy, covering both the public and private sectors, based on voluntary guidelines which collective bargaining would broadly operate, could help to get a climate of market realism and inhibit inflationary settlements in pace-setting industries or companies. But even so, one has to admit that the guidelines may be too loose and could be breached in ways that would allow private-sector pay once again to fuel inflation, even with high levels of unemployment and unused plants and machinery. We can draw little encouragement from the experience of 1981–5 in the private sector.

In 1978, the voluntary 5 per cent overall guideline for pay settlements was shattered by a 17 per cent rise awarded by the Ford Motor Company. Ford claimed that a 17 per cent settlement would not be passed on in increased prices for their cars and could to some extent be absorbed by revised productivity agreements. Yet it was obvious to all that if such a large increase, so far above the guideline, was paid it would influence the whole pattern of private-sector pay-bargaining. The dam would burst: rising inflation would force the Government to counter with rising un-employment. The whole economy would suffer from the actions of a tiny minority of the workforce. The Government's proposed ban on public-sector purchases of Ford vehicles had neither statutory authority nor Parliamentary approval. The sanctions were seen to be arbitrary and unfair and did not deserve to succeed. But the Ford problem was real. It will arise again, and an incomes strategy that has no reserve power will run the grave risk that rising inflation in the private sector will totally undermine any mechanism for comparability in the public sector, since it will escalate inflationary pressure from the private sector through to the whole economy.

This is the situation again today. First, it is clear that pay pressure in the private sector – with average manufacturing earnings rising at 8–9 per cent in 1985 – is far outstripping productivity gains, thus increasing unit costs and fuelling inflation. Second, public-sector pay, though held down at, or below, the current underlying rate of inflation of approximately 5 per cent, is nevertheless being pushed up where comparability mechanisms exist, for example the nurses' award. When this happens it in turn triggers a growing and justified sense of unfairness, which leads to a readiness to disrupt services in those parts of the public sector where there are no comparability mechanisms currently operating – as manifested in the teachers' action.

Thus the crucial question is not what to do about public-sector pay, but rather how to restrain private-sector pay pressure if it starts to move above the levels justified by productivity increases. This is where a counter-inflation tax would provide the mechanism whereby private-sector pay could be prevented from provoking inflation. It does not have to be invoked; indeed, it should only ever be a last resort. If private-sector pay-bargaining is realistic, no statutory disincentive should be needed. An inflation tax must, though, be enacted in legislative form and then held in reserve for use if market bargaining fails. Experience has shown that effective sanctions need the legitimacy of Parliament behind them. The threat of invoking an inflation tax should be sufficient to ensure greater realism in private-sector pay-bargaining.

If ultimately required, an inflation tax would apply only to medium-to-large companies with over one hundred employees and then only if they went beyond the inflation limit declared by Government. This is where pay and price pressures can be most acute and least sensitive to the market. This limitation would effectively restrict the coverage of the tax to about 20,000 companies and 75 per cent of the total workforce. Since small businesses and new firms would be outside the scope of the tax, most of the fastest-growing high technology and service firms would be unaffected. Far from being a penalty on success, as some have mistakenly argued, the inflation tax is a mechanism which allows the Government to maintain the most favourable economic climate for the growth of output, employment, profits and living standards – a climate in which fast-growing firms inevitably benefit most. Because the tax would be levied on the increase in the average hourly earnings of all the workforce, it still allows a large degree of flexibility within that average. Hiring twenty additional, highly paid and talented people does not much change the average pay of a thousand.

It is clearly essential that the greatest encouragement should be given to those industries where, through restrictive practices or inefficiencies, there is considerable scope for sizeable increases in productivity. A good example has been the 8 per cent productivity increase at Austin–Rover in 1984–5. If the inflation tax on pay rises which are above the inflation limit is not to penalize such improvement, it must allow an exemption for any payments to workers which result from an increase in the company's profits. Profit-sharing and the inflation tax, were it needed, can thus work hand-in-hand.

In order to qualify for the tax incentives for profit-sharing and for the exemption from the tax, companies would be obliged to register with the Inland Revenue any profit-sharing agreements before they take effect. If these agreements could be introduced at any point, they would merely become a disguised way of paying wages unsupported by profits. For similar reasons, it is important that payments which only increase the employees' share of profits remain subject to an inflation tax, while payments which arise from an actual increase in profits are exempt. This arrangement would ensure that the just rewards for increases in productivity are properly shared with the employees, without the need to install costly, bureaucratic ways of checking whether such increases are genuine or not. If these increases resulted in higher profits there would be a prima facie argument for saying that they are genuine.

A company could also take advantage of the profit-sharing exemption to pay the profits due to its employees in the form of shares, for which there are already sizeable tax benefits under the 1978 Finance Act. In the case of Ford, it would have been able to share its increased profits with its employees, beyond the inflation limit, without any penalty under the inflation tax while taking advantage of new tax incentives – especially given to encourage profit-sharing schemes – which are outlined in detail in the next chapter on industrial partnership.

Another form of tax-based policy which has recently been advocated would reduce the tax bills of individual companies that gave pay increases below the inflation limit.[2] It involves a payroll incentive – consisting either of a remission of corporation tax or National Insurance contributions – for a company which increases its labour force by more than a threshold percentage ; or keeps pay per head down to a certain amount; or does both, effectively the belt and braces approach. The incentive is a bonus rather than a penalty. Thus, problems of definition and demarcation would not be crucial and the onus would be on employers. This has the advantage over an across-the-board reduction of employers' NICs in that, by definition, it would not apply where the concession is eroded in pay increases.

The drawback is the cost. If, for instance, the incentive is applied to enterprises and firms employing a total of 2 million workers, with a rate of £500 per head, the annual cost would be £1 billion. Furthermore, abuses could accumulate if the scheme became permanent, and corporate reorganizations were designed to establish fictitious increases in employment, or artificially low pay increases.

Until a more competitive and decentralized labour market can be established the payroll incentive could be a useful transitional measure that would eliminate the need to introduce an inflation tax. It would encourage an important change from the current preference for higher pay to more jobs. It would also be far better for jobs than any possible basic-rate tax cuts or threshold increases in the next Budget, since it would confine tax reductions to companies 'which favoured jobs over pay, irrespective of increases in productivity'.

The link with the public sector, since the inflation tax would be confined to the private sector and the nationalized industries, is through comparability. If comparability is to be developed and used as an argument for fixing pay levels in public-sector pay-bargaining, then any scheme which helps curb inflation in the private sector contributes to solving the problem of public-sector pay.

What one has to do is to avoid leap-frogging and escalation. That is why a historic element in any comparability calculation is essential. For example the teachers' dispute in 1985 was over their 1984–5 pay claim, when the average inflation rate was only 4½ per cent. Yet the teachers' claim was often discussed in terms of the 1985 inflation figure of 5½ per cent. This ensures inflationary awards. What is needed is an acceptable frame of reference to cover public-sector pay negotiations on the one hand and a formula for public-sector pay awards on the other.

A suggested frame of reference for negotiations, which would therefore not be binding and would allow for negotiations over productivity and efficiency payments, could be that public-sector workers would get last year's 'real', i.e. productivity-adjusted, private-sector earnings – unless their own productivity and efficiency agreements were worth more – in which case they would get the excess. In 1984–5 'real' private-sector earnings rose by 4.6 per cent which could have been taken as the basis for public-sector pay negotiations which would start after that fiscal year.[3]

This could then be modified in two important respects. First, to allow extra increases for Government employees whose occupation was in shortage. Secondly, for an increase if their comparison-group had grown faster than the private sector average on perhaps a three-year cycle. This would help those who could not easily negotiate any productivity arrangements. Such extra payments would normally be deducted when calculating the catch-up element. In such a way it would be possible for average pay in the public and private sectors to grow together while encouraging increased productivity and greater efficiency in both sectors. Such a frame of reference could not replace the separate review bodies where there are no negotiations; they cover at present the armed forces, doctors and dentists, nurses and top salaries.

A suggestion worth considering, as a way of dealing with these and other groups, would be to offer a fixed-comparability formula with no provision for bargaining. Under the fixed formula, pay rises would be awarded which automatically follow last year's actual private-sector earnings. In Britain in 1985 these increased by 7 per cent. That represented a 2.4 per cent increase above the 'real'-earning increase justified by productivity. To ensure that this formula did not get out of control, the independent Pay Information Board would have to look periodically at the comparative position of the different groups. In any year covered by such a review the automatic fixed formula would not apply, and the review's comparative adjustments, either up or down, would apply using the present safeguard clause in the different review bodies' terms of reference, which relate to exceptional circumstances. This is justifiable, as the guarantee of continuity of service to the consumer is vital. This formula would best suit those in the public sector, whose jobs do not easily fit into productivity arrangements and who have no clear comparator in the private sector. It might appeal to teachers, social workers and people working in the emergency services who are not covered by existing review boards but who, in return for such a formula, might be persuaded to settle for a no-strike agreement. Such an agreement could justify a formula which runs the risk of being inflationary if public-sector pay ran above inflation level and was not constrained by an inflation tax.

In effect, the alternatives are: an increase limited to the rate of 'real' private-sector earnings growth and collective bargaining over additional productivity increments, or a higher increase linked to actual private-earnings growth, but with no provision for collective bargaining. This type of incomes strategy is an ambitious objective. It is a mental switch-off for those who are resigned to living with present levels of unemployment. It is, however, a necessity for those who are not prepared to tolerate the waste and despair of high unemployment. Success has so far eluded every political party. Yet to abandon the search for an incomes strategy that links the private and public sectors together is either to accept high unemployment and falling public-service standards or to let public expenditure absorb revenues that ought to be put into capital investment. We are all dependent for our export earnings on the commercial sector, but the commercial workforce depends too on those who work in the public service.

The public sector employs nearly 27 per cent of the working population in Britain. To put it crudely, that is a large number of voters. It also contains 48 per cent of all trade union members. The armed forces aside, the public service is covered by a variety of bargaining arrangements. Until the early 1970s, it did not matter greatly that these largely operated independently of each other. The public services – health, education, defence and government – which made up 68 per cent of the sector were, excepting, perhaps, the doctors, far from militant in their attitudes to pay and conditions of employment. Public sector pay broadly kept in step with, if not a little behind, its private sector counterpart. There was rough *de facto* comparability.[4]

It was when inflation began to raise its ugly head and necessitated efforts to raise public-sector efficiency that the passivity of the public services ended. In 1974, by contrast to 1972, it was public-sector pay pressure and the commitment to index-linked pay that was inflationary. The Conservative administration's reorganization of local government and the NHS resulted in substantial restructuring, and with it sizeable salary and wage increases. The one-off Halsbury pay award for nurses in 1974 and the Houghton award for teachers in 1975 meant that public-sector pay awards moved sharply ahead of private-pay increases by 1976. Public-sector pay fell back somewhat by 1979 and then moved ahead again in 1981. Since then it has steadily fallen behind. In marked contrast to the 1960s, the public sector has accounted for the majority of all working days lost through strikes in the 1980s. Most of these strikes have been over pay levels or employment reductions. Despite its avowed devotion to decentralize pay decisions, the present Government has felt obliged to intervene, often covertly, more frequently than ever before.[5]

The absence of a coherent public-sector pay-strategy has meant that efficiency has suffered and disruption in the public services is with us yet again. The problem of public-sector pay-pressure goes very deep. We see this with the teachers' strike on the one hand and the consequential effects of the nurses' pay settlement on the other. A solution must tackle the perennial problem of the measurement and management of public services. In private industry, if new equipment or work practices serve to double output per worker, this will show up in figures as a 100 per cent increase in productivity. But in public services, we measure the price of input, not the value of output.

If, for instance, a hospital rearranges its wards with the result that one night nurse can watch over the same number of patients that previously required two nurses, that would tend to show up in the figures for current public expenditure as a drop in the cost of nurses, but it would be accompanied by cries of 'cuts in nursing numbers'. Similarly, if volume is increased by using more day surgery, which requires extra staff – perhaps in the administration of out-patients – this is seen as an increase in expenditure on staff, perhaps accompanied by lurid descriptions of 'burgeoning bureaucracy'. If the out-patient surgery is successful and demand for in-patient cold surgery drops and a ward is closed as a consequence, this again can, and usually is, represented as an example of a 'collapsing NHS'.

These perhaps over-simplified examples nevertheless demonstrate a critical problem. In private industry it is such productivity increases that finance real pay rises and ensure that the cost in wages is not passed on by an increase in the cost of the product. In public services, however, pay cannot rise in 'real' terms or – to put it another way – exceed the overall rate of inflation without simultaneously increasing the real cost of public spending.

This offers a harsh choice to any government attempting to stabilize public spending, and most western governments have been struggling to do just that since the mid-1970s. Either government can try to hold the real pay of its own employees constant and maintain employment levels, in which case they will fall further and further behind private-sector employees' pay – unless the latter are to be deprived of some of the fruits of their productivity by statutory pay controls. Or government can pay more, while reducing staff to offset this and hope efficiency changes will maintain standards of service. To allow rising pay to absorb more and more of public spending is to ensure increased taxation and that, apart from the electoral consequences, all too often contributes to a stagnant economy and higher unemployment.

In practice, governments pursue a mix of these policies. Since 1980, the present Government has held public pay roughly constant in real terms. For the public services as a whole, pay rose just 0.1 per cent faster than prices from 1980–1 to 1984–5; some 7.2 per cent slower than the economy as a whole. The nurses fell behind inflation by 2.5 per cent while the police roared ahead by 15.9 per cent and the teachers went up by just 1 per cent.[6] Of course all trade unions measure their pay against the most favourable position they have previously been in in the comparative-pay league. In the teachers' case this was immediately after the 1975 Houghton Award, since when they have lost considerable ground.

This comparative lobbying often identifies groups of public-service employees with party-political preferences. It has considerable dangers, as one can see at present – the police and soldiers believe they will do better with Conservatives, for example. Local-authority manual workers, despite being influential in Labour's 1979 election loss, feel they will get a better deal from a Labour Government. As the election draws near politicians who want to pick up votes make promises in order to buy support. The loser in all this is the public, who not only ultimately meets the bill for rising real public-sector pay, but also feels the consequences in the form of a reduced range and quality of public services. To find a better way of settling public-sector pay is vital if we are to retain the concept of public service, retain the virtues of a non-political public service, and enhance its standards of integrity and objectivity.

Disillusionment with *ad hoc* comparability in the public service drove the Labour Government to introduce cash limits in 1976, after an inflationary wage-explosion aggravated by the failure of the 'social contract' in 1974–5. Yet cash limits were, and remain, a very crude mechanism for control, as indeed is the whole Treasury approach with its emphasis on a single fiscal year and the separation of capital and revenue. In 1979, on taking office and having unwisely – though inevitably – committed itself to implementing the Clegg awards, then feeding inflation by the decision to double VAT, the new Conservative Government attempted a different form of control in addition to cash limits. It set a series of 'pay factors' (i.e. targets), which allowed for a 17.5 per cent rise in pay over the next four years. In practice there was considerable overshooting and a 31.5 per cent increase resulted. Low 'pay factors' are clearly one method, though not a very effective one, of trying to lower the inflation temperature. The critical question is whether they are also a way of stimulating productivity. The evidence suggests not.[7]

When inflation was declining after 1981, the 'pay factors' turned out to be less severe at the end of each year than they had seemed at the beginning. In addition, there was always the reserve built into public-spending plans to help bridge the gap. The real test has now arrived, however, since inflation has risen beyond its target level, and the Treasury is grimly determined to limit the damage to their contingency reserve from unjustified payments early in the 1986 pay round.

Meanwhile the public sector lacks the incentive to achieve productivity gains without rekindling inflation. Cash limits or 'pay factors' can be met more easily by cutting services than by increasing efficiency, which is harder for public service managers to achieve. In short, any government needs more ways of measuring and rewarding efficiency in the public service.

Even the attempt to inject a significant element of market forces into the settlement of public-pay problems will not be enough without output measurement. Market criteria are a useful improvement to gauge the claims of public-sector workers and to counter pressure-group politics. The market mechanism does provide an indication of whether individuals think the job is worth doing for the money. It tells us, for instance, that plenty of people want to train as nurses, but that some of the trained nurses prefer to leave for better-paid private medicine. But it cannot provide all the answers. If there are plenty of college leavers willing to become teachers, that is no guarantee of quality, or of commitment, or even of capacity to teach. Responsible, senior teachers will be 'locked in' by years of specialization and it is not in the nation's interest to see good classroom teachers exploited. To maintain professional standards, public servants must feel their skills are valued and that this is recognized financially. If market pressures indicate that we should pay public employees more and we respond, then we must find a way of introducing some form of internal-market pressure to ensure efficient use of personnel, more flexible working arrangements and an improved output.

The difficult question is how to measure and evaluate the 'output' of public service, in health or education as well as in administration. Until that is achieved to a greater degree, governments will either fail to cut spending, to improve services, or both. The present Government is in serious danger of falling into this trap. It is widely recognized that a more 'productive' approach is needed to tackle the root problems of public-sector pay.[8] The key to a long-term solution is to link this productive approach with new methods and procedures for pay comparability. Comparability, provided it is not inflationary, would be more than a useful proxy for the market. It would aim to provide new ways of evaluating public-sector 'output' which, in short, would mean less money for the inefficient and more for the most productive employees. It would also give public-service managements the stability and incentives that would enable them to motivate employees and manage them better.

Much of the preparatory work for a coherent public-service pay-strategy based on comparability has been done. The 1982 Megaw Committee on civil service pay argued that labour market forces were necessary, but insufficient to deserve detailed comparisons. Instead it emphasized that civil-service pay should be determined by the so-called 'inter-quartile' range of outside earnings, or the band of pay between the top 25 per cent and the remaining 75 per cent of the range of relevant private-sector wages, which are loosely linked to private-sector productivity performance. A non-inflationary comparability system for the public-service sector as a whole is credible along the lines of the Megaw blue-print for the civil service. The essential requirement would be a single and independent pay information board covering all the public services, developing 'inter-quartile' comparison with jobs outside. The results of this work would not be imposed by compulsion, but would be determined by a system of independent arbitration.

The Treasury has recognized the 'important role of arbitration' in its current attempts to revise the system of civil service pay determination, and has pledged to give full, written explanations to the unions if and when it is refused. The Treasury's proposed system is for annual surveys of pay movements in the private sector, with negotiations for civil servants then being constrained within the upper and lower quartiles of such outside settlements – between settlements of the top 25 per cent and bottom 25 per cent of workers. But this was rejected by the civil service unions, since the system would still constrain the overall annual cost of civil service pay below the upper quartile, so that there would be no practical way, even over a fixed period, to make up the significant erosion of pay and salary levels since 1981.[9]

The detailed task of comparing productivity between public and private sector organizations would involve a regular, perhaps yearly, efficiency audit of the public service – as undertaken by the new pay information body. How this audit is conducted and how public service 'output' is measured would need to be anchored to the data yielded by the comparability studies. The concept of factor analysis, which the Megaw Report recommended, would be used to widen the scope of comparability beyond the Civil Service. As the Report argued, 'factor analysis methods of job evaluation permit comparisons to be made between jobs both in the same organization and in different organizations, in both public and private industry, taking full account not only of the various tasks involved but also of the difficulty of the work, responsibility and the accountability involved'.[10]

Factor analysis was first devised as a concept and procedure by Hay-MSL management consultants and developed in the second volume of the Megaw Report Research Studies. The Hay 'Guide-Chart Profile Method' of job evaluation and efficiency is now used by many firms for job comparability exercises involving different industries in the private sector. The key to factor analysis is the measurement of the work of an entire industry in terms of job evaluation – involving such factors as job recruitment and retention, salary grades and seniority of service – for individual firms in the industry. The number of such job-evaluation schemes in the private sector has grown rapidly in recent years. There is no reason why, in principle, the Megaw Report should not be adapted to introduce factor-analysis methods of output management and job evaluation for the public services as a whole.

Comparability would, of course, be an inappropriate mechanism for pay determination in the nationalized industries which deal in publicly traded goods. For some, mainly those facing international competition such as British Steel, market forces may be sufficiently strong to determine the outcome of collective bargaining. But for nationalized industries in natural monopoly positions, such as gas, electricity and the Post Office, competitive forces provide little discipline and excess pay settlements could simply be passed on in prices. In these cases, formulae embodying an appropriate degree of price-constraint are needed, elaborating on the RPI-X approach adopted for Telecom, with the 'X' factor determined by the rate of growth of productivity in the industry concerned.

The Government could reduce the uncertainty under which the public-sector negotiators have to operate, by bringing greater synchronization of settlement dates. It has been argued that if the public-sector pay-settlement 'season' came in the early summer, at the end of the private-sector pay-bargaining calendar, it would meet both the CBI's desire to prevent pace-setting by public industries and also make historic comparability exercises more valid for the public services covered by them. A government that wished to take economic planning at all seriously would see that a tidying-up of public-sector settlement dates would make it feasible to bring pay and employment considerations into line with broader policies on, say, fuel, power and transport.[11]

Unless a new interrelationship is established between salary levels in the public and private sector – based on non-inflationary comparability – there is a real danger that history will repeat itself and public-sector pay will become a major issue again in 1987–8. Not only is the cohesion and unity of the nation threatened by the widening gap between private affluence and public squalor but also economic decline will never be tackled effectively without a comprehensive incomes strategy underpinned by, and reinforcing, the emergence of a new political consensus.

7 *Industrial Partnership*

For industry to prosper and succeed, unions and management have to see themselves as partners in a common enterprise in which they both have a share and a stake. The old class divide – the 'us-and-them' instinct, the mutual suspicion on the shopfloor – must end if our nation is to become more competitive. Structural changes in industry that ensure more information and greater participation can help, but far more important are changes in attitude.

There are encouraging developments and signs of increasing realism in some industries, but it is all happening too slowly. The trade unions face their biggest crisis of the post-war period. Their membership has fallen after a long period of steady growth. This is, for the most part, a result of the dramatic changes in the economy that have reduced employment in heavily unionized manufacturing and increased it in the less unionized service and non-technology industries; it is also the consequence of economic policies that have damaged employment prospects generally. But union members are also asking, 'Why should I continue to pay for union membership when I get so little back in return?' It is doubtful that trade unionism will ever recover its former power and influence after this setback, though it could become a constructive influence.

The traditional white, male, manual workers who dominated the old trade union image have now been joined by women workers, white-collar workers and black and Asian workers. This new membership has brought with it new attitudes. Rising standards of living, greater leisure time and wider expectations lead union members to demand new responses and new approaches from both their trade unions and the collective bargaining system. They want modern, efficient services from the union: services that keep them in touch with what the union is doing, that provide efficient staff back-up at short notice when problems arise at the workplace and that offer comprehensive advice on even more complicated issues such as pensions and health and safety.

Trade unionists are becoming sick and tired of long disputes and fruitless strikes. Even when they fully support the objectives of their union, they have been less willing to see the strike weapon used. As strikes come more and more to disrupt their lives and those of their families, they question the morality as well as the effectiveness of disruption. All too often the consequences of such industrial action are felt more widely than in the particular employer's business alone. Strikes frequently contribute to unemployment, to lack of investment. When teachers strike, why should children suffer? How can it be justifiable to single out for strike action the constituency of the Secretary of State for Education, when the children in that constituency do not even vote? If doctors take disruptive action, waiting lists grow longer and patients, not the Government, suffer. If dustbins are not emptied, it is not the local councillors who are inconvenienced but the old and disabled. If Social Security staff work to rule and delay payment of child benefit, it is not the Government but poor families that are hit the hardest. What is becoming all too clear is that certain people are unaffected by strikes: those who send their children to private schools, who do not draw benefits, who will not empty their dustbins when there is a strike, who are covered by private health schemes – they are all virtually immune when a public-service strike occurs. The strike weapon is unselective and affects trade unionists and their families more than most other sections of society.

The average trade unionist is clearly becoming impatient with the old decision-making procedures, procedures that are often clearly unrepresentative and obviously undemocratic, that give too much power to small groups of activists and not enough to ordinary union members. The trade union reforms introduced by the Conservative Government in 1980, 1982 and 1984 should therefore, in most respects, stay. They deserve to do so, for they were broadly a sensible response to a national mood; after the 1979 'winter of discontent', it was felt that union power needed to be curbed. The SDP demonstrated that it was a new political force when the overwhelming majority of its MPs, formerly mostly Labour, voted for changes in the law affecting the closed shop, a law that they had helped vote on to the statute book during the Labour Government. It was necessary to show that we could admit to error and to learn from our mistakes.

The Conservatives' handling of trade unions has, however, had a deeply unattractive side. Mrs Thatcher misread the public mood when she banned trade unionism at the Government Communications Headquarters (GCHQ) at Cheltenham. This establishment has a crucial security role to play, and it is in the national interest that it should maintain continuous operations. GCHQ is answerable to the Foreign Secretary and had never taken strike action until 1979. During the 1979 Civil Service pay dispute one of the reasons why I crossed the Foreign Office picket-line was to demonstrate solidarity with those in GCHQ and in other sensitive establishments who wanted to work and were at that time exercising their right to do so. Yet Mrs Thatcher, having rightly insisted that there could be no repeat of the previous disruption at GCHQ, refused to lift the ban on trade-union membership when the unions offered a virtual no-strike agreement. She appeared then to be acting vindictively against the very principle of trade unionism. Even more important, she gave the impression that trade unionists could not be trusted with top-secret information. This was regarded as a slight against the patriotic commitment of hundreds of thousands of trade unionists. It is a decision that will be reversed by any Government formed or influenced by the SDP/Liberal Alliance.

It is, however, the 1984 legislation on trade-union democracy that will prove to be the most far-reaching in its consequences. The SDP was, in fact, the first political party to champion the return of the unions to their members, at our first Party Conference in 1981. It is not the first, nor will it be the last political party to see its policy initiatives stolen by rivals in government. But at least this meant that the reform, when it came, had a breadth of support that made it more likely that the initial resistance from the Trades Union Congress (TUC) would fade. The TUC is now wisely bowing to the new mood of its members, who think it absurd to go on rejecting the offer of state funding of their postal balloting. This change of heart among TUC leaders towards the new legislation indicates that British politics is being perceived in a different way by many trade unionists whose political commitment hitherto has been automatic support for the Labour Party.

One of the most significant manifestations of the shifting foundations of British politics is the wish to establish new patterns of partnership at the workplace. The 1980 agreement between the Electrical, Electronic, Telecommunication and Plumbing Union (EETPU) and Toshiba in Plymouth was an early example of a new partnership, with an agreement covering 'pendular', or 'final-offer', arbitration and equal status for all employees. Since then, there have been many similar agreements. The Amalgamated Union of Engineering Workers (AUEW) agreement at Nissan's new plant in the north-east; the EEPTU agreements in newspapers; the establishment of the Union of Democratic Mineworkers (UDM) and the realism that has been forced on the National Union of Mineworkers (NUM) in the aftermath of the miners' strike – all these are part of the same process. They are not just a rejection of all that Scargillism has come to mean – intimidation, mass picketing and revolutionary zeal; they are a search for a new structure, a recognition that the old patterns and attitudes have failed.

This point was confirmed decisively by the outcome of the miners' strike. A victory for Arthur Scargill would have been a ghastly defeat for the nation. It would have set back any chance of reversing our decline for many years. But it was the peculiar character of Arthur Scargill's leadership that defeated itself. Never prepared to accept any compromise, he was incapable of claiming the victory that was his on all too many occasions during that dispute. The National Association of Colliery Overmen, Deputies and Shotfirers (NACODS) initiative, to name but one proposal, came within an ace of being accepted by the National Coal Board (NCB) and the Government. Had the NUM settled for it, it would not have been NACODS's victory but a victory for Arthur Scargill's tactics of intimidation, a victory for the Labour Party's condoning of violence and refusal to advocate the pithead ballot. Eventually the strike was defeated, but it left, after months and months of picket-line violence, a sour taste.

There was no national mood of satisfaction, let alone rejoicing. That old-style confrontation, worse even than the 1925–6 strike, should never have happened in a sophisticated democracy. The Government had rightly seen that a strike was inevitable under Scargill's presidency of the NUM. For anticipating the need to build up coal reserves it deserves more credit than for its handling of the dispute. A more sensitive Government would have been able to rally the working miners earlier and more comprehensively, particularly if it had been seen to be trying hard to create jobs in areas likely to be affected by pit closures. A more competent Government would not have come so perilously close to losing.

At the time of the mass picketing outside the British Steel coking plant at Orgreave, the British Steel Corporation (BSC) should have taken action against the NUM. That would have nipped in the bud the increasing need to use the police physically to hold the line against the pickets. The Scunthorpe steel works nearby was desperate to keep its furnaces going. The steel-work unions were at odds with the NUM. Whereas it might have been sensible to withhold civil action against the NUM in the early stages, by then the Nottinghamshire miners had voted to continue working and would not have stopped in sympathy.

Despite all the SDP's reservations about some aspects of the Government's handling of the strike, by holding firm in that crisis the SDP established an approach to industrial relations and other areas that could bode well for the future. That this approach can come through, even within the present political system, serves to nail the lie that only Mrs Thatcher and the Conservatives can give firm leadership.

Traditionally the NUM has been hostile to partnership in industry. Under Joe Gormley's leadership in the 1970s it was prepared to operate a tripartite mechanism with the NCB and the Government, but there was a distinct separation of trade-union, management and Government responsibilities. A partnership that meshed the three together and involved mutual responsibilities was a threat; the separation of roles within the tripartite structure was necessary if confrontational industrial relations were to continue. It will be interesting to see whether the emergence of the UDM forces a change of attitude in the NUM on this and other issues.

New attitudes are emerging everywhere in the trade-union movement. There are many signs of a classless readiness to engage in, and create, different structures and different lifestyles: the frustration that can be witnessed by trade unionists when, as parents at a parent–teacher association meeting on a council estate, they argue about standards of education at their local comprehensive school or rally around a project of self-help for painting a classroom; the resigned acceptance of the semi-skilled worker who joins a company-based private health-insurance scheme because of the waiting lists in the local hospital; the growing exasperation of a trade-union manual worker at the indignity and insensitivity of separate canteens, separate car parks and separate time-keeping arrangements, particularly when his white-collar sons and daughters are working in the same factory but enjoying different privileges; the anger of trade unionists experiencing the humiliation of the bureaucracy at a Job Centre when, for the first time, they find themselves unemployed; the readiness of trade unionists to dip into their pockets to help finance a local sports field, or to be ready to contribute to funds for a local hospice.

Managers too are changing attitudes. Management is not experiencing the same crisis that has hit the unions. There is a more self-confident image, a greater readiness to manage. However, this is the time not to sit back but to introduce more far-reaching changes in management approaches. Employees want a greater say at work. Whether it is called participation or industrial democracy, the demand is to be more involved at the workplace. Trade unionists want more democracy at work, not just within their own unions.

Employees want management to work in partnership with them and their unions to bring in new technology, to improve skill-training; generally they want management to play its full part in modernizing British industry. They are tired of standard management attacks on the opposition to change from unions when at the same time they see outdated equipment, lack of support for new skill-training and crude status barriers between management and workers. The petty *apartheid* of the workplace has to go. Unless modern management recognizes this, we will pay a heavy price with divisions and conflict at work, when there should be co-operation and partnership. What is more, as Japanese management has shown in the UK, partnership at work is also more efficient than conflict.

It is easy for the SDP to identify with these feelings because they are fully represented among its membership. Moderation in policy does not mean endorsing the *status quo*. Social democracy can have more passion, commitment and strength than any ideology of the extreme left or right. The SDP must never allow itself to be set in the concrete of the old vested-interest politics. Our new party already represents both miners and management; as they work together within the SDP, they see themselves as social partners, not as two opposing sides of industry. We want neither Labour's institutional links with the unions nor the Conservatives' dependence for finance on business donations. We have built the party on the firm base of one member, one vote, through postal ballots using the single transferable vote, and we want it to represent all sections and all parts of the UK.

The desire of trade unionists for sensible ways of settling disputes at the workplace is beginning to be met by 'strike-free' agreements. These agreements often provide for a new mechanism, 'pendular' or 'final-offer' arbitration, to settle differences without strikes. But they also include single status at the workplace: the end of separate canteens and car parks for management and workers. They provide for proper consultation on all aspects of work with a powerful employee council. They provide for proper training in new skills that managements have neglected for too long. In short, they constitute a comprehensive package that meets the modern needs of both trade unionists and managements, and they are here to stay.

At the same time, some unions are pioneering new approaches to skill-training, which other unions must follow if they are to meet the changing needs of modern industry. The new system of apprentice training in electrical contracting, which replaces the old time-served apprentice system with a modern approach to training, has paid off handsomely, with more apprentices who are better trained than ever before. Likewise, the EETPU tripartite approach, involving the Government, management and unions in new training schemes, shows how co-operation can provide the new skills that are needed. Other unions and the TUC should stop sniping from the sidelines and adopt the same approach.

Pendular arbitration has the great advantage over old-style 'split-the-difference' arbitration of being less prone to inflationary settlements. Split-the-difference arbitration encourages employers to put as their final offer something well below what, in the last analysis, they would settle for and the unions to table a 'final' bid that they know is pie in the sky. It is no wonder that such arbitration often ends with an award that bears little relation to the financial position of the individual company. When employers and unions know, as under pendular arbitration, that the arbitrator can choose only the final offer or bid and cannot split the difference, this concentrates the minds of both. In most cases, bid and offer draw so close that arbitration is not needed and strike action becomes a thing of the past. Strikes over recognition should be avoided with the aid of new statutory recognition procedures that guarantee all employees the right to union representation, if a majority of the workforce so votes in a secret postal ballot.

It is, however, the unions themselves that need to do much more to rid the British trade-union movement of outdated, haphazard and harmful structures and inefficient and poorly funded methods of work. The SDP has always recognized that Governments can help this process. All union contributions need to be made tax-deductible, just like the tax deductions for professional subscriptions. This would be fair in principle and would break down another petty status barrier. But it would also help encourage unions to raise their contributions, as the cost to members for the increases would be less. This would give them more resources to improve their services.

The SDP has also pressed for a trade union development fund to be established. Unions can finance many of the new services they need from their own resources. But just as Governments regularly help industry to make changes and to introduce new equipment and technology, they should also help unions in the same way. Thus, a fund could help facilitate union mergers where there is a financial barrier to overcome. It could help unions to install modern computer equipment, not only to keep membership lists but to run many other activities. This Government has shown too little interest in making unions work better and serve their members more efficiently; yet there is an important constructive role for a Government in this area. The services that unions provide for their members and the work that unions do in the industrial relations sphere are too important for Governments to ignore. The Government can bring about, through funding, much needed reforms here, just as in other fields, and could transform many unions' levels of efficiency and effectiveness.

A new attitude of partnership in industry also requires partnership between the Government and each side of industry. The one-sided nature of Labour's 'Social Contract' approach and the Conservatives' refusal to have a serious dialogue with the TUC are in marked contrast to the actions of most other European Community countries. One does not have to return to the discredited corporatism of the 1960s and 1970s, but a totally 'hands-off' approach to industry is folly.

It is quite clear that an industrial system that places control with small groups of managers, cut off from those who work with them, and that encourages polarized battles between trade unions and management cannot compete because it does not co-operate. The task is to seek methods of industrial organization and ownership that bring together both competitiveness and co-operation.

A clearer understanding of the different roles of private enterprise and public services would help. With acceptance of the profit motive in the one and attention to economic efficiency in the other, a truly socially progressive economic policy could be forged. In the light of advancing new technologies and new patterns of financial management, it is absurd to fail either to recognize the divorce between ownership and control or to understand the need to give priority to strengthening worker participation, to extending democracy within industry. The need for a more competitive industrial and commercial base means that we must avoid imposing bureaucratic structures that suffocate innovation, inhibit flair. To overemphasize control and regulation is to provide a recipe for absolute economic decline. A high-wage, high-value-added, high-productivity and risk-taking economy will be easier to achieve within a framework of profit-sharing and worker share-distribution schemes. We are far more likely to move towards the aim enshrined in the SDP's constitution of an 'open, classless and more equal society' this way than by perpetuating monolithic state enterprises and imposing a minimum wage by statute.

It is the SDP, not the Labour Party, that is trying to explore new directions in redistributive social policies. In the debate over equality the SDP is paying increased attention to the philosophy of John Rawls.[1] The force of the Rawlsian advocacy of justice as fairness arises from two key principles: the requirement that all inequalities be justified to the least advantaged, the difference principle, and the 'priority of liberty', i.e. that a less than equal liberty must be acceptable to those citizens with the lesser liberty. In highlighting these principles, we should not forget Rawls's underlying assumption of a society with the property of 'close-knittedness', which he also explores by reference to the concept of 'social union'. It is hard to avoid concluding that without a basically harmonious society, the principle of social justice will be unstable and difficult to apply. The deepening of economic, social and racial inequalities within Britain is damaging our tradition of close-knittedness, putting social unity under constant strain and acting as a source of disharmony.

The Labour Party, as well as the Conservative Party, has much to answer for, as it has tolerated the inefficiency of the nationalized industries. It is this inefficiency that has contributed to the present public indifference over moves towards privatization. There is no sense of public outrage over denationalization, and the Labour Party, still stuck with Clause IV, seems unable to adapt to the changed public mood. As each privatization takes place Labour tries to minimize its 1983 manifesto commitment to renationalize all privatized firms, with compensation related to the price of the original sale. This formula, devised to scare off

investors and, hopefully, to sabotage the privatization of Britoil, British
Telecom and British Gas, has failed. It is also manifestly unjust. Labour
now expects to compensate individuals properly but not corporations –
an impossible distinction to make in any legislation. Over 2 million people
applied for Telecom shares, which doubled overnight the number of
shareholders in the country, from 4 per cent to 8 per cent of the adult
population (though the number has now dropped to 6 per cent). This
means that with the addition of British Airways and the sale of more
government shares in British Petroleum, there will be a huge group of
individual shareholders with a vested interest in preventing the return of
a Labour Government. The SDP/Liberal Alliance will not seek to restore
public ownership but will instead make these large private concerns,
many of them in a monopoly position, live under greater competitive
pressures to ensure that they are more responsive to consumer needs.

The old Labour slogans sound so outdated. A nationalized steel industry, far from holding the commanding heights, visibly plunged, in the
mid-1970s under Labour, into the depths of the economy. Guided by the
1975 report by Lord Beswick,[2] the Labour Government refused to let
BSC rationalize to reflect its realistic market level, thereby ensuring that
the eventual restructuring, when it came in 1980, was far more savage in
its social and economic impact. A contributing factor was the steel strike.
Exactly the same can be said to have happened with the NCB. The Coal
Board management had become too used to the Central Electricity
Generating Board's purchase of the bulk of its output, and though it had
tried to keep up its market share, it needed political authority to reduce the
number of pits following the productivity schemes that were eventually
pushed through in 1978. In neither industry was the workforce particularly loyal because both were publicly owned.

The key to reform is the individual citizen's desire for a meaningful
stake in society, most crucially in the place of work and in the home.
The biggest vote-winner in the 1979 election was the Conservative pledge
to sell council houses. In some cities, like Plymouth, this had been
happening in principle without Labour Party objections for years. The
obvious attraction of this measure in the eyes of many people was that
they were free to improve and to own their council houses, without having
to leave their housing estates. Its popularity was confirmed in the 1983
election, and now Labour at last accepts council-house sales. But, like
its current acquiescence in trade-union reform, its activists' conversion

owes almost everything to votes and little to an understanding of why the public feels as it does. For the next decade or two Labour seems destined to be a follower, not a leader, of public opinion, unable to comprehend the motivation behind either the small businessman and entrepreneur or the new trade unionist. Now it is the Conservative Party, not Labour, that is promoting a wider public distribution of asset and property ownership. There are many flaws in the way this is being done; the prime motive being not wider competition but the reduction of the Public Sector Borrowing Requirement (PSBR). However, as judged against the *status quo*, privatization can claim some advantages in improved management and a greater commercial orientation. There will in any event be little public enthusiasm for reversion to state control, except from the leaders of the large public-sector unions.

Predictably, the unions concerned oppose the privatization of British Gas, but their own members will take up their share options – as happened in the case of British Telecom. Many of their members will not want these organizations renationalized. Once successive Governments openly used their power to force British Gas to raise prices to provide extra revenue, the consumer was bound to question state control. The real question raised by the privatization of British Gas is: How can competitive pressures on such a large private monopoly be ensured? Giving the shares, free, to every adult citizen would, besides giving a massive boost to share ownership, leave the Government free progressively to dismantle the corporation's monopoly position without facing the charge that it was reducing the value of an asset in which people had bought shares on a stock-market valuation. The SDP is clear that changes will need to be made to widen competition. A free issue of shares would be a better way of freeing up other monopoly state industries and giving everyone a stake in their future. It would mean that the short-term motive of reducing the PSBR would be absent. If a limitation were to be imposed on the size of any institutional or individual shareholding to ensure a wide spread of ownership, it would mean that many more citizens would start to think in terms of assets and of building up capital; that in turn would start to change the national attitude to commercial enterprise, which must become more influential within British culture.

The employee-owned sector is growing faster in Britain today than in any other country in the European Community; in the middle of 1983, for instance, four new producer co-operatives were being registered every week. The number of registered worker co-operatives has increased from just over 300 in 1980 to nearly 1,000 today, with the creation of 8,000 new jobs in the process. In addition, growth is accelerating, with new registrations now running at over 200 a year.

More widely, the number of employee share-ownership schemes approved by the Inland Revenue has increased from 33 to 433 since 1979–80. If savings-related share-option schemes are added, the total comes to nearly 800. By any standards these are impressive rates of growth. And though the essential character of these schemes can no doubt best be seen as a form of deferred profit-sharing, they should not be criticized for that. Like new measures to promote wider share ownership or general citizen ownership, they are transforming from within the character of the market economy and conferring the benefits of capital ownership on a wider number of people than entrepreneurs alone.

Worker co-operatives are emerging as an important part of the British economy. But they need a new, devolved framework in which to expand further. A priority is to develop strong co-operative support organizations that offer a range of services, along the lines of the Caja Laboral Popular, or people's saving bank, in Spain, which has helped to foster the Mondragon group of co-operatives. The Caja provides up to 75 per cent of the finance for new co-operatives, with the remainder provided by the employees themselves and the state at a low interest rate. Nowhere else in Europe are financial resources and management expertise so effectively combined for the development of employee-owned firms.

The kind of support agency we need in the UK would be similar to the industrial co-operative associations or employee stock-ownership trusts in the USA, with specific powers to give matching grants for employees' investment in their own companies, to make available loans at preferential rates of interest and to provide a loan-guarantee scheme for commercial investment in employee-owned enterprises. Government support should be given to co-operatives on terms that are at least equal to those offered to conventionally owned companies. The conventional company structure should not be seen as the only one available to people starting up new businesses. It is ludicrous, for example, that, compared with companies, co-operatives are currently at a tax disadvantage when issuing bonus-share provisions to employee-members. In addition, Business Expansion Scheme finance should be channelled to employee-controlled companies as well as to conventional companies, and they should receive tax deductions on the same terms.

Creating this sort of new framework will encourage more radical innovations, particularly leading towards employee buy-outs. It should be possible, when a company is facing closure or liquidation, for the employees concerned to be given the first option to buy the whole or part of the enterprise. Employees should be enabled to rent a failed company from the receiver or liquidator. This would help to revive companies that have failed as a result of incompetent management rather than adverse market conditions. However, if we want to help employees rent a failed company we need to reform our bankruptcy laws. At the moment the receiver has an overriding aim: to liquidate the company in order to pay off creditors. That is his duty under the law. We need to replace this system of 'death at dawn' with the procedure used in the USA known as 'Chapter 11'. A company pending closure can put together a rescue plan and go to court to stop any single creditor from demanding payment. As the new survival scheme is put into force, the company can slowly pay off its creditors one by one.

We need the equivalent of the 1980 Small Business Ownership Act in the USA, which provides loans of up to $500,000, administered through the Small Business Administration, to finance employee buy-outs of closing firms and employee ownership of new firms.

Employee-owned enterprises taking over parts of the public sector is an interesting development. The classic example is the National Freight Corporation (NFC) employee buy-out. There strong and committed internal leaders were able to persuade substantial numbers of fellow employees to subscribe for shares in the proposed successor business, and both the Government and the City were reasonably helpful. Of course, an NFC-style buy-out is easier to bring off when the price of the business is substantially lower than one year's payroll. It would be easier still if the Government were to offer the same favourable terms to public-sector employees as it does to council-house tenants.

A capital-intensive state industry may be beyond the reach of an employee buy-out, but not all the remaining nationalized industries are of that kind, nor do they necessarily have to be privatized as single units. The National Bus Company is a useful example of both points. The relationship between its workforce size and its balance sheet's net worth is not very different from the NFC's. There are clearly opportunities for employee ownership here. The same is true if one examines some of the diverse operations of the local authorities and the regional and district health authorities that are due to be privatized. In Spain, for example, the socialist Government is establishing a number of co-operatives of the existing public-sector workers to 'contract out' a range of services, including hospital laundry and ancillary services, local garbage collection and energy-maintenance supplies. In Britain the present Government has agreed to a co-operative running the catering service at The Royal Navy Hospital Haslar in Portsmouth.

A measure of tax relief to promote incentives for start-up co-operatives should be established and implemented through the existing Co-operative Development Agency. This could include relief from income tax for members of co-operatives in respect of their contribution to the enterprise's capital (in the same way as pension contributions are treated), relief from a proportion of corporation tax during a start-up period and provision for employees who are made redundant to claim up to six months' unemployment pay in advance for investment in a new co-operative. Employee buy-outs could be encouraged by offering relief from capital transfer tax or capital gains tax for sellers of shareholdings to employee owners.

The thinking of the American economist Martin Weitzman is helping to recast the argument for new forms of partnership and participation in industry. Also the British economist James Meade is arguing for an end to the still deep-seated sense of alienation, saying that this will require 'different arrangements for workers' participation in decision-making as well as new arrangements for their participation in the enjoyment of the fruits of the firm's success'.[3]

The arguments of Meade and Weitzman are far-reaching in their consequences. The central point of the Weitzman thesis is that we should move from a wage-orientated economy to a share income economy.[4] In other words, a substantial part of the average person's take-home pay should be expressed not as a regular wage but as a share of the profit earned by, or value added to, the company to which he or she has contributed. What is required is a new system of reward, introduced by tax incentives, to express part of a worker's pay as a personal share of a firm's overall profitability, in bad times as well as good.

Such a development could build in the right incentives to resist both unemployment and inflation. A share system, Weitzman argues, has a

built-in drive towards absorbing unemployed workers, increasing output
and lowering prices that does not cease until all available labour is fully
employed. He summarizes his thesis thus:

Were just one firm alone to convert from a wage contract to an equivalent
share contract (initially paying the same compensation), that firm would increase
employment and output by lowering its price, lowering its revenue per worker,
and decreasing the pay of each worker. But if all firms (or a significant number)
convert to a share system, something like a balanced expansion of the economy
would take place, with the increased demand from higher spending of newly
employed workers feeding back to keep prices, revenues per worker and labour
remuneration more or less steady but with the economy automatically going
towards a higher employment level.[5]

There is a risk that in Weitzman's share system extensive participation
in decision-making, together with revenue-sharing developments, could
encourage firms to reduce either investment or employment opportunities. Paradoxically, this could mean a poor deal for the unemployed.
Unless sufficient flexibility in the shares allotted to labour and capital
could be ensured, a share economy run in the interests of the existing
capital shareholders (that is, the existing workforce) would tend to be
expansionary in its investment decisions and very cautious about its
employment decisions, to the disadvantage of the unemployed. This is
because, under the share system, the percentage shares of the value of
the firm's net product – as divided between the owners, managers and
workers – remain fixed and unchanged.

The wage contract has merely been replaced by a wage-plus-profit-
sharing one, which could introduce new and direct conflicts of interest
between the 'share partners' and jeopardize the firm's plans for employment and capital investment.

To counter this James Meade has put forward a more flexible pattern
of 'labour–capital partnerships' based on the issue of share certificates to
all existing workers, managers and owners in proportion to the incomes
that they were formerly deriving from the firm. The dividends paid on
the capital share certificates for the managers and owners would be the
same as the dividends paid on the labour share certificates, with the
consequence that any decision that is to the advantage of one 'partner'
will also be to the advantage of the other. The division of the shareholdings
in the value of the firm's net product can thus vary without damaging

the interests of any of the 'share partners'. Meade's intriguing thesis is this:

By the issue of additional capital share certificates, new investment could be financed whenever it was jointly agreed that such investment would add more to the value of the firm's total net product than to the cost of raising the new funds to finance it. The same principle could be applied to decisions to expand the employment of labour. Once again, the total of the firm's distributable income would go up proportionally more than the number of claims on it; and all existing claimants, both capitalist and labour, would gain by expansion so long as the cost of attracting the new labour was less than the new worker's net addition to the value of the firm's product.[6]

The Meade solution sounds very simple – and indeed it is. There appear, however, to be some important drawbacks to the scheme. Meade has not completely succeeded in removing potential conflicts of interest. One example would be a decision to devote part of the firm's resources to the provision of social amenities or fringe benefits for the workers; this would not confer any direct benefit on the capital shareholders. Another conflict could arise from a decision to promote a worker from one grade of work to a higher-paid grade, a development that would involve the issue of additional labour share certificates to the promoted worker. The inevitable unequal allocation of capital share and labour share certificates among individual workers, managers and owners respectively would have awkward consequences, as Meade partly recognizes. For instance, strict adherence to the principle of 'equal pay for equal work' would have to be abandoned, with *new* employees being taken on without qualifying for their share certificates until after a set period of employment. But, as Meade argues, in an age of high unemployment a period of admittedly lower-paid work leading to eventual participation in profits is surely preferable to stagnation in a dole queue.

Both Weitzman and Meade recognize that a whole new share system, or set of labour–capital partnerships, cannot be introduced overnight by a series of legislative enactments. Changes are possible and should be encouraged by the Government, primarily through the introduction of a new stepped system of tax concessions and incentives: the further each firm is prepared to go towards the 'share economy', the greater the tax incentive should be.

An experimental first move of some substance need not be prohibitively expensive. In the first place, it would probably be limited to corporate employment, excluding the small business, the self-employed and the public services. Thus it might cover about half of total employment. Let us suppose that an income tax rate of 20 per cent, instead of the normal 30 per cent, is to be charged on profit-related bonuses up to a maximum of 20 per cent of total pay. Then let us assume that the take-up rate is initially only 50 per cent. On these assumptions, the gross cost is less than 2 per cent of all income tax now levied on employees, or say between £0.5 billion and £1 billion per annum, about the size of the Chancellor's 'fiscal adjustment' in the spring 1985 Budget. The modest take-up of the modest benefits of the 1978 profit-sharing scheme – with between 300,000 and 400,000 workers covered today, still fewer than 2 per cent of all employees – is a reminder of the necessity for a real breakthrough: any tax concession must ensure that the profit bonuses, employee shares and labour–capital share certificates become significant parts of each individual's total remuneration.

It is realistic to assume that, particularly in the early years of a new share system, a large proportion of workers will wish to take all or most of the capital component of their remuneration as immediately spendable income each year. Lower-paid workers do not have enough income left over at the end of the week or month to enjoy the option of saving. Hence, the first tier of a new tax-incentive structure might be the option to take all or part of one's profit share or capital share as a tax-reduced cash bonus. Possible models here would be Japan, where workers in many large manufacturing companies receive a quarter of their total pay in the form of profit-sharing bonus, or the New Zealand system of employee partnership, as pioneered in the mining industry in the 1960s and 1970s, which involves the issue of 'labour shares' of no capital value to employees and the limitation of the return for, as well as the liability of, capital shareholders so as to make the enterprise a partnership of those working in it. In the UK a useful model would be the John Lewis Partnership, where all the profits go to the worker-members, or 'partners'. In 1983–4 the Partnership Bonus of £25 million was up by 49 per cent and was a significant proportion of the pay of the 25,000 worker-members of John Lewis.

The second tier could be more ambitious: encouragement to workers to retain as much as they can of their profit-shares so that they can grow as company equity. The first tier could build on the profit-sharing scheme established under the 1978 Finance Act. The second tier could build on

Save-As-You-Earn (SAYE) share-option schemes: the money would be held in, say, a building society or bank savings account. After a fixed number of years, or at intervals such as those that apply to equity warrants, the individual could choose between taking the money in the form of shares or, if the share price had not risen, as a cashable building society or bank savings account. The longer the employee delayed taking the profit, the greater the likelihood of capital gain. It might be appropriate to increase the incentive the longer the employee held the shares and increased their individual stake in the equity.

Tax concessions that enable companies to give shares to their employees free of income tax, or taxed at a reduced rate, should be linked with a corresponding reduction in corporation tax. In 1982 a Green Paper was published on the creation of a new form of industrial enterprise to be called an 'incorporated partnership', but nothing was done subsequently. A further reduction in corporation tax, designed to encourage the conversion of companies to an incorporated partnership basis, with shareholders getting higher but limited dividends, could lead, as Weitzman has argued recently, to employees gradually becoming the part-owners of the productive resources with which they work, both through investment and through bonus-share issues. That is to say, an 'explicit link' should be established between increases in company dividends and the issue of bonus shares to employees, followed by corporation tax changes aimed at encouraging new forms of partnership.

The third tier of incentives would be arranged for people not working for companies with capital share schemes and for those who would welcome an opportunity to expose part of their capital to the rewards, and risks, of owning company shares on a wider scale. The 2 million small investors in British Telecom and the £16 billion invested with unit trusts suggest that these individuals are more numerous than many suspect. Direct equity-owning incentives could be like Loi Monory schemes, introduced in France in 1978, which enable a fixed percentage of shares in firms of 200 employees or more to become available to small investors at reduced margins and lower premiums. The attraction of investing in unit trusts would be the wider spread of equities, the daily research, the administration carried out by the trust managers and the simplicity, for the investor, of the whole scheme. In West Germany, for instance, lower-income citizens can purchase shares at up to 50 per cent less than the market price, provided they hold them for six years in a savings fund or pension scheme. It is entirely possible that the UK unit trust system could be adapted in this way, taking the West German system of tax relief on share-price discounting as a useful model.

For individual workers the prospect of annual cash bonuses and/or a growing share in the capital value of their company in particular, and UK industry in general, would gradually give them the equivalent of a 'second wage'; that would initiate the age that Anthony Crosland anticipated over twenty years ago and termed the era of the 'two-wage worker' – the person paid for his labour but also enjoying personal share ownership and dividends on a significant scale.[7]

All of these proposals are part of the range of ideas that is being debated by both Social Democrats and Liberals. This debate is passing Labour by as it soft-shoe shuffles its way through its in-built ambivalence and its ideological heritage. There is no intellectual depth outside the avowedly Marxist wing, which is at least thoughtful even though ideologically blinkered.

At the heart of the debate about how to unite the goals of social justice with market prosperity is the concept of social partnership. New methods of industrial organization, participation and ownership are essential to encourage both competitiveness and co-operation. Neither will work without the other. Partnership, rather than polarization, is a critical ingredient for the success of a long-term strategy designed to reverse our economic and industrial decline.

8 Urban Regeneration

In the inner-city riots we are reaping the harvest of the polarization of our politics over many decades. We see a stark division between suburban citizens who commute into work in the inner city and those who live in the cities and have no work. This is a critical source of tension at the very centre of our financial and commercial life. A feature of Mrs Thatcher's Government has been its readiness to ignore the social consequences of its economic policies, even though some of the industrial restructuring and rationalization it has undertaken has been necessary and right. Instead of tempering the harsh effects of readjustment, the Government has claimed that there is no alternative. It has failed to build a constituency of people, particularly among civic leaders in many cities who are ready to adapt to change and lead the process of renewal.

Instead the constituency of those who wish to resist all change has grown. The Labour Party has irresponsibly allowed the likes of Derek Hatton in Liverpool, Ted Knight in Lambeth and Bernie Grant in Tottenham to drag the reputation of good local government down to its lowest point this century. But people like this would have found it difficult to remain in power and achieve notoriety if the Government had not given them such powerful grievances to exploit.

The need for proportional representation in local government elections has never been greater. It would immediately help to create a local political system based on consent and co-operation rather than confrontation. It would enable new partnerships to be forged between business and the community at local level, and between national government, local authorities and the private sector so they could work towards the economic revival of inner-city areas. Such partnerships are now the only way to revitalize the inner cities.

Somehow the Conservative and Labour parties must be persuaded of this truth. Sadly, however, the Conservative Party sees a political return from the exploits of Militant Tendency. Mistakenly, the Labour Party believes that its turn will come and it will once again wield absolute power. The first-past-the-post system suits the interests of both the old parties. But it does not, and will never, serve the interests of those who live in cities dominated by political extremists.

The prospect of early change, even when Labour has expelled some of the most flagrant offenders, is remote. These extremists are not just the household names. They are entrenched within the Labour Party in a number of our cities, and they work behind the scenes in many more. They damage police authorities and weaken the police when they try to grapple effectively with crime prevention. They injure employment prospects in cities where unemployment is already far too high. They make it easier for the Conservative Government to justify its neglect of the inner cities.

The tragedy is that Government's neglect has been reinforced by the irresponsible ways of Labour councils stretching from Lambeth to Edinburgh, with many in between. These councils abuse their powers only because they are elected on a minority vote and are unresponsive to majority needs. The Labour Party cannot escape its responsibility for the present low standing of local government, or for the ease with which people overlook the Government's appalling record over local government finance. Both the Labour and Conservative parties remain adamantly opposed to introducing proportional representation for local government.

Conservative councillors tacitly agree to concentrate council houses in safe Labour areas, while Labour councillors tacitly accept the concentration of private housing in safe Conservative wards. There is a conspiracy between Labour and Conservative politicians in the town hall as much as at Westminster. They conspire together to freeze out SDP and Liberal councillors, to deprive them of information, to keep them off key committees, to reduce their influence and thereby (it is hoped) to reduce the threat they pose.

One of the refreshing aspects of the dominance of the SDP/Liberal Alliance in seven county councils is that proportional representation is being implemented over the membership of committees. The SDP/Liberal Alliance is refusing to follow the pattern of the old parties in excluding opposition councillors from open involvement in decision-making. It is interesting, though, how often they refuse to participate and share responsibility, preferring to retain the old confrontational style on the surface and conspiracy beneath the surface.

Only when councillors are elected by proportional representation and are genuinely seen to be representative of the communities they serve will the authority and integrity of local government be restored. This is essential if central government is to target more resources to the areas of deprivation and need, and then allow local councillors to decide how those resources are to be used. Proportional representation is therefore one of the keys to decentralization, for only if there is confidence in local decision-making will central government be cajoled into giving up its powers.

Government policies to revive the inner cities in the 1960s and 1970s, such as the Urban Programme and Inner City Partnerships, at least recognized some of the problems of structural economic change and the decline of unskilled jobs in inner cities. But these programmes have suffered from being too centralized and too inflexible to deal with the problems. Too often central government has been far too slow to respond to the failures of its policies. There was considerable evidence by the late 1960s that the huge multi-storey housing estates that had replaced traditional streets were themselves creating social problems; yet they were still being built well into the 1970s. Much of the driving force for these developments came from central government. Central government prevented local authorities from exercising enterprise and initiative, and its policies were insufficiently sensitive to the need to encourage the creation of new enterprises over a wider area than the small pockets of deprivation in inner-city areas.

Inner-city economic policy must be refocused so as to encourage new industries and businesses. But to rely solely on this will not be enough. Small businesses will be more likely to succeed where there is already a dynamic economy in which other businesses are expanding and where more people are employed and therefore spending money. At present the prospects for business expansion have been set back by the Government's across-the-board expenditure reductions in urban aid. Total urban spending in 1986–7 will be £225 million, compared with £224 million in 1985–6, which represents a 5 per cent reduction in real terms. This will be especially damaging to the Inner City Partnership authorities and the twenty-three Urban Programme authorities, which include the most deprived inner-city areas in Liverpool, London, Manchester and Newcastle.

Economic federalism, discussed in Chapter 5, has some interesting lessons when one compares Glasgow with Liverpool. One sees a contrast between a more traditional, commonsense, Labour-controlled Council in Glasgow, and the Militant-dominated Liverpool Council. But there are deeper differences than this. In Strathclyde, Glasgow has an effective regional authority. The city and regional council has worked effectively with the Scottish Development Agency – for example, over the new Scottish exhibition and conference centre, which was built on schedule and to budget with the support of both the public and private sectors. Glasgow also gained from the weight of the Scottish Office, the independent Scottish banks and the feeling of nationhood. The similarity between the two cities – both lacking new major industries, both having large Irish-immigrant populations, both suffering from urban decay, extensive clearance and new town development – is such that one can point to the success of economic federalism and its potential for the English regions.

Within the disciplined reflation of the economy to which the SDP/Liberal Alliance is committed, we have suggested measures to be taken of direct and immediate assistance to the unemployed in the inner cities. An extra £1 billion on infrastructure investment, to build and improve housing and roads, is a sensible measure and can be concentrated on those areas of greatest decay. A job guarantee under the Community Programme for those unemployed for over a year could be of direct help to unemployed unskilled workers in the inner cities. Local authorities' current expenditure could be given a £1 billion boost through the existing rate-support grant mechanism and distributed so as to acknowledge inner-city needs. We would help local authorities to finance their own economic development activities, both directly and in consortia with local businesses in local enterprise trusts. In the medium term we would transfer non-domestic rates to the centre as a national tax, and we would use the powers given to central government to introduce preferential non-domestic rates in inner-city areas to help industries already there and to attract new ones.

Setting up regional development agencies in parts of England, with the task of promoting economic renewal in their regions, would be an important additional stimulant. Local authorities would also be given a specific statutory power to spend money on economic development. Many authorities have already devised initiatives designed to help local communities to cope with economic decline. They are, however, increasingly stymied, not just by lack of resources from the centre but also by restrictions on the amount they can raise themselves under the 1972 Local Government Act.

The aim must be to create an environment within which the public and private sectors can work together to renew our inner-city areas. This process could become self-generating as improvements proceed.

The other essential task for an SDP/Liberal Alliance Government serious about its economic policy towards inner-city areas would be to ensure that ethnic minorities are able to participate with equal opportunity in the jobs market. In 1976 the Race Relations Act established the legislative framework that would enable equal opportunities policies to be pursued. It did not require that specific proportions of people from ethnic minorities must be recruited; nor did it require employers to recruit ethnic minority applicants in preference to white, all other things being equal. It merely enabled positive action to be taken in training. Special courses were to be set up only for black people to enable them to compete on equal terms with white, and special publicity was to be provided for vacancies in jobs where ethnic minorities are significantly underrepresented.

These provisions can be implemented fully only if the proportion of people from ethnic minorities in the community and in employment in firms and other organizations is known. This will require the monitoring of the ethnic composition of the existing workforce and a commitment by people within organizations who are responsible for recruitment to make decisions without discrimination. Yet even these very mild provisions of contract compliance have not been implemented, except by a very few local authorities that are equal-opportunity employers and that make sure that contracts are let only to private companies that are also equal-opportunity employers.

If we want our ethnic-minority citizens to know that they are equal citizens and have an equal contribution to make to our society, the very least we should do is ensure that current legislation is implemented. Home Office Ministers say that proposals for contract compliance are under consideration. Department of Employment ministers, however, oppose contract compliance, and do not agree with the Act even though it is on the statute book.

In the Civil Service the Government directly employs 600,000 people, but fewer than 1 per cent of these are non-whites, compared with the proportion in the general population of 3 per cent. The very minimum a good Government needs to do in support of equal opportunities policies is to require all public authorities to be equal-opportunity employers and all private contractors in receipt of public contracts to demonstrate that they too are equal-opportunity employers.

The situation of the ethnic minorities in relation to the white majority is a complex one. While Asian self-employment was lower than that of whites in 1974, by 1985 18 per cent of Asian men and 14 per cent of Asian women were self-employed compared with 14 per cent and 7 per cent for white men and women respectively. For West Indians, on the other hand, the figures were much lower: 7 per cent and 1 per cent respectively. Special Enterprise Trusts need to be created specifically to help black people to set up in business on their own. Also the existing powers conferred by the Race Relations Act for special training should be used in particular to train for enterprise and to train more black teachers and more black policemen and women.

It is in our inner cities that one sees derelict sites, empty industrial and commercial buildings and squalid and deteriorating housing. New industry will not be attracted in these circumstances. At times it has looked as if the Conservative Government, with its political base in the south, was ready to abandon the inner cities in the north. To his credit Michael Heseltine, when Secretary of State for the Environment, tried to dispel this image in relation to Liverpool in the early 1980s. But a policy of benign neglect not only wastes the resources that are already there but also leads to disastrous and unacceptable further deterioration in the quality of life and opportunities for those who must continue to live in the inner cities. It also puts pressure for more housing development on the smaller towns and rural areas, some of which are already encroaching too far in their surrounding rural environment.

The regeneration of the inner cities is in the interest of the whole country. We all bear some responsibility for the huge housing developments of the 1950s, 1960s and 1970s. It was central as well as local government planners and architects who were responsible for the concrete jungles. The people who live there did not choose this environment. It has been imposed on them, and they have no realistic choice but to stay. Many will never get a housing transfer, and many could not afford to buy their houses even if they wanted to. As an urgent priority the environment of these huge estates must be changed; walkways and common areas that have become havens for muggers must be redesigned.

Whole blocks need to be demolished and small homes built that recognize the principles of privacy and security that are commonplace in the design of owner-occupied housing.

There is, too, a clear dimension of racial inequality in housing. While 46 per cent of West Indians rent from the local council, only 19 per cent of Asians and 30 per cent of whites do so. Compared with whites, black council tenants tend to live not in houses but in flats at higher levels and with less room space. Surveys of the economic and social conditions of black people show that the properties they occupy are, overall, markedly inferior to those occupied by white people. A quarter of all black council tenants have applied, and are still waiting, for a transfer to another property.

While higher government spending to renew the infrastructure of our cities, particularly housing, will help, this alone will not achieve the turnaround needed. The infrastructure investment required is huge: it has been estimated at £3.5 billion extra per year for the next ten years. This level of direct public investment will just not be possible within the constraints of sound economic management. In any event, a total dominance of public investment would be undesirable; the inner-city economies are already far too dependent on the public sector. We must encourage private-sector investment, not just because it generates greater economic activity than public sector investment but also because it offers a choice to people that the public sector hitherto has failed to offer.

There is also scope for co-operation in the field of rented housing. Home ownership is not everyone's choice. There are stages in most people's lives when renting is the better option, and for some this situation is permanent. However, although local authorities and housing associations receive subsidies that enable them to provide housing at moderate rents, government restrictions on public-sector investment, particularly since 1980, have resulted in supply not keeping pace with demand. What the Government needs to do now is to offer to finance a lower interest rate for building societies and other financial institutions that will invest in long-term, index-linked mortgages to finance new housing developments.

We need to develop a new sector of social housing for rent, with new incentives to encourage a larger volume of investment in such housing from private financial institutions. A number of building societies have found it possible to attract 'index-linked' finance from pension funds and to on-lend it at a real rate of interest of 4 per cent. With the help of a fifty-year, index-linked mortgage at a 4 per cent real interest rate, a dwelling that costs £30,000 can be economically let at a rent of £44.50 per week. Although this is higher than a 'fair rent' for the same dwelling, it is still less than the £70 per week that would be needed to service a mortgage of £30,000 at 12.5 per cent interest. Index-linked mortgages are ideal for financing rented housing because rents rise with inflation. The objective must be to stimulate an increase in building-society financing of housing for rent, using both their own resources and institutional finance.

A government premium to cover 25 per cent of the cost of the interest and principal repayments would reduce the weekly rent from £44.50 to around £36. A simpler form of finance would be a one-off grant of 25 per cent of the capital cost. But an annual grant would prove to be fairer and more flexible, and would provide an opportunity to adjust the level of the premium in line with changes in mortgage tax relief.

Social housing would have to be developed within a decentralized system. Local bodies – primarily housing associations, but also private companies, housing co-operatives and local authorities – would be empowered to provide this new form of housing for rent. But there is a cost to pay. In most urban areas even a reduced rent of £36 per week for a house costing £30,000 would be a great deal more than a 'fair rent' or a council rent for the same property. Tenants on housing benefit would have to find up to 40 per cent of the difference. To enable assured tenancies to contribute to meeting priority needs in areas of severe housing deprivation, it would be necessary to extend the high-rent provisions of the housing-benefit regulations so that tenants on low incomes would need to find only 10 per cent of the difference. The householder would, in addition, have the safeguard of knowing that the co-operative or corporation owning the property operated under the sort of social framework that Parliament has handed down over the years for building societies.

Local government would be helped by such a change, for it would be able to look at ways of passing control of some housing estates and tower blocks to the people who live in them. Neighbourhood housing trusts set up, owned and managed by the people who live on the estates would be able to make use of the new legislation to encourage private finance into their estates, and to develop a wider range of tenures.

Governments, whether Labour or Conservative, have hitherto found no objection in principle to part-financing council houses for rent. Public–private partnerships will only work now if the Government is prepared to invest in the scheme. Public funds could provide leverage to attract private capital through tax-free bonds. Governments have never objected to helping the mortgage payer through special tax allowances. There can be no objection, therefore, to their part-financing housing for rent that is either co-operatively or corporately owned.

Another area for reform is our system of urban development grants. They are too restrictive and inflexible and are still confined to the most deprived metropolitan and city authorities, whereas the American system of urban development action grants has cast its net more widely and creatively.

The UK system gives priority to urban areas with 'serious social needs'; the American system, on the other hand, increasingly stresses the stimulation of economic activity. The evidence suggests that the share of American projects involving commercial and industrial development, as opposed to housing and environmental concerns, is nearly double that of UK projects.[1] There are good grounds for widening the scope of the UK urban development grants to include local economic development as well as social need, and increasing the number of 'mixed-use' projects involving private capital. In addition, if smaller cities and urban districts outside the major conurbations qualified for grants – like the 'Labor Surplus Area' or 'Pocket of Poverty' criteria used in the US[2] – the UK urban development grant system could become an important lever in economic regeneration.

The facts speak for themselves. Between 1982 and 1985 in the USA over 1,250 projects, involving $1.7 billion of urban development action grants, received preliminary approval. These projects are estimated to account for 208,000 new jobs, stimulating nearly an extra $1 billion in private-sector funding, and a projected $250 million in extra tax revenues. The UK has fared relatively worse, with over 170 projects – involving nearly £45 million in urban development grants funds – accounting for only 10,000 new jobs and £175 million in leveraged private finance. The UK urban programme is now set to decline from £338 million in 1985–6 to a planned £324 million in 1987–8 – in cash terms, a reduction of £14 million in two years.

The American experience also emphasizes the need for more entrepreneurial local government in order to maximize revenue and undertake initiatives. The 'first generation' of local public–private partnerships evolved in cities such as Baltimore, Pittsburgh, Minneapolis and San Francisco, where the local authorities took the lead with new initiatives.[3] A similar role is possible for our local government. The 1985 report of the Audit Commission concluded that a more flexible approach is necessary, one that would allow local authorities to do more to help themselves. The Commission suggests they should be able to generate more funds internally and work with private companies without circumventing central government public-expenditure controls. At present, however, the Government controls the total amount of capital spending of local authorities, from whatever source the money is found, and has used this power to reduce the total amount of investment in real terms.

Three particular sources of additional funds for capital expenditure cited by the Commission are improvements in operating efficiency, increased charges for services to the private sector and further sales of under-utilized assets. Local authorities currently have £5 billion of receipts from assets that they are not allowed to spend. In 1985 councils could spend only 30 per cent of non-housing receipts and 20 per cent of housing receipts.

The Audit Commission contrasts the UK situation with American case studies in which local authorities have devised complex sales of assets on a leaseback basis; for example, Westinghouse Corporation purchased the New York City Subway cars and then leased them back to the City. In the Bay Area of San Francisco firms have been able to negotiate arrangements with the City for the purchase of capital facilities that are then leased back, including local roads and highway maintenance. To introduce such schemes into the UK we need a longer-term central and local government framework within which capital expenditure can be assessed. It means a three-to-five-year planning horizon for capital so that programmes and projects are not subject to abrupt changes and the year-end 'rush to spend'. There should be adequate provision for the depreciation and replenishment of fixed assets in accounting treatment and spending programmes; more encouragement to local authorities to fund their capital programmes with private participation, as in leaseback deals, and to rely less on new borrowings as a source of capital finance; and minimal central government involvement in the details of local programmes and projects. This will necessitate a substantial change of attitude and a more open-minded and stable political atmosphere in local and central government.

The concept of leveraged finance – public seed-capital attracting larger private funds for investment that would not otherwise have taken place – goes much further in the USA than in the UK. The Federal Government's major contribution to the financing of urban infrastructure (other than highways) by state and local government is through tax-exempt bonds, amounting in 1984–5 to nearly $7 billion in lower interest costs on local loans, and community development block grants used exclusively to 'lever' private equity and loan capital in mixed-use projects. In this way public capital can attract not only private finance but also a wider spread of private financial institutions involved in joint projects. For example, this approach has been used by the US National House Improvement Corporation in Pittsburgh, which has been able to recycle mortgages, guaranteed by the City, on improved houses as a means of tapping longer-term money put up by insurance companies.

The instigation in the UK by central government of a system of leveraged finance and tax-exempt bonds – in place of the annual grants and subsidies that make up the largest portion of the existing Urban Programme – would help to release private-sector funds. There is also a need for the Government to encourage a network of consultants who would act as intermediaries in packaging projects financed mainly by private institutions. The Scottish Development Agency has recently brought in a US consulting firm, America City Corporation of Baltimore, which has been involved in privately developed waterfront projects in Baltimore and Boston harbours, to package the 'Inverclyde Initiative' in Greenock. Many companies and banks in the UK are engaged in the work of enterprise agencies and trusts, which are forms of public–private partnerships that have evolved successfully in the USA. Many agencies also have local government involvement, ranging from financing to the provision of rent-free accommodation, although their priority is to help new and existing small firms.

The Government, in the 1982 Budget, authorized tax relief on corporate contributions to some, but not all, enterprise agencies. This was a wise step forward, but more needs to be done through new tax incentives. In the American equivalent, the Small Business Revitalization Corporation, local authorities take equity participation in many projects, and companies are able to write off against tax their involvement with the particular

Small Business Revitalization Corporation concerned with urban renewal. Similar treatment could be offered to those UK enterprise agencies and trusts operating in inner-city areas. Significantly, the London Docklands Development Corporation has offered financial incentives to encourage a move in this direction by Enterprise Trusts, such as the 'Project Full-employ' workshops for new businesses, operating in the docklands area.

The Neighborhood Housing Services Program in the USA is a national network of locally funded and operated self-help schemes that are success-fully revitalizing declining urban neighbourhoods. The British National Home Improvement Council, impressed by the American experience, has recently initiated a similar scheme, Neighbourhood Revitalization Services, which is a working partnership of residents, local officials and representatives of financial institutions whose brief is to tackle housing renewal problems.

Progress has been slow, however, with only two Neighbourhood Revitalization Services operating in 1985 (in Sheffield and Bedford) and a third in Oldham in 1986. The start-up costs are not high – less than £60,000 initially – but most local authorities in the UK have been reluctant to participate unless central government makes some funds available. But the government is making it even more difficult for local authorities to support such activities through further reductions in the Urban Programme.

The situation is different in the USA, where some limited Federal funds are available, and a new Neighborhood Reinvestment Corporation has been established by Congress to encourage more private-sector finance for schemes run by voluntary agencies and charities. By contrast, in the UK there is some doubt whether the embryonic Neighbourhood Revitalization Services can get off the ground.

A far more imaginative approach is needed in the UK, drawing extensively on other countries', and not just on American, experience. Small but additional central funding for home-improvement schemes is needed to encourage greater local government interest and involvement. New types of loan schemes, which local authorities could make available to certain categories of households for improvements, are essential. The loans could be financed from part of the capital receipts from the sale of council houses if the local authorities were allowed to act in this way. This could be complemented by allowing the building societies to enter the unsecured lending market and start to create a secondary market in house mortgages, which has long been the principal American method of creating low-cost finance for home buying in inner-city areas, with local banks in place of U K building societies.

There are good grounds for hoping that with such new thinking and new attitudes we could reverse our present urban decay. This will, however, require far more imagination and drive from central and local government, far greater readiness to construct a sound relationship between public and private sectors and, above all, the introduction of proportional representation, which is the only way of changing the present political stalemate that stultifies thought and initiative in so many of our cities.

9 Educational Standards

One of the more provocative and troubling documents to be produced on our education system is *Competence and Competition*, commissioned by the National Economic Development Office and the Manpower Services Commission (MSC). The report compares our system of education and training with that of three of our more successful competitors: Japan, West Germany and the USA. It makes it clear that our greatest educational failure is not with the high-flyers, the academically strong who end up in higher education, but with the bulk of our population. Our class-ridden society has never expected enough, or realized the full potential, of that majority. We are not going to flourish either socially or economically, let alone reverse our relative decline, until we do.

In the UK half the school population leaves full-time education at sixteen; in Japan 90 per cent stay on longer. In the UK one in three has a recognized vocational qualification; in Germany two in three. In the UK one in fifteen adults has a degree; in the USA one in five.

How can that state of affairs have come about? The factors that have contributed are numerous. But the single largest factor is the failure to ensure the matching of pounds to performance, resources to standards, investment in education to quality of education. In the present atmosphere of discontent and disillusionment, one of the most objective sources is Her Majesty's Inspectors' report on the effects of Local Authority Expenditure Policies on Education Priorities in England in 1984. This is densely written and packed with information, but it tells us much of what we need to know about the state of our schools in the two fundamental areas of investment and quality. The HMI's 1984 report says: 'Complex as the relationship is between levels of resources and quality of work, the fact that there is a link between them is clear.'

The political use to which the figures on pounds and performance have been put is depressingly typical of the current polarized political climate. Labour spokesmen quote the figures to show that insufficient pounds have been invested and tend to talk as if money alone can solve the UK's educational problems. On the other hand, Sir Keith Joseph and Mrs Thatcher concentrate on poor performance, on the deficiencies in quality and management. The problem is both insufficient investment and poor quality. Parents, taxpayers and educationally committed non-specialists must force politicians, teachers and educationalists to concentrate on both investment and quality. We need to invest more in education and yet we need, urgently, to ensure that extra investment leads to improved quality. The combination is critical, the investment is considerable; and to persuade taxpayers to fund such an investment they need to be convinced that there will be a return.

The most worrying finding is on the quality of education in the schools that Inspectors visited during 1984. They found that there was poor leadership in 46 per cent of schools. The quality of work was least satisfactory with the able pupils. The organization of pupil learning was unsatisfactory in some lessons in nearly 50 per cent of schools. Individual pupil needs were inadequately identified in 50 per cent of schools visited and better preparation for lessons was considered necessary in 30 per cent of primary and secondary schools and in 40 per cent of special schools. Improved management of resources by head teachers was identified as necessary in 25 per cent of primary schools and in about 12 per cent of special and secondary schools.

The message of the Inspectors' report on investment shows clearly that without investment we will not achieve quality. They found that materials such as books and equipment were unsatisfactory in 35 per cent of local education authorities; that the state of repairs was unsatisfactory in 59 per cent; and the decorative state of schools unsatisfactory in 68 per cent. The budget for maintenance and decoration has been reduced in 57 per cent, and in some schools parental contributions exceeded the capitation allowance. The induction programmes were found to be unsatisfactory in almost 50 per cent; the range of specialist curriculum coverage in the advisory service was inadequate in 60 per cent; the provision of classroom ancillaries was unsatisfactory in 29 per cent, of librarians in 71 per cent, of technical assistants in 50 per cent, of foreign-language assistants in 51 per cent and of clerical assistants in 43 per cent. Only eleven local education authorities were satisfactory in all the major aspects of provision, and thirty-one were unsatisfactory in the majority of aspects of provision. This devastating critique emphasizes that on both quality and investment the educational record in our schools is profoundly disturbing. It is a situation of which teachers, as well as the parents who use the system, are only too well aware. Yet there seems to be a depressing reluctance to face the nature of the challenge, which is far more deep-seated than many recognize; at the root is a devaluation of the esteem and status of the teacher in society.

The Government's relationship with the teaching profession is now deeply strained. The teachers' strike action, in some places persisting throughout three of the last four years, has meant a disastrous disruption to children's education. This was well documented in a Secondary Heads Association survey, which showed that the withdrawal of good will by teachers was more damaging than the days lost. Truancy went up while standards went down. Extra-curricula activities were particularly affected. All this was predictable, but nevertheless tragic in its effect. The teachers' pay dispute has provoked a bitterness that means that the problem of morale will not disappear even with a settlement.

Teachers' pay represents 75 per cent of the educational budget, so the step-like increase that I believe to be necessary will be very expensive. The NUT claim of a 25 per cent increase, which would give each teacher an extra £1,200 a year would cost £632 million in 1986–7. Unlike the Houghton award of December 1974, which would involve a 34 per cent pay rise, this time any big pay award must be conditional on structural changes designed to improve standards and efficiency. Many teachers feel that the inadequacy of their pay is the culmination of a long series of keenly felt insults and deliberately inflicted injuries to the education service generally. They cite the cutback in university places, the squeeze on the science budget, the doctrinaire hostility to the Open University with its poor funding, the closure of skills centres and the abolition of the Industrial Training Boards. Educationalists feel, with some justice, that these represent not merely 'efficiency savings', but a deliberate policy decision to downgrade the importance of educational and training opportunities.

The place of education and training within the nation's spending priorities is now a contentious issue in British politics, and will become even more contentious in the future. The Government conveys a sense of mistrust, of a low valuation of the country's schools and further education colleges. This is not helped by the fact that too many Conservative local and national politicians' families use the private educational system and want to give greater support through tax and other financial concessions to the private sector.

There has been a reduction in education spending over the last seven years. Public expenditure on education and science in real terms has fallen from £13.2 billion in 1978–9 to £12.4 billion in 1985–6 – at current prices, a reduction of £0.8 billion, or 5.6 per cent. The harsh reality is, however, that if greater priority is to be given to the needs of industry and employment over the next seven years, the scope for making substantial additional resources available for all forms of education will be limited. In education, as in other areas, there will have to be selective choice as to what should be given the highest priority for extra spending.

A sensible objective for a government pursuing a disciplined reflation of the economy (with the growth in overall public expenditure held to 2 per cent per annum in real terms, and achieving a sustained 3 per cent growth of output each year – which would be impressive compared with past British performance) might be to aim to restore in real terms the level of education expenditure to its 1978–9 position as early as possible in its first term of government.

Alarm about the fraying fabric of local schools is being felt far beyond the teaching profession. Although the Government boasts of rising unit-cost spending and the improved pupil–teacher ratios, in reality teachers and parents know that Government policies have trapped spending below what is needed to keep educational standards high. It is difficult not to have a sense of impending tragedy about the school system in which so many of us, as parents, teachers or politicians, have pinned our hopes for the future. Education falls between two stools. It lacks the benefit of local autonomy, since central government funds the greater part of its budget and has the decisive influence on the national, not local, negotiations over teachers' salaries. Nor does it have the clarity of responsibility where the Secretary of State is wholly in control. Decentralization offers the best way forward for education, but if that is to be done, the national pay-negotiating procedures need to be reformed and an element of local autonomy introduced.

To outsiders, the tortured language of the teachers' pay negotiations means one can easily get lost in its coded intricacies. Terms like assessment appraisal, evaluation or career development all have an inner significance. What parents and the public want to be assured about is that in exchange for higher salaries teachers accept both an effective system of monitoring for improving the quality of their teaching and a pay structure that rewards and keeps those talents where they are needed – in the classroom. Parents know that a headteacher whose commitment and quality falls off very quickly becomes a liability, and the school suffers. There must be a way of ensuring that those few headteachers are retired or move elsewhere. Also, we need a career structure designed to ensure that good teachers are encouraged to stay. To attract good teachers, most parents accept that teachers must be paid more. The problem is convincing those not involved with schooling as taxpayers and ratepayers to finance the increase. Independent assessment of teachers made by the profession on objective criteria is essential. There is much to gain from new and substantial extra financial rewards going to good teachers. Not every teacher deserves the highest salary. The teachers' unions cannot expect the government to find more money if they resist sensible contractual changes aimed at attempting to reward effort, efficiency and excellence. The Family Doctors' Charter in the 1960s gave a step-like increase in general practitioners' pay, as did the Junior Hospital Doctors' Charter in the 1970s. Both were, albeit too tentatively, geared to improving the standard of service. Teachers' holidays are, as judged by all other professions, very long. It is not unreasonable to expect that extra training should take place in some of that holiday period. Teachers prepared to undertake extra-curricular activities, as most are, should have that financially recognized.

It is no fault of the younger teachers that the pay structure of teaching has clearly been damaged by falling rolls in primary and now secondary schools. Greater incentives should be introduced to hold the enthusiasm of the young committed teacher. It will be difficult to hammer out what should or should not be in a new teacher's contract and to devise a new pay structure to last into the next century. But none of this work will repay the effort unless it brings about a new spirit within the Government towards the teaching profession and within the profession itself. Any Government can act, as this Government has done, in such a way as to undermine the self-respect of the teaching profession. But no Government can legislate for a profession to command respect – that is something that only the teaching profession itself can achieve.

School teaching badly needs a professional body that commits itself to certain professional standards, advises government on educational matters and plays a major role in maintaining quality in its entrants and practitioners. Such a body could, if it operated effectively, help to give the profession the status and self-respect it needs. It could also defend the political independence and neutrality of the profession – a matter which, in the current mood of intervention from both extremes of the political spectrum, is increasingly important. Professional bodies of this sort are commonplace in medicine. Lawyers have the Bar Council and the Law Society; nurses have, in addition to many unions, the Royal College of Nursing. Some of these bodies have a reputation for conservatism and the pursuit of vested interests, and this could be a danger for any similar body for teachers. But these professional bodies also provide a cohesion and independence, and, at their best, a defence of standards from which the teaching profession would benefit.

The minority who move on to higher education enter a system with a high international reputation. Efficiency, as measured by graduations per unit of economic input, is almost the highest in the world. Where the UK suffers by comparison with other countries is not so much in quality, but in quantity. There is not enough higher education. Only 14 per cent of those eligible to take part in higher education do so in the UK, and this is far too low. The participation rate in Japan is 40 per cent, while in the USA it is 50 per cent. The Government is aiming for a 15 per cent participation rate in the UK by the 1990s. The nation needs more, rather than less, higher education, and if the eligible population for higher education does decline, we should recruit a higher proportion of it. Our academic standards are so solidly based that the fear of 'dilution' is bogus. The allegation that 'more means worse' was always profoundly wrong. More people should stay in full-time education after the age of sixteen, and there should be a broader base to that education. The provision of an educational maintenance allowance to encourage those in poor families to stay on should be a high social priority; we are missing out on the considerable talents of those who prefer to leave school and bring in extra money to their families, even if they are only claiming YTS allowance and then social security if no jobs are available. The Government is ready to pay out on the MSC budget what it refuses to pay on the education budget. The case for bringing the MSC under the responsibility of the Department of Education and Science is very strong.

Expenditure on desirable educational objectives obviously cannot be unlimited, but it is this Government's narrow, malevolent and incompetent general attitude to higher education that is so wrong. The Government admits in official documents that the economic return on higher education is definitely high, but it contradicts that admission in tone and substance in virtually every ministerial pronouncement.

Two interesting plans have recently been put forward to widen access to higher education, and to promote greater flexibility and competition. Neither plan is worth serious consideration. The essential difference between them is that the first is institution-led, whilst the second proposes a system which is consumer-led.

The *institution reform plan*[1] is based on four separate steps that, in practice, would occur together. It is argued that this plan should be implemented for the universities, but polytechnics and other institutions could be brought into any scheme.

– First, a scale of full-cost fees to be charged to all students, rich or poor, would be calculated. The fees would be designed to keep the institution solvent, provide for replacement of capital and pay interest on private loans (which it would have the power to raise) for expansion if needed.

– Second, the entire local authority grant system for student maintenance would be abolished and the money clawed back to the Exchequer. This total sum would then be handed to the University Grants Committee (UGC), which would be instructed to divide it into two parts: research and teaching.

– Third, the UGC would be left free to distribute these separate allocations among institutions according to peer-group evaluation of the aggregate research and teaching potential of their individual departments, also taking into account plans submitted for future research and teaching capacity. In addition, universities and polytechnics would be encouraged to raise far more outside money from gifts, grants or contracts than is currently UK practice.

– Fourth, universities and polytechnics would set up student-aid offices that would receive funds for various forms of student support on an income-related basis; funds would be decided by the institution and drawn from the research and teaching allocations. This could include remission of fees and maintenance grants. It could include subsidies for the interest charge on bank loans arranged through the institution – which might even go into the loans business itself.

A controlled amount of public money would go to all higher education institutions, but they would then be allowed to add to it in various ways from private sources; this is, of course, already being done with considerable success by many higher education institutions, Salford

University being one of the best examples. This plan, rather like proposals for an internal market in the NHS, is workable, not least because the entire arrangement, including student aid and general financial planning, actually works in many US state universities, though because of autonomy from the federal government it has been left to each state to provide its own selection of incentives for moves in this direction.

In a *consumer plan*[2] the changes are more radical, but the costs would be higher. It has been called an adult learning entitlement for the equivalent of two years' full-time study to all men and women aged eighteen, which they would be entitled to use for full-time, part-time or periodic study, or a combination of all three, at any time beyond their eighteenth birthday. The entitlement would comprise a study grant-support element and a fee element, both calculated at whatever levels were in operation at the time, where fees were calculated to cover in aggregate the average costs of teaching and facilities used.

Adults enrolling on a course that led to an award or qualification offered through higher or further education would draw the appropriate amount of entitlement. Students on other courses recognized by a Registration Board would also draw the appropriate amount of entitlement. Thus, a day student would be empowered and entitled to study when, where and what he chose until the entitlement was used up. Where a student wished to study away from home, the student would be required to bear additional costs, except where it was necessary to be a resident student.

Special entitlements would be available for those studying in priority areas, say engineering, technology, medicine, but these would vary from time to time, depending on priorities established for occupational needs. Institutions would offer special entitlements through bursaries or scholarships. Employers would be able to sponsor students through awarding their own entitlements, as is the case at present with industrial sponsorship. Individuals who used up their entitlements and who were unable to obtain special entitlements would be responsible for covering their own costs if they wished to continue.

The entitlements could be supplemented by an associated loans scheme. Students would be able to take out loans for part of their costs, for fees in excess of two years. Students would also be able to take out loans for topping up basic social security levels of support; this could well be means-tested or brought into the overall taxation/benefit structure. The fees element of the student funding would be paid direct to the student to spend on the desired course. Student maintenance could be paid through the SDP's Basic Benefit system, which would take the consideration of maintenance awards for the post-eighteen sector out of the education system. While it would be possible for people on Basic Benefit to study after they had exhausted their fee entitlement, they would have to meet course costs themselves.

Similarly, the funding arrangements for institutions need revision to enable them to be more responsive to student requirements than at present, and to give them financial incentives to do so. Institutions would have three sources of income: a core grant to cover the general public service contribution and a 'background' level of research; research contracts for grants for specific projects; and student fees, covering in aggregate the average cost of the teaching hours and facilities used. This last would be derived from deducting students' fees from institutions' current block grant. In a social market system, the fee would not have to represent the full economic costs of the course, as it would be accepted that core running costs of an educational establishment are the responsibility of the state. Institutions would then make up their income by recruiting students. If they wished to innovate and needed pump-priming in order to recruit students, an innovation/development fund would be available, for which they could make bids.

Two other measures would enable and encourage institutions to be more responsive. Within the core-funding budget limit, institutions would be free to offer whatever length and level of courses they thought appropriate to sustain their admissions. Some institutions might choose to change the balance between full-time and part-time study, between three- and four-year degrees and two-year courses. No additional core funding would be available to support these initiatives, but application could be made to a national development fund.

A national higher education development fund would be created by deducting an appropriate figure from the overall core grant. Institutions could apply for funding from the development fund within its criteria, which might be varied from time to time, while upholding the intention of encouraging colleges and universities to extend the range of their services. For instance, institutions proposing to run weekend programmes or extend the teaching year from thirty-six to forty-eight weeks could be eligible for additional funding from the national development fund.

Another policy implication of a more efficient higher education strategy would involve a rethink of the Government's whole stand on overseas students. This is one of the most short-sighted of all the Government's decisions. It has lost the UK immediate commercial business, but unquantifiably more in long-term commercial orders, overseas markets and trade. A different approach would be to encourage the untapped earnings potential that, even under realistic restrictions, almost certainly exists. For example, financial incentives and fee flexibility could be provided for institutions that perform well in attracting foreign-student income without lowering standards. Foreign students are good for Britain. They create the decision-makers of the future who will have good will and affection for us.

It is self-defeating for us not to increase substantially the science budget. Japan, France, West Germany and the USA are all increasing their investment in science. The UK, which was actually cutting its science budget in 1985, at least started to aim again for level funding in 1986. But even this is to budget for relative disadvantage, to budget for losing out in the highly competitive scientific and technological drive that will fuel other nations' prosperity.

The revised expenditure plans involve new allocations of £614 million in 1986–7, £628 million in 1987–8 and £647 million in 1988–9 for the science budget. This represents an increase of £15 million in 1986–7, and a further £15 million per annum in 1987–8 and 1988–9. In total, it amounts to a 7.5 per cent cash increase that, on the basis of the Treasury's lower inflation forecasts, is designed to maintain 'level funding' in real terms over the next few years.[3]

But this increased funding amounts only to what the Advisory Board for the Research Councils' report calculated as the minimum required. Taking account of the past erosion of the research councils and the future costs facing them, the report actually recommended total increases of £15 million for 1986–7, £30 million for 1987–8 and £40 million for 1988–9, a cash increase of £85 million. This would have allowed for 1 per cent per annum real growth in the science budget over the next three years.[4]

The House of Commons Select Committee on Education and Science's report, *The Future of the Science Budget*, concluded in 1985 that the research councils, the British Museum and the Royal Society as a whole were facing increased costs of at least £20 million, or 3 per cent above the inflation rate. The Committee recommended that annual increases in the science budget 'should be at least 3 per cent above the general movement of prices indicated by the GDP price deflator'. This would amount to a total cash increase of £110.5 million over the next three years, allowing for 3 per cent per annum real growth.

Sir Hans Kornberg, President of the British Association, warned in 1985 that the morale of the research community was lower than it had ever been, and that there was an urgent need to increase the proportion of our gross domestic product devoted to research.[5] Ten years ago, it could be argued that national strength in basic research was not essential for economic success. Japan, for example, achieved spectacular rates of growth by importing and adapting technologies that had been developed overseas. But since then, it has become clear that many of the new industries of tomorrow will be based on technologies that are highly dependent on pure science. This is the main reason why the Japanese, French and American governments are all currently restructuring their support for research and development, with much greater priority being given to investment in new areas of research at the expense of applied programmes.

Even at current levels of provision, we are losing ground to our industrial competitors, and this underlying trend will continue. In the natural sciences and engineering, for example, our expenditure as a proportion of our GDP is only just over half that of the USA, Japan, France and West Germany. Without a higher volume of investment in science to strengthen our economy, we will continue to fall behind at a time when the world is moving into an era where basic research is playing a critical role in generating the scientific winners on which will be founded the industries and markets of the future.

If we are to reverse our economic decline, we will have to raise the level of skill training. Teenagers who leave school at sixteen, for the most part, do not participate in any further education or training. In the USA and Japan, over 90 per cent of their teenagers remain at school until eighteen. In West Germany 90 per cent of those who leave school at sixteen go into jobs with formal apprenticeship training schemes.

The contrast in Japan is not just in formal education. Employees are trained extensively by the firm they work for. They can often be trained six or seven times during their working life and taught completely new skills to prepare them for new jobs. In the USA, although it is mainly the individual rather than the employer who funds further education and training, the ethic for self-improvement and higher and further education has become a way of life. Those in Britain who pour scorn on the American higher education system do so without realizing that the average American is far better educated than his British counterpart.

In Britain, education and training are not given enough priority. Government estimates put employers' spending on training at less than 1 per cent of turnover. This is well below comparable levels in Germany and Japan. Yet an educationally qualified workforce, able to adjust to new techniques and new machinery, is essential to our economic survival.

We need to develop new concepts like Open Tech, where the key to success is flexibility. If we are to succeed in changing people's attitudes to further education and training in the urgent timescale required, then we will have to devise a way of fitting the education to their needs. The courses must be accessible to all. In rural areas flexibility is necessary where the population is evenly dispersed, and a lot of people live a long way from educational colleges. We need flexible arrangements for those who work long shifts or unusual hours, and so find it impossible to attend a college course.

Open Tech can meet those needs. It produces many learning packages on a variety of courses. It has local field offices that are widely dispersed and ready to deliver study packages and personal tuition. It aims to give effective access to the education and training that exist in colleges and adult education centres. Its accessibility is proving an incentive for employers to enlist employees on the scheme. The Government should give grants to the unemployed, so they too can renew their skills and training. The more people able to join Open Tech, the more opportunities there will be for adults to update their skills. The potential advantages for individuals, employers and government are enormous.

It is better to try some of these new techniques for generating efficiency first in the field of higher education. This is the area where it is vital that standards are maintained and improved, and where new investment must be found and used to the best advantage. It is an area that has suffered from constant government interference, which has led to a serious loss of confidence in the UGC. Students have seen the value of their grants cut by 20 per cent over the last seven years and have suffered from arbitrary changes in travel regulations and now in social security regulations, which have had a savage impact on those with high housing costs. The higher education sector has no obvious interest in clinging to the *status quo*.

It might later be possible to take some of these techniques into secondary and primary education, particularly if in the meantime the salary dispute is settled in a way that both improves standards and raises the teaching profession's morale. It is very difficult, however, to persuade teachers to consider new ideas for the school sector while they feel so dissatisfied. Yet parents are frustrated and perplexed by much of what they see happening in our schools. The costs of a teachers' salary increase, and of educational maintenance allowances to help children in poor families stay on in school past the age of sixteen, will be very expensive. Those who determine the educational budget will have to examine ways of improving standards. This country must make it a political priority to think afresh about education, and that can best be done in an atmosphere where all concerned sense a deeper political commitment to the underlying purpose and value of education.

10 Health Care

Looking to the 1990s, the thrust of NHS policy should be towards ensuring better service for every patient. It should be obvious that the consumer interest has to become more central to health provision. New policies should first be tested out on an experimental basis in co-operation with local managers rather than imposed right away through the whole service. The NHS has suffered from too many 'appointed days', with a national reorganization imposed from the Department of Health and Social Security (DHSS). In future Ministers should be advised less by civil servants in the DHSS, who have no direct experience of NHS management, and more by people with experience of administering the NHS at local and regional levels. What is sad to see is the diminished role for professional nursing advice in the running of the NHS.

There are many research findings, suggesting new policy themes, that have not received adequate attention from the present Government. The most important is evidence about the quality of care. Much health-service planning in the past has been concerned with inputs (how many staff and how much money should be spent on buildings) rather than outputs (how much post-operative infection there is, how many hours people wait before being seen by their local surgeons). This was perhaps understandable when the differences in input between regions and client groups were so marked. But there is a strong case now for moving on to find new ways of assessing the quality of care. These should include consumer surveys, since the voice of the consumer and patient is too weak in the NHS while the power of the medical profession is still too strong. Peer review of medical records chosen at random by fellow doctors is essential, as is the independent assessment of new evidence on the effectiveness of treatment and operating procedure, such as the recent study on heart transplants. Equally important is the quality of care, particularly in areas such as those for mentally handicapped people where there are still very few services genuinely run on the social as distinct from the medical model. Each specific policy needs to be assessed in terms of its contribution to raising the quality of actual care and actual services to consumers.

There have got to be new ties and new relationships between primary care and the rest of the NHS. The family doctor service is now in a much better state: it has attracted able recruits in the last ten years in a way that it never did before. Now 50 per cent of medical students put general practice as their first choice. Family doctors are working as members of primary-care teams that include health visitors and district nurses and employed nurses. The 10,000 employed practice nurses represent a new and considerable resource in terms of skilled patient care. The General Practice Finance Corporation's cost-rent scheme has been a success, and the standard of premises has risen. General practitioners are now doing more active diagnosis and treatment. Their pathology requests amount to 20 per cent of the total workload of the hospitals and X-ray requests to 10 per cent. All this has already had a major effect in reducing the demands on hospitals. The referral rate of new out-patients from general practice is half what it was in the early 1960s. GPs are now referring only 155 patients for each 1,000 on their list, compared with 320 then.

The question is whether this investment can be turned into really effective high-quality primary care. In spite of the successes, we are a long way short of this. The recent evidence of poor coverage on cervical cytology is very clear. Less well known is that some diseases that ought to be prevented through immunization are now far too common. There were still 100,000 cases of measles and nearly 7,000 notified cases of TB in 1983. Immunization rates nationally may be reasonable but in some inner-city areas, they may be only half the national rates – so low, in fact, that there are serious risks that diseases such as polio may recur. There is still duplication between the family doctor's role and that of the school health service, and we are still not providing an effective developmental service for children.

For adults, the care available to people with long-term illnesses such as diabetes, epilepsy or hypertension is sometimes haphazard and, on the research evidence of the Royal College of General Practitioners and others, often downright poor. We are maintaining both the family-doctor service and one of the world's most extensive systems of repeat out-patient clinics at a cost of £1 billion per year. At a practical level it would seem quite incredible to outsiders that GPs and hospital doctors can be treating the same patients with as little contact between them as sometimes still happens. We must look at the contractual arrangements for doctors, whether GPs or consultants, and see if there cannot be a greater integration of service obligations. We need new forms of co-operation between family doctors and the rest of the NHS.

A first practical step would be to create an NHS development fund on which family doctors and NHS general managers could draw.[1] At present the development margin in general practice is locked into the family doctors' own incomes. The more they do in terms of providing new services and taking on work, the greater their loss. We have got to find new and positive incentives which will lead to co-operation and to extra service. There are many family doctors who are now ready to grasp the new opportunities, if they are presented in an attractive and satisfying way. Just as joint funding unlocked doors between the NHS and the social services, so a new kind of primary care funding would provide the focus and structure for better forms of regular co-operation and planning between family doctors and the rest of the NHS. Pilot schemes for a primary-care organization that crosses the present administrative boundaries need to be designed, since the present arrangements leave a lot to be desired. It should be possible to devise a better pattern than the existing one, in which the Family Practitioner Committee is separated from the district health authority, which employs the community health staff.

Doctors in an area might agree to take over routine care of people with diabetes, to undertake more minor surgery, or to provide special help for very elderly patients, in co-operation with district nurses. Such programmes would entail clear definitions of aims and costs, and clear commitments on both sides. In order to fund the programmes, development money, both capital and revenue, should be available. It would be particularly useful to develop new forms of co-operation between doctors and the nursing profession as part of this programme. The development fund might eventually take a sizeable share of all development money available to the NHS, but it would be better to build it up gradually, starting with an investment fund of £25 million for the first year, £50 million for the next year and so on, and, while fully expecting to climb up to over £150 million, to do so only at a pace that can be properly absorbed.

The fund could also sponsor pilot schemes on intensified ante-natal care, for example, where the patients themselves would select their admission time, which would demonstrate the extent that it is possible to reflect consumer wishes. The fund could encourage innovation and experimentation between districts and then promote the practice proven to be the best, which would be universalized through conviction rather than by a DHSS circular.

The second main area for new policy development is that of local inequalities in the NHS. The issue of equality must play a greater part in NHS policy-making: there is little point in having a national service if it simply follows the contours of social advantage. The greatest indictment of the present Conservative administration in its handling of the NHS is that it has done virtually nothing to follow up the Black Report on inequalities of care.[2] Differences in the quality of service provided by local areas are still immense. Yet the difference in cost and the difficulty of providing services vary greatly between different groups. For example, it requires much more managerial drive and more resources to deliver a high immunization rate in inner Liverpool or to provide a good service for the over-seventy-fives in Hastings. The NHS is not doing a very good job in areas of severe social deprivation, and we need new techniques to improve that record. There is a strong case for a 'deprived district' policy in the NHS, whereby specific targets are set for improving certain services and special funds are available for meeting these targets. But such centralized interference on the narrow but important area of correcting inequalities of care cannot be justified, and will not work, without making radical changes in the method of financing all district health authorities. The first priority is to establish a far greater degree of decentralized management for the vast majority of district decision-making.

In May 1975, as Minister of Health, I established the Resource Allocation Working Party (RAWP) to review the arrangements for distributing NHS capital and revenue with the aim of securing a pattern of distribution that was responsive to relative need objectively, equitably and efficiently. Even at the time we knew we were embarking on one of the most profound changes in the development of the NHS. In September 1976 the Working Party reported. The amazingly rapid growth rate that the NHS had just experienced – a full 1 per cent extra of GDP in just over two years – was about to end because of the expenditure cutbacks imposed by the IMF. We knew that in future the redistribution of resources was going to have to take place against a less buoyant economic background, within both the NHS and the country. Nevertheless, RAWP was structured as a response to an objective analysis of facts, although its creation owed almost everything to a political stimulus. The Working Party was deliberately designed to provide an apolitical way forward that would withstand changes in Ministers and in Governments. I am thankful that it has proved to be that.

The RAWP recommendations have been implemented despite the powerful protests of the London teaching hospitals, though at a varying pace reflecting, in part, worsening economic circumstances. There has, however, been measurable progress in correcting inequalities. Given the rigidities and inequalities existing before RAWP, such progress has been perhaps the most far-reaching recent development in the NHS and far more beneficial to the NHS than all the varying reorganizations of its administration. In 1979–80 the poorest region was 9 per cent below its RAWP target allocation, the richest 13 per cent above. There have been quantifiable improvements in the services provided in the East Midlands and the North-East as a direct result of RAWP. The RAWP formula has rightly been modified over time, and while, in theory, it compensates for regional cross-border flows, there are still a number of distortions and disincentives. The 'Service Increment for Teaching' has helped compensate for the extra service cost per medical student and has to some extent drawn the teeth of the London teaching hospitals' criticisms, but relying on standardized morbidity ratios as a proxy for mortality data was inevitably a somewhat rough-and-ready expedient. What is remarkable is how well the criteria have withstood the test of time.

Joint financing was introduced around the same time as RAWP, to break down the financial disincentives in order to encourage co-operation between the local authority social services and district health authorities. As long as health care is narrowly defined and there continues to be a physical separation between the authorities responsible for the NHS and the social services, it is crucial to have cross-financing arrangements. A large part of the motivation for introducing joint financing was to provide the financial spur to co-operation and in that it has had considerable success.

Overall financial support for the NHS has to be increased in real terms in order to be able to cope with the demographic pressure of the elderly and handicapped. Over the past decade OECD studies comparing the level of spending on health care in the UK with those of other Western industrialized countries have consistently shown the UK to be at, or near, the bottom of the league, both in terms of the proportion of GDP and per capita. The latest OECD survey reveals that, since 1974, the UK has experienced, in real terms, the slowest rise in health expenditure per capita of all Western nations except Greece and Ireland.[3] In 1984 the UK's absolute level of spending on health care, at 5.9 per cent of GDP, was the lowest in the OECD, apart from the Netherlands (5.6 per cent) and Belgium (5.8 per cent). All our other major competitors, such as the USA (9.8 per cent), West Germany (8.2 per cent), France (8.1 per cent), and Italy (6.7 per cent) were ahead. The Health and Personal Social Services (H&PSS) share of the planning total of gross public expenditure has risen only slightly from 11.2 per cent in 1975–6 to 12.2 per cent in 1984–5.

The harsh reality is that the relatively low UK expenditure on health care has been masked by the efficiencies that initially came with the structure of the NHS. Now, as a result of relatively poor economic performance and slower growth than most other countries in the OECD over the last fifteen years, the NHS is seriously under-funded.

It will be very hard to catch up on the funding or to alter substantially, over the next decade, the percentage of GDP devoted to health. It upsets me personally to admit it, but given other high-expenditure priorities like science and skill-training to strengthen our industrial base, the scope for a significant improvement in health expenditure in the future, relative to other public expenditure programmes, is likely to remain very limited. A target of 1½ per cent of inflation-proof growth is as much as can be hoped for, and that will barely meet demographic pressures. Regardless of the way in which public health care is provided and financed, the resources available to provide such care are almost certain to be less than the demand. Expenditure on health care is greatest among the young and the aged. During the period 1981–94, the Government forecasts that the under-fifteen group, as a percentage of the population, will be relatively stable, declining in the 1980s to around the 1981 level (20.5 per cent) by 1994.[4] A similar trend is envisaged for the group aged fifteen to sixty-five. However, it is the old, particularly those aged seventy-five and over, whose number and expenditure implications pose a major problem for government. The over-seventy-five group is forecast to rise from 5.8 per cent of the total population in 1981 to 6.7 per cent in 1994.

The Government is now planning to prevent any real increase in personal social services (PSS) beyond 1985.[5] Yet increased demands for PSS from the aged, if not met, will be translated into further pressures on hospital services and 'community-care' facilities. The evidence indicates that this is already happening at a time when money for joint financing is, in some parts of the country, becoming scarce. For many years the norm for geriatric beds has stood at ten beds per 1,000 population aged sixty-five and over. It has been calculated that 20 per cent more beds will be required over the next twenty years to provide a pattern of care similar to that provided at present.

We have been able to absorb such demographic changes in the past: in the period 1972–82, a 23 per cent increase in the population aged sixty-five and over resulted in a 33 per cent increase in the number of elderly admitted to hospital. Effectively managed units can provide good service with small numbers of beds. But with more rapid discharges there needs to be adequate support in the community.

The reduction of bed numbers is acceptable only if community services improve – but this is unlikely. The DHSS's own figures confirm that the provision of home-helps and meals-on-wheels is falling behind the demographic trends;[6] while the evidence suggests that there was a fall in the provision of local authority residential places in the six years leading up to 1984. These homes are already struggling to cope with heavily dependent people, for whom they have neither the number nor the level of trained staff to cope effectively.[7]

In the next decade a good turnover of geriatric beds may be achieved by a more efficient use of beds and good discharge planning. Those people requiring long-term institutional care are in the age-group that is now increasing most rapidly. Discharge could be encouraged if long-stay patients received stronger community support through, for instance, more widespread voluntary care, adult-fostering schemes and even a modest increase in funds for local authority personal social services.

The effects of demography, technological change and the pursuit of greater equality in the provision of health care will put varying degrees of pressure on health authorities in the next decade. If the inaccuracy of past wage- and price-effect assumptions persists, it seems almost certain that NHS funding will remain in a state of 'perpetual crisis'. With sluggish economic growth and severe constraints on the distribution of resources between different public-expenditure programmes, it will become even more important than hitherto to gain the maximum benefit from health budgets.

The House of Commons Select Committee on Social Services, during its review of last year's public expenditure White Paper, established that much of the 19.5 per cent real increase in NHS expenditure since 1978 has been swallowed up by cost increases embodying the relative price effect – that is, the extent to which the cost of health care rises faster than costs in general – that has reduced the scope for improving patient care. If that is allowed for, the rate of increase in real terms is reduced to 9.5 per cent, which over the last seven years has represented an average increase of only 1.4 per cent per annum. Even this adjustment does not allow for demographic trends, the increasing numbers of people aged seventy-five or over or technological innovation. If these factors are taken into account, the average increase is only 1 per cent per annum in real terms.

There are some changes that could make a great difference to the effective use of scarce resources. The first would be to give the district health authorities greater freedom to plan their expenditure over a period of time. There is more scope to carry over expenditure into the next year than there was in the past, but this does not go nearly far enough. Health authorities should have the freedom to defer consumption, to engage in savings and to build up balances, and they should be encouraged to experiment and innovate. All of this can and should be done within the existing structure. It is not necessary to raise the issue of efficiency in the privatization debate over health care, for there are techniques for evaluating and improving efficiency from within. There is also positive merit in having certain aspects of our lives that are not dominated by costs and economic value, and this is particularly applicable to health care. Medical need should predominate in the allocation of health care. An external market in health care, if encouraged to grow, could reach such a size that its impact on the NHS as a competitor for scarce skills would start to distort the health allocation. There are, however, strong arguments for introducing internal market disciplines into the NHS. A crucial change of philosophy in managing scarce NHS resources would acknowledge openly that there is no virtue in achieving a situation in which each district has to be self-sufficient.

One way to bring greater efficiency to health care that interests me personally is to create an internal health authority market. Decentralizing would encourage a district to buy-in services which it does not have, or sees no advantage in providing; this would encourage those districts that have particular specialized services, or spare capacity, to sell their services to other districts. Usually, in such an internal market – though not invariably – out-of-district services are undertaken by authorities that are close by. This cross-district activity already happens to a limited, but unstructured, extent, and most authorities are determined to move to self-sufficiency, irrespective of whether that makes economic sense.

Negotiation over prices between districts would concentrate the minds of both managers and doctors on cost effectiveness, provided there were also some incentives to earn extra revenue by allowing the savings made to be applied to development in other aspects of a district's health-care activity. This must occur without an automatic and matching fall in previous health authority allocation totals. In such an internal market there would have to be proper costing systems, and there would have to be a far greater degree of cost sensitivity for both the buying and the selling districts than there is at present.

An internal market for health authorities would make it possible for a Minister of Health to insist that waiting-lists above a certain length would no longer be tolerated. For the first time, within the NHS, patients could be given the right to monitor the minimum time they would have to wait for surgery or treatment instead of feeling that they were lucky to be given any attention. Standards would be systematically compared across districts, and fluctuations in service evened out.

The internal-market model is not 'privatization', rather, each authority would act like a small nationalized company. Alan Enthoven, who has advocated the internal-market model, describes the concept as being 'a kind of market socialism'.[8] It would be sensible to start now with demonstration projects in districts that are keen on the idea, rather than to impose one national blue-print.

Districts with a shortage of beds would buy services from those with too many, and this could help teaching hospitals attract more patients and more revenue; rather than by central decree, it would be through competitive pricing. By and large the teaching hospitals' range of services is larger, matched by higher in-patient costs, but they might not lose out to other districts, as they may be able to guarantee a shorter stay, owing to less chance of complications or better results.

An internal-market model could serve patients' interests better than the present model. Although they would have to travel more, patients would no longer be victims of the vagaries of national capital-expenditure cutbacks in local hospitals or the consequences of arbitrary central controls on local consultant numbers. The internal-market model would, as today, enable authorities to purchase services from the private sector and vice versa. To win acceptance for the internal-market model it will be necessary to convince staff and, particularly, the health unions that this is a sensible development, wholly within the ethical principles of an NHS whose remit is to provide care on the basis of need, not the capacity to pay.

An internal market within the NHS would depend on each authority having far greater financial and managerial autonomy than it does at present. Each district would receive an allocation based on per capita revenue and capital allowance, drawing on criteria for needs such as those outlined by RAWP. After allocation the greatest possible degree of autonomy would be crucial for the success of this venture. The districts would have the freedom to carry over funds, to plan spending over longer periods and to make transfers between capital and revenue. Consultants' contracts would be with the authority, and, one would hope, GPs would also be prepared to change their contracts to fit in with any new primary-care organization that might develop along with more autonomous districts. A degree of decentralized wage-bargaining for all staff would be helpful, though it might take time to win acceptance. Present capital and manpower restrictions would be lifted progressively, whether these came from the region or the DHSS. The Minister of Health and the DHSS would continue in their roles as leaders of the Health Service, predominantly through the creation and control of the development fund. This would allow Ministers and Parliament to withdraw from the day-to-day running of the NHS and to concentrate on the progressive eradication of inequalities of care. They would also be able to make a priority of community and primary care.

Ultimately, as the district health authorities built up their autonomy they would be allowed to raise part of their revenue locally. If local income tax had, as one hopes, become the norm for providing over 50 per cent of local government finance, a separate health assessment would be possible. Perhaps, too, direct elections by proportional representation to the health authority would be accepted and eventually even the merging of health and social services. These are, however, elements that are not essential for developing an internal-market model. They should certainly not be imposed quickly – the NHS now needs time to evolve.

The priority for health care in the early 1990s is not further administrative upheaval, nor an ideological debate about private or public medicine. Instead, there is scope for a sensible partnership where the public –private health frontiers need defining and where it makes sense to avoid duplication. We have all suffered from the sterility of a polarized public–private debate about health care. The sensible priority is more effective management of the existing structure in the interests of the consumer. Putting patients first must become not just a slogan for politicians to espouse, but an aspiration for the NHS to live up to. It can be an achievable reality provided that health care is reorientated away from a centralized position towards a decentralized pattern. Health care must also concentrate on providing a better measurement of output, in terms of standards and accountability of health care, than it has at present.

What we do not want to see in the 1990s is the same divisive debate about the role of private medicine that we saw in the 1970s. Although I believed wholeheartedly in the considerable theoretical merits of separating private medicine from NHS hospitals, in retrospect I admit that the overall impact of the policy and the doctors' disruptive action was such that it was not worth the price that we had to pay. It was destructive to NHS morale and seriously added to the waiting-lists. A somewhat similar debate, this time about private medicine and the role of the family doctor, may now be in sight, now promoted by a Conservative Government. Again, it is safe to predict that the outcome will not be worth the controversy. Promoting private medicine to the extent where its size ensures competition with the NHS will not only be damaging to the National Health Service; it will also, perhaps imperceptibly, damage the cohesion of the nation. The family practitioner service is one of the most popular aspects of the NHS: over 95 per cent of the population use it. There are all too few services that are genuinely national, that bind the nation together. Those of us who want to see the NHS give better value for money and a better service to patients are entitled to warn this Government not to try and promote a private family practitioner service. We need to build on what we have that is good, to improve existing family practitioner services. Primary care needs to be strengthened by integrating family medicine with hospitals and social services. It cannot be done by separating family medicine from the NHS and stimulating an alternative private family practitioner service. To make health care more efficient is in the interests of patients and all who work in the health and social services.

11 Social Responsibility

If we could only achieve greater harmony within the personal relationships that make up the United Kingdom, we would be taking a major step towards creating a unifying force that would bind us all together. Such a sentiment, though easy to express, is very hard to achieve because such relationships are individual, personal and not always susceptible to external influences. It is also open to question how far governments, local or national, should go in attempting to be such an external influence. However, it is in the area of rights and responsibilities that politicians have a role.

This Conservative Government, strangely, has failed to recognize its responsibility to give a lead in promoting the link between rights and responsibilities. It has, less surprisingly, failed to promote racial justice in those areas where there are concentrations of ethnic minorities. It has been careless in protecting the environment, particularly that in the inner cities, which is deteriorating rapidly. It has shown no imagination in creating opportunities for the unemployed to contribute to society. As a result, the level of alienation among some of our citizens has probably never been so high. Black citizens in particular feel and experience discrimination in almost every aspect of their lives.

After the 1981 riots in Brixton Lord Scarman warned of the consequences of ignoring these problems in the future. The recurrence of trouble in Brixton, the riots in Tottenham and the burning shops in Handsworth in 1985 are grim reminders of the problems and harbingers of our future.

When the Conservative Government no longer wants to listen and is content to deride – the impression given by the ministerial response to the Church of England report, *Faith in the City – a Call for Action by Church and Nation* – then the outlook is fraught. When too many in the Labour Party stand by and acquiesce in anti-police propaganda, which is levelled not just by militants, then the atmosphere becomes even uglier.

The police have too frequently been seen to take the heat, to bear the brunt of the inner cities' burning resentment. We are in danger of allowing the police to become the scapegoats for the failings of our society.

The social, environmental and economic conditions of our cities contribute to despair and bitterness that in turn have created tensions and conflict between the police and the community. Lord Scarman, in his report on the Brixton disorders in 1981, wrote:

The police do not create social deprivation, though unimaginative, inflexible policing can make the tensions which deprivation engenders greatly worse. Conversely, while good policing can help diminish tension and avoid disorder, it cannot remove the causes of social stress where these are to be found, as those in Brixton and elsewhere are, deeply embedded in fundamental economic and social conditions. Any attempt to resolve the circumstances from which the disorders of this year sprang cannot therefore be limited to recommendations about policing but must embrace the wider social context in which policing is carried out . . .

It would be folly not to reflect on these measured words, for they carry a dire warning on which we have so far hardly begun to act.

. . . In analysing communal disturbances such as those in Brixton and elsewhere, to ignore the existence of these factors is to put the nation in peril.[1]

Unemployment among the young and the difficulties of growing up in a society dominated by a selfish philosophy of materialistic greed contribute to the sense of despair. Yet responsible and responsive national and local government can act in the interests of the whole community to help create employment and foster partnership with private enterprise. The Conservative Government has shown an insensitivity to employment needs and has starved cities of resources, so that even with good management and the best will in the world, job prospects have dimmed and standards – whether on housing estates or in social services – have slipped, all contribute to growing hopelessness.

It is no exaggeration to state, for instance, that the United Kingdom is now in the midst of a drug epidemic. For an epidemic to occur, two factors are crucial: availability of the drug and a vulnerable population. We have both factors operating today. The prevalence of drugs, particularly heroin, is dramatically illustrated by the total amount found by the Customs and Excise, who seize about 90 per cent of all drugs found. What is important is the relative availability. Most drugs can be bought easily; for those below sixteen, perhaps more easily than a bottle of alcohol. The cost of staying 'high' on drugs over a weekend is less than the cost of getting smashed in a pub. Even with heroin, a 'bag' sufficient to keep a youngster high for a weekend can be bought for between £5 and £10. The vulnerability of the population is harder to prove. Historically, heroin has always been depicted as the drug of despair, and there is certainly much despair and hopelessness about in parts of Britain today.

The Government, however, vigorously denies that there is any link between drug addiction and unemployment. Hitherto, the evidence of a link has been one's common sense rather than objective study. It has certainly been an unfortunate coincidence for the Government that the availability of heroin in particular has increased over the last six years, at the same time as the strong growth in unemployment. The Conservative Government bears a considerable responsibility for increasing the unemployment figures, but it is ridiculous to pretend that they bear a major responsibility for the growth in drug offences or narcotic addicts. Apart from some very foolish cuts in the Customs and Excise Services, their main political sin has been to react too slowly, and with too little research and thought, to the drugs epidemic that has developed around us all.

What we now know is that as most of us assumed on the basis of observation and sense, the link between drugs and unemployment does exist.[2] A four-year follow-up study of 1,036 school-leavers, who were aged between fifteen and sixteen in 1979 and nineteen and twenty four years later, shows a strong link between drug use and unemployment. The contrast between the unemployed and other young people when aged nineteen and twenty is striking. Amongst males, the levels of those who had used illegal drugs were 54 per cent (unemployed), 33 per cent (employed/students). Amongst females, the corresponding levels of drug use were 35 per cent (unemployed) and 22 per cent (employed/students). The association does not by itself mean that there is any cause-and-effect relationship. Drug users come from all sections of our society, the rich as well as the poor, in rural communities as well as the run-down inner-city areas. The appeal, for the young unemployed, of illegal drugs is that the drug scene in the inner city does provide a supportive haven; a social milieu in which the strains and stresses of unemployment can be forgotten; where such an escape can be bought at less cost than escaping through alcohol.

Drug misuse will remain a major problem for some years, probably it will continue at epidemic proportions. What is odd about this epidemic is the paucity of research, the way that political actions are taken without a sustained strategy which is deeply rooted in medical and scientific evidence.

A classic example of political prejudice triumphing over objective fact is the development of a strategy to deal effectively with alcoholism. Most people spend less on alcohol and tobacco during a recession, when their incomes fall. Unemployment is inversely related to alcohol and tobacco use. What we do not, but should, know is whether expensive alcohol being made more expensive enhances the appeal to use illegal drugs. The Chancellor of the Exchequer raises the tax on alcohol in successive Budgets with no scientific advice on its effect. The medical profession has virtually withdrawn amphetamines, and we know very little about the possible enhancing effect of this action on illegal drug-taking. Indeed, it is still, in government, unusual to discuss alcohol and drug problems together; also, to discuss legal medical drugs and illegal drugs together. Yet we are in the midst of a 'poly-drug epidemic' and we know all too little about the interaction and interface between all of these chemical substances that have addictive properties. The real price of alcohol and tobacco has gone up since 1979 while the street price of heroin has been cut in half.

We do not know if there is a hydraulic effect between legal and illegal drugs. The Government has launched into a drugs media campaign against expert advice and in the face of warnings, and even some evidence that such a campaign could do harm. Available evidence and necessary experience are not being brought into the decision-making process. Drug policy and drug research are inadequately linked. We do not effectively monitor the changing patterns of drug misuse, nor do we sufficiently evaluate the response to treatment and education.

The burden of treatment and care for drug users falls on GPs, hospital staff, community workers, district nurses, health visitors, psychiatric social workers and other social workers, all of whose numbers are restricted by Government cutbacks and whose budgets, whether through the health authorities or local government social and educational services, are being severely squeezed. There is, despite the new £10 million central DHSS funding for action over drug addiction, no sense of an overall strategy to grapple with the problem. Meanwhile it is often left to the police to deal with the casualties of the worsening drug scene.

It is in policing policy above all that a new concordat must be built between police, local councillors and the public. Any proposals must lie within our national tradition of policing by consent, but they should also demand greater responsiveness by the police and participation by the community. More concerted action is also needed to organize crime prevention in the community. An independent standing commission is needed to review specific operational incidents in which the police have been involved; it could inquire into incidents at the request of a Chief Constable, police authority, Home Secretary or on its own initiative. This is a desirable addition to the present powers the Home Secretary has under the Police Act 1964 to inquire into specific incidents, such as accidental use of firearms. An independent complaints procedure could also be introduced by amending the complaints provisions in the Police and Criminal Evidence Act 1984, if the structure in that Act proves to be ineffective.

To increase public confidence in the police is also to increase their effectiveness. The recruitment of far more black officers into the police is essential so that, as Lord Scarman recommended 'the composition of the police fully reflects that of the society the police serve'. There is no doubt, as the lessons from America show, that in a multi-racial society, a multi-racial police force is essential. It is not just property and people that have been under assault in Tottenham, Brixton and Handsworth. It is the fundamental principle of policing by consent. It is this principle which has been central to building the unique and previously much-envied quality of our police. It is this principle which must be restored if we are to have peace in our cities.

Nothing can excuse the fact that nearly 800 crimes were committed during the two days of the Brixton riot; that nearly 2,000 police had to be deployed into the area, and of the 216 people arrested, 109 came from outside the area. Criminal behaviour can never be justified; even though one wants to expose the underlying strains and stresses, it is important to avoid making the mistake of appearing to excuse criminal behaviour. The police have a thankless task during these disturbances and though mistakes will be made, we must always remember the circumstances in which they try to protect the community. The people in the affected neighbourhoods were often terrified by the violence and are immensely grateful for the efforts that the police make on their behalf.

Yet, when all that is said, establishing police forces which more properly reflect the racial balance in the community is not a marginal issue, to be left low on the agenda and allocated little in the way of funds. It is one of the most urgent priorities of urban policy. We will not create fully representative police forces by accident or chance. If we make no effort, we will get no results. And so far, we have made precious little effort – intermittent, half-hearted national campaigns that no one remembers, no one has evaluated and which have manifestly produced no results. The Metropolitan Police have so far carried out no research to find out why their recruitment efforts have failed to find a response amongst the ethnic minorities.

In 1981 only 132 officers in the Metropolitan Police were black – 0.5 per cent of the total strength – and for England and Wales as a whole there were only 326 – 0.3 per cent. By 1985, there were 271 black officers in the Met., nearly 1 per cent of the total strength. Unlike so many dimensions of the urban problem, this is one for which there are straight-forward remedies which can be applied immediately. Research into why communities respond differently to recruitment drives should be carried out, both locally and nationally. All of our police forces should be basing their recruitment efforts on the results of such research. A wiser Government would have made it clear to the police authorities that it expected police forces to establish a proper racial balance as an urgent priority before the Brixton riots. Had this not been done, certainly after the riots it should have become unavoidable. The positive action measures permitted by the Race Relations Act must be used to the full to recruit more police from the ethnic communities. Racially representative police forces will not solve the problems of our urban areas, but those problems will certainly be more difficult to solve without them.

Lord Scarman recommended special training courses for blacks to enable them to meet the existing entrance standards of police forces – as is possible under the Race Relations Act 1976 – and for vigorous selection procedures to be enforced to prevent racially-prejudiced people being recruited to the police. Both these policies are absolutely essential and Parliament should insist that police authorities implement them and report back to the Home Secretary so that he can report to Parliament on the progress being made. To avoid creeping towards a national police force by piecemeal extensions of the Home Secretary's powers, Parliament could itself take a monitoring role. If need be it should summon local police authorities to give evidence, at all times preserving their autonomy and independence. A decentralized police force is a democratic safeguard as well as being more responsive to individuals.

Policing, after decades of all-party consensus, is now being undermined by the constant criticism of police decisions by left-wing extremists, some serving on police authorities, others prominent as Labour councillors. Over the past few years, this has combined to undermine community support for the police and strain police confidence in the community. The police have made mistakes and have adopted too defensive a position. Some senior policemen have reacted by becoming less and less willing to listen to, and adapt to, fair criticism. The result of all this is that the principle of policing by consent, which has been responsible for ensuring our personal security, is now at risk. It is the most vulnerable in our society who will be the most damaged if policing standards deteriorate.

It is the combining of rights and responsibilities that holds the key to higher police standards and improved crime prevention. The responsibility for containing and reducing crime cannot be shifted to the police, nor can it be shifted to judges and magistrates, despite the absence of a commonsensical, easily understood sentencing policy.

Crime has risen under successive governments. One doubts that there is any relationship between the rise in crime and the government in power at the time. It is the exceptionally high number of crimes committed by young men which present society with its greatest challenge. In 1983, 47 per cent of all those convicted for crimes against the person, 68 per cent of those convicted for burglary, 58 per cent of those convicted for theft, and 64 per cent of those convicted for criminal damage were males under the age of twenty-one.

The SDP/Liberal Alliance has quite deliberately tried not to exploit party divisions over law and order. We have done our best to rescue crime and policing from their current position as a political football, kicked between Labour and Conservatives. One way of achieving this is to use the authority of the all-party Select Committee to establish a new special committee which will cover police affairs for a period, separately from the Home Office Select Committee. This has been done in the past through a special Select Committee on Race Relations, and it effectively defused a delicate situation where race was being given an undesirable party political flavour.

Each local authority should set up a crime-prevention unit. The unit would be able to ensure that crime prevention was a relevant factor in all decision-making; heighten public awareness of the need and potential for limiting physical opportunities for crime; encourage communal action; exploit that potential and co-ordinate action to mobilize both official and voluntary expertise and action in crime protection and prevention activities.

Local authorities can and should take special steps to ensure that the distressing results of criminal damage, particularly graffiti and damage to lights and lifts, are cleared up. This must be treated as a matter of urgency. We know that if graffiti stays and damage remains without repair, the morale of local communities suffers, thereby reducing individual pride and responsibility.

On the estates with high crime rates, there should be caretakers on twenty-four-hour patrol. Blocks of flats with a crime problem should have caretakers and entry-phones should be installed to control access. With such provisions, close informal links can be established between caretakers and local police officers on the beat to identify troublemakers. Greater self-management among tenants in council-housing estates, and more investment, would create a greater feeling that their environment was worth protecting.

In schools much more attention should be given to showing how destructive crime and vandalism are to community life, and more resources must be found to make available special places for schoolchildren whose parents have given up attempting to control them at home.

The theme which links all these ideas is that crime prevention is a community responsibility. We can no longer set the police apart, and expect them, and them alone, to tackle crime. Community leaders, especially in local government, have a vital role, complementary to that of the police, to try and contain, and therefore reduce, crime.

The inner cities are among the areas of the country hardest hit by the structural changes to the economy of the past two decades, which have produced a severe decline in the UK manufacturing industry and in unskilled jobs. The recession of 1980–82 compounded the problems. The expansion in public-sector employment of the '60s and early '70s which created thousands of jobs, many taken up by immigrants, has long been over. City centres have retained service employment, but they tend to employ people who commute to work from suburban areas – they do not employ enough people from the inner cities to counteract the effect of job decline in those areas. New industries are sited in pleasant environments with easy access to long-distance motorways – in and around smaller towns along the M4 and M25 for example – rather than in the traffic-clogged and decayed inner cities.

These general economic problems have the most severe impact on people from ethnic minorities, who are concentrated in inner-city areas. 83 per cent of West Indian men and 73 per cent of Asian men are manual workers, compared with 58 per cent of white men.

This concentration of black men in manual work has meant a disproportionately high vulnerability to unemployment. In 1985, the rate of unemployment for West Indians was 25 per cent, for Asians 20 per cent, compared with 13 per cent for whites. Amongst the young, the figures are even more disturbing. Over 50 per cent of black unemployed men had been registered for over a year, compared with 33 per cent of white. Twice as many black women had been unemployed for over a year compared with white women. These discrepancies were not merely due to the high proportion of blacks who were unskilled – they were also due to discrimination. Discrimination is revealed, too, in the statistics within the same socio-economic categories. In the skilled-manual and foreman group, 25 per cent of whites have people working under them, compared with only 17 per cent of West Indians.

While the majority of families in the UK are white, it is clear that black families face particular difficulties. Some of them are still separated by our immigration laws and others suffer considerable discrimination, as well as higher unemployment and poverty. Any family policy which fails to take into account cultural variations hides the considerable differences in the composition and size of families between whites and blacks – and the further differences between Asians and most West Indians. The average Asian household (4.5 persons) is larger than that of West Indians (3.4 persons) or whites (2.6 persons). This is due in part to the fact that more Asian households contain children than do West Indian or white, and that a larger number of Asian households contain more than two children (31 per cent) than do white (5 per cent) or West Indian (12 per cent). This pattern of larger households amongst Asians has important implications for housing policies which have largely been ignored.

The striking variations in household patterns are affected even more strongly in two further areas: the headship of households, and single-parent families. Only 7 per cent of Asian, and 25 per cent of white, households are headed by a female. Among West Indians, this rises to about 33 per cent. Not all of these, however, are single-parent households. Nevertheless, the data on single parentage reveals that a much higher proportion of West Indian households consist of a single parent with children under sixteen (18 per cent), than Asian (4 per cent) or white (3 per cent). This means that over 30 per cent of all West Indian households with children are single-parent households, which is a dramatic increase from 13 per cent to 36 per cent, in the proportion of West Indian single-parent households since 1974. The comparable proportions for whites and Asians are 10 per cent and 5 per cent respectively. The Policy Studies Institute reports that 'these significant differences in household patterns between groups suggests the need for a more sophisticated policy approach in dealing with family matters than displayed by a return to "Victorian values".'[3]

Black families in Britain face three different forms of racism: overt and intentional, disguised but deliberate, and unintentional but adverse. Why, for example, has the Government not moved more quickly to restore the investigative powers of the Commission for Racial Equality, which were lost through a misreading of the 1976 Race Relations Act by the Law Lords? Parliament quite clearly intended that the Commission should be able to look at areas from which there had been no individual complaints. Otherwise, important inquiries, such as those looking into the housing policies of the Labour-controlled London Borough of Hackney would never have been carried out. There were no individual complaints because it needed a systematic examination of the council's housing-allocation procedures, by the Commission, to expose the extent of discrimination which was being suffered by black families. Almost half the Commission's forty-seven investigations would have been impossible without the power to investigate without a preliminary complaint. The Law Lords having quashed this power, the Government has still made no commitment to restore it.

Rights and responsibilities come together more in relation to family policy than in any other area of policy. The family is a collective unit where rights cannot exist in isolation, and where responsibilities to each other are an essential self-discipline. Responsibilities are the bridging factor without which the family unit soon crumbles. Family policy is nevertheless a double-edged sword. The wise politician treads warily in this field, not wanting to moralize or to intrude into relationships that are intimate, diverse and difficult to define. Just as law and order can never be the preserve of one political philosophy or party, so family policy becomes more suspect and results harder to achieve if it is advocated in a fiercely partisan manner. It is also the classic area in which in other countries governments, both of the extreme right and extreme left, have abused their power.

If family policy is to be more than political rhetoric, it has to be rooted in the reality of present-day Britain, not in nostalgia for the past. We must be careful not to use the term family only in its traditional sense of the nuclear family: father, mother and children. The reality is that one in eight of all families have a single parent. Divorce has risen by 45 per cent since 1973 and is still rising. Within that figure, the number of divorces for marriages lasting less than four years has risen from 15 per cent to 21 per cent, which should caution us against creating a climate in which early marriage is encouraged. In one-parent families divorce is the major factor, 34 per cent being divorced, 22 per cent being separated, 17 per cent being widowed and only 16 per cent being single.

This Conservative Government has found itself more comfortable talking about the family on the basis of Victorian mythology. Whenever it has had to put a price tag on its policies, it has chosen to keep the words but refuse the action. Family policy has provided a respectable cloak for some of its more regressive policies. Firstly, by emphasizing its support for such an all-embracing group as the family, the Government has been able to hide its lack of support for particular families within the group. It has also been in the interests of a Government which does not give a high priority to helping those less well-off to emphasize the general, in the hope that it will divert attention from the particular. For this Government, which has shown itself so markedly resistant to promoting women's rights and equal opportunities, talking about the family has meant that it has not had to defend its beliefs. The Government has been able to perpetuate what it sees as the natural order of life, requiring women – not men – to give up or interrupt their careers for children and disabled or aged relatives.

A sensible, wise Government is one that acts in ways that enable a responsible society to emerge. It does not dictate, but encourages an assertion of good neighbourliness, of respect for others, while being robust in the defence of necessary rules and obligations. It encourages more caring and understanding, and draws and builds on the strengths of a multitude of family units up and down the land. It wants to strengthen the role of women, not just as mothers and as wives, but as citizens; at the moment their voices are still too weak in all of our decision-making forums. Family-orientated policies in a responsible society are not authoritarian, but recognize and encourage an interrelationship between the rule of law in the community and self-discipline within the family.

For over a decade, social reformers have talked about the need for a more integrated approach to social policy. Joint action on social policy was current in 1974, when I started as Minister of Health. We were aware then of the dangers of the compartmentalized welfare state. The Maria Colwell case and others had shown the dangers of a fragmented approach to family problems. More than a decade later the Jasmine Beckford case showed that we need to be conscious of the pitfalls of separate attitudes, even though we have separate departments for education, health, housing and social services, whether at central- or local-government level. Case after case of child abuse shows that we need more integration of social policy, and that includes the police, who must not become isolated from the prevention of social disorder. For almost a decade, the Standing Commission on the Family, now renamed as the Family Policy Studies Centre, has been wisely, though fruitlessly, pressing successive governments to develop a strategic approach that would require every legislative proposal to include a 'family impact statement', plus an annual report on how families have fared during the year.

In 1986, well into the second term of a Thatcher Government, we have mounting crime statistics, growing violence, increasing drug addiction and evidence of an irresponsible society where the values of selfishness and independence seem to be triumphing over the values of unselfishness and interdependence. Much of this is not the fault of this Government, although the Labour Party endlessly tries to blame them. The roots of crime are longer and go deeper than Mrs Thatcher's period of government and it was foolish of them to pretend otherwise when in opposition in the 1970s. It is also a mistake for Mr Tebbit to claim a superior set of values for the Conservative Party. The truth is that the values of society and the role of the family are not set by political parties. All the parties can do is to enable, not dictate, responsible patterns of behaviour to emerge.

In July 1982, Mrs Thatcher set up her Family Policy Committee, a secret committee of eight Cabinet Ministers, herself as chairman, the heads of the Think Tank and the No. 10 policy unit, to develop both short- and long-term policies under her chairmanship. She was only too eager then to declare that the Conservatives were 'the party of the family' and she, particularly when in opposition, had a tendency to depict the Conservative Party as the party of 'law and order'. We can now begin to see how empty these claims really were.

The intention was to make 'the family' one of the central issues of the 1983 general election. In the event, the idea was abandoned, in part because the 'Falklands factor' made it unnecessary, in part because policy plans which had been extensively leaked proved to be unattractive. It is worth recalling the themes, ideas and questions that the Family Policy Group posed. How does the Government get women to stay at home to look after the elderly and disabled? Does the Government need the Equal Opportunities Commission? Should the Government continue to allow unemployed sixteen-year-olds to be eligible for welfare? How could the Government redefine the minimum 'safety net'? Was the Government being too generous to one-parent families? A Conservative Government's potential for social engineering was demonstrated most vividly by a proposal from Sir Geoffrey Howe, then the Chancellor of the Exchequer, suggesting that children should be 'trained to manage their pocket-money better'.

A second, and later, batch of papers leaked from the same committee provided an even better guide to this Government's political values. These papers looked at ways in which the largest single group of people living in poverty – low-paid families with dependent children – could be helped by the tax system. They noted the most effective way would be to redistribute resources from childless couples to couples with children, and pointed to the best mechanism – removing the extra half allowance, which all married men receive over and above a single person's tax allowance, and redistributing this sum, then £3,000 million, but now £5,000 million, to couples with children. They also noted that this sensible proposal was then and remains today an SDP policy. The paper went on to say 'its supporters include, at one extreme, the Child Poverty Action Group and the National Council for Civil Liberties and, at the other extreme, Mr Sam Brittan in a recent article in the *Financial Times*.'

It is symptomatic that anything which could command such widespread support was automatically viewed with suspicion by that group of ministers. As well as being just, such a redistribution to families would also help end an historical anomaly. The married man's allowance was introduced four decades ago when only 10 per cent of married women worked. Now, over 50 per cent of married women work. Moreover, half the men who receive the married man's tax allowance, with its extra half allowance, do not have dependent children.

So, what did Mrs Thatcher's Family Policy Committee conclude? Sir Geoffrey Howe warned his colleagues that the losers would make more noise than the gainers and his advice was accepted. The votes of six million childless couples were ruled more important in the run-up to the 1983 election than the needs of six million families with dependent children. Exactly the same considerations have presumably applied during the 1985 Social Security Review. Instead of linking the tax and benefit system, the Government has kept them separate with the exception of the proposed Family Credit. This potentially important step towards integration of tax and benefit has, however, been damaged by the method of implementation. Instead of being paid to the mother, it will be paid to the husband and so, whereas a reduced child benefit will still be available to the reasonably well-off mother, the less well-off mother receiving Family Credit will have to persuade her husband to make it available for the family budget. Also, the married man's tax allowance will stay and so there is no 'new' money to float off the inevitable losses that accompany any restructuring of social security. Far from signalling a major reform, capable of eradicating the worst of family poverty, the Government has deliberately ducked out of introducing a major social reform. The reason is not hard to find. They do not want to redistribute money from their potential voters to the poor, whose votes they feel they can ignore.

The SDP's anti-poverty programme has rightly won tributes from across the political spectrum. At one end Frank Field, the Labour MP and former director of the Child Poverty Group, said 'Socialists have important lessons to learn from the SDP's proposals. We now have a serious challenger for the poor's votes.' The *Financial Times* thought it was the most original policy idea to be placed before the electorate in the 1983 election. The SDP programme has now been updated and integrated even further with our tax reforms. We would achieve a substantial redistribution of resources to one of the biggest groups of people now in poverty – low paid families. Some of the lowest paid families, on a gross income of £30 a week or less, would receive an extra £27 per week.

Pensioners would benefit particularly. The single pensioner with a net income of £57.65 a week, paying £16 a week in rent and rates, would receive an extra £20.96 a week. This major increase is only made possible by being selective and making the benefits income-related. The Labour Party will never be able to achieve such widespread help if it remains determined to stick to universal benefits.

The SDP programme involves the abolition of the four main income-related benefits – Supplementary Benefit, Family Income Supplement, free school meals, and housing benefit – and the replacement of these with a new Basic Benefit, payable through an integrated tax/benefit system. The Basic Benefit would contain a personal credit, a child credit, and a housing credit. It will be payable to anyone who has a low income for whatever reason, whether it is low pay, dependent children, old age, sickness, disability or unemployment. Because the Basic Benefit would be integrated with tax, the take-up problem of existing income-related benefits would end.

To pay for the Basic Benefit, we would phase out the married man's additional tax allowance and use the saving as the principal source of extra revenue to boost Basic Benefit significantly at the lower end of the income scale. Instead of the current £9,740 million (1984–5 prices) spent on the four major income-related benefits, we would spend £13,900 million on the Basic Benefit. We could afford to do this because we would be phasing out the married man's tax allowance at the same time as phasing in the Basic Benefit and using that £5 billion which the Chancellor loses in tax to fund the Basic Benefit scheme.

The main beneficiaries of this extra expenditure would be the poorest households. A couple earning £60 a week, paying £26 a week in rent and rates, and with two children under the age of eleven, would receive an extra £26.64 a week. Families with children would continue to gain significant additional income under the Basic Benefit until their gross earnings rose above £180 a week, at which point no extra benefit would be payable.

The present Government was too timid to integrate their proposed social security changes with the tax system. They avoided the central challenge. The SDP's new tax proposals draw on our social security proposals and are designed to fit together closely. The tax and social security system is crying out to be made fairer, more efficient in distribution and more effective in redistribution.

The new Family Credit Scheme is little more than a half-hearted step towards the Basic Benefit. The Government boasts that it would help an extra 200,000 families, whereas the Basic Benefit would reach over six million families. More ominously, the modest gain from Family Credit for low-income families will be scaled back by the Government's decision that every household must pay at least 20 per cent of their rates, irrespective of means, resources or family size. The result, according to the Government's own figures in the technical annexe which accompanied the Social Security White Paper, is that although 2 million households will gain from the benefit changes proposed, 3.8 million will lose, including nearly 800,000 families with a gross income of less than £120 per week.[4]

There are six myths still held by Mrs Thatcher and her Ministers and contained in the leaked papers and policies of the Family Policy Committee.

The first Conservative myth is that families no longer care. It was stated quite explicitly in the leaked papers: 'What more can be done to encourage families to reassume responsibilities taken on by the state, for example, responsibility for the disabled, the elderly, or the unemployed sixteen-year-olds . . .' According to this, the modern family, unlike earlier generations, stick grandmother into a home and forget about her. But only 5 per cent of the elderly are in institutions at present, and this proportion includes hospitals and psychiatric units, as well as old people's homes. Of course, the total number of people in institutions has gone up as the number of elderly has increased. But then, so has the number being looked after by families. There are now over 9 million pensioners, compared with 2.5 million of an equivalent age in 1900. But the proportion of over-sixty-fives who are in institutions today is no higher than it was eighty years ago. Even before the existing squeeze on the social service budgets, surveys suggested that only 11 per cent of the elderly were getting any visits from the district nurse, only 9 per cent received a call from a home-help, and a mere 3 per cent received the occasional meal-on-wheels. Compare this intermittent help from the local and central government with the consistent, comprehensive and systematic help from the family, which a survey for Age Concern showed: one in six elderly people with surviving children lived with them; two in six elderly people lived within six miles; four in six elderly people saw their children at least once a week.

Another myth is that there was a cosy, stable community in the Victorian era with people being born, brought up and dying in the same community. This looms large in Mrs Thatcher's wish to return to 'Victorian values'. The reality was quite different, however, as the historians have demonstrated. The chance of having many relatives in the same village was low, right into the twentieth century. It has been the policies of rent restrictions, council housing and a fall in population growth rates which produced stable communities. The Edinburgh historian, Michael Anderson, has suggested that in many areas, this has produced 'more stable communities than have probably been found for hundreds of years'.[5] His studies included putting the 1851 census on computer. This showed that in the last century, 16 per cent of children had moved by their second birthday, 40 per cent by their fifteenth and well over half the adult population were not living in the community where they were born. True, people did not move as far as they do today, but the telephone and the motor-car make 150 miles in 1985 shorter than fifteen miles in 1885.

Nor has the advent of mass divorce had the profound effect that some believe. Death created roughly the same proportion of single-parent families in the early nineteenth century as divorce does today. There were probably even more single-parent families with dependent children in the early part of the nineteenth century, as divorce today is disproportionately high among childless couples, whereas the high mortality rate in the last century did not distinguish between couples with children and the childless.

Nor is there much truth in the image of a warm, Victorian, extended family, with older children helping the younger, all under the same roof, with the grandparents there to babysit. The reality was quite different. The average household contained 1.8 children in 1750, two children in 1850 and 1.1 children in 1970. One reason that families were not as big in the past as is often assumed was the high infant-mortality rate. An even more important factor was the number of children leaving home to go into service as servants, live-in apprentices, journeymen or shop-workers. The average family did have more children – the peak was 3.59 in 1801 – but family size was not nearly as large as popularly believed. Moreover, there were not nearly as many grandparents living with families in the nineteenth century as is commonly supposed. In the 1850s, only 8 per cent of households contained three or more generations, yet some 4 per cent still contained three generations by 1970.

A more insidious belief is the idea of the moral purity of earlier generations. This is a very glib and easy view to propagate, but there is no evidence to prove it. Computer research has shown, by linking the date of marriage with the date of birth of the first child, that about 60 per cent of women in the nineteenth century conceived out of wedlock, roughly the same proportion that admit, in recent social surveys, to engaging in pre-marital sex with their future husbands. Illegitimacy rates, even at today's levels, are only a little higher than in the mid-Victorian era.

There is no evidence either that parental love is any less today than a century ago, perhaps the converse. The Victorian analogy that does carry conviction is one that compares the 1985 bed-and-board supplementary benefit regulations for the under-twenty-six-year-olds with those which required the poor to move on from parish to parish seeking relief, a harsh reminder that patterns of life imposed in the last century can still be forced back in this. Similarly, the Government's proposals in the Social Security Review to cash-limit the Social Fund and to end all right of appeal is to bring our social security system back to nineteenth century relief. At that time, when the poor-law box was empty, there was no more help for the poor. Now, when the Social Fund ceiling is reached, towards the end of the year, no more emergency applications can be considered.

Everyone likes to romanticize the past but there is less excuse for it today, when the proportion dependent on welfare is almost one in seven – the same proportion as in Mayhew's Victorian London. We should not forget what life was like in those times: the huge proportion of the elderly who relied on poor relief; the large numbers in institutional care; the small minority of the elderly living with relatives; the battered wives and neglected children; the high infant- and maternal-mortality rates – with some four out of ten children dying in infancy.

Today's 'happy families' no longer follow the card-game pattern of Mr Bull, the butcher, with his non-working wife Mrs Bull, plus their two young children. Divorce, dual-career marriages and step-families have been endlessly examined by the media and increasingly scrutinized by the social scientists in the last decade. We know the Bulls today account for about 15 per cent of the twenty million households in the country.

We know Mr and Mrs Bun, both of whom go out to work to support their children, account for another 15 per cent. We know the number of one-parent families has increased sharply in the last two decades and now number about one million. About one out of every three new marriages is now expected to end in divorce. In the USA it is one in two. One out of five children in Britain today will experience the divorce of their parents before the sixteenth birthday. We know the number of elderly people and single people living on their own has doubled.

Step-relationships are partly replacing the predominance which direct blood relations like cousins, uncles and aunts once had. This is hardly surprising. One out of three marriages today involves one partner who has been married before, and in one out of six marriages, both partners have been previously married. These 'reconstituted families', as the social scientists have named them, have, for all the strains which preceded their formation, extended family networks and are often very successful, giving a better quality of family life than that which they replaced. Despite the depressing divorce statistics, the most recent evidence suggests that only 8 per cent of women and 14 per cent of men will never marry, although many more couples are cohabiting before marriage.

The area of family policy which presents the most dramatic and new change is the growth in the number of elderly people. The number over sixty-five has increased by one-third in the last two decades. Total numbers will not now increase until the next century, but the number over seventy-five – the group with the largest demand on our health and social services – is rising rapidly. Only one person in every seventy-six was over seventy-five at the turn of the century; today, one in sixteen is over seventy-five and this proportion will drop even lower. The over-sixty-fives require three times as much health expenditure as the typical sixteen- to sixty-five-year-old; the over-seventy-fives require six times as much. These cost differences are even more dramatic for the social services. Yet between 1976 and 2001, the number of over-seventy-fives will increase by 900,000.

The response to this must be to ensure that within the NHS budget there is sufficient growth in these sectors to cope with the demographic challenge, and that sufficient resources are available for caring for the elderly in local authorities' personal social service budgets. Whereas shortage of money presents a serious problem, the problem of outdated attitudes to the elderly is also immense. Our health, education and social services have been predominantly constructed with the 'cereal packet' family in mind. Yet we know from surveys that over one-third of all pensioners living on their own have no children to whom they can turn for support. We also know that the people to whom the elderly have turned in the past, women aged between forty-five and sixty, now go out to work. About 70 per cent of women in this age group are working. Demographic trends suggest that there will be fewer such women in future. In 1900, there were eighty-three women aged between forty-five and sixty for every 100 women over sixty-five. Today, there are only forty-five in this age group for every 100 over sixty-five.

Although families continue to provide the great bulk of care for the elderly, the disabled and the sick, these families are increasingly overburdened and the exploitation of married women in the care of the elderly and disabled is a disgrace. Unlike single women or married men who give up work to look after an elderly or disabled relative, the married woman is not eligible for the invalid-care allowance. The Government has resisted all pressure to extend this and *The Economist* noted before the last election that any government which was serious about the family would end this anomaly immediately.[6] It remains, in 1986, indefensible that a married woman is not eligible for the invalid-care allowance, and that there is no tax relief for the extra costs of caring within the family home.

The Labour Party, in contrast with the Conservatives, have more generous and sympathetic policies towards the family, but they are prohibitively expensive. Labour's weakness is that they cannot face up to the need for a more realistic approach and cling to universal benefits which are so cripplingly expensive that they are kept down to levels which cannot alleviate real hardship. The other serious lesson for Labour's family policymakers is the oldest one in the book: social engineers need to proceed with even more caution than nuclear engineers because the results are far more unpredictable.

How then should a government, committed to enabling a responsible society to emerge, proceed? Firstly, it should examine the impact of policies on the family, sector by sector. In education, for example, researchers have shown that by the age of seven, there is already a four-year reading gap between children from professional families and some of their contemporaries from unskilled workers' homes. The former have a reading age of nine by the age of seven, while many of the latter are still stuck at five. In her days as Education Secretary, from 1970–74, Mrs Thatcher committed herself to the Plowden Committee's goal of a nursery place for 90 per cent of four-year-olds. That commitment was given in 1972 with the target for achievement being set at 1982. Ten years later, Mrs Thatcher as Prime Minister decided that the 40 per cent of children in nursery school should be cut down to only 36 per cent. Yet what she said in April 1973, as a member of Mr Heath's Government, is no less true in 1986, even though the social attitudes of her own Government are very different.

If a child has any handicap – a reading difficulty, a difficulty in talking or a difficulty in being with other children – the earlier you can spot it, identify it and deal with it, the most chances you have of overcoming it . . . nursery education should give a child a much better command of language right from the start and I would think that you should be able to get a command of numeracy earlier in a primary school than you would otherwise.[7]

A wise government would also concentrate attention on the social class differences in health standards, which still show that unskilled workers in social class five die younger, suffer from more diseases such as bronchitis, tuberculosis and lung cancer, have fewer of their own teeth and lose more of their wives in childbirth and their children in infancy. None of these differences is small. Maternal mortality is twice as high as in social class one; the death rate for bronchitis is five times as high, and for tuberculosis, it is ten times as high. Of course, the cause for this last inequality is much wider than the health service. Housing, education, income and unemployment all play a part.

Another area where government action could help family life relates to divorce. The pressures facing families in the 1980s emphasize the need for more marriage guidance, more funds for the conciliation service for separating couples, and a family court for divorce and the wide variety of other domestic and child-care cases. This Government's attitude to conciliation is as shameless an episode as any in its sorry record on family policy. It has been inexplicably reluctant to support the new conciliation programme. Family conciliation is based on the same principles as industrial conciliation. A neutral negotiator attempts to identify and expand areas of agreement with the aim, not of producing a reconciliation, but reducing the conflict, bitterness and distress caused by separation. It is the best protection that children caught by separation can be given, and has been shown to dramatically reduce the number of 'tug-of-love' disputes over access and custody.

The Bristol scheme, which was the first full-time service, was launched with charitable funds six years ago. But in spite of winning the support of a long list of distinguished experts, including the senior judge of the High Court, it was almost allowed to die by the Government. A succession of officials' reports, including the Finer Committee, the Lord Chancellor's Advisory Committee on Legal Aid and the Law Commission's Report on the Financial Consequences of Divorce, have all supported conciliation, but the Government continues to drag its feet, though we now know that they are contemplating legislation.

Fewer than 5 per cent of separating couples are offered out-of-court conciliation at present in the UK. Yet in several parts of Australia, Canada and the United States, every separating couple is offered the service. Since compulsory conciliation was introduced in California, the number of contested cases has dwindled to a fraction of the earlier caseload. Yet it took this Government several years before it was ready to provide some 'research money' into conciliation, and another year from making that commitment to announcing which research team had been selected.

Divorce reform has been an issue from which successive governments have shrunk. Despite the six-fold increase in divorce since 1960, it is still regarded as abnormal, yet in the next decade some three million adults and over two million dependent children will experience it. It is now more than ten years since the Finer Committee first proposed the idea of a family court, and over seventy years since the first family court was set up in Ohio in the United States in 1914.

The defects of our present court system were set out by Finer and a succession of subsequent reports. The first and worst defect is the two-tier system of justice. The comfortably off can use the county and High Courts, but the poor have to turn to the second-class substitute for matrimonial relief, the magistrates' court. Finer's plan would have made the choice of court depend on the complexity of the case, not the wealth of the applicants. Other defects in the present system include ludicrous procedures under which different issues in the same case have to be heard at different levels, inconsistent judgements between the separate levels, and an adversarial procedure which requires a 'winner' and a 'loser', rather than a compromise on which both sides can agree. In 1980, only fifty out of 165,000 divorce petitions resulted in a defended hearing. The concept has the support of the British Association of Social Workers, the Law Society, the Justices' Clerks and the magistrates.

A family court would not just be involved with divorce but with all the many other domestic legal issues – adoption, guardianship, wardship and care orders. It is good to see that the recommendation of the Select Committee on Social Services, that parental rights in future should only be transferred by the courts, rather than by a resolution of the local council is likely to be introduced by private members' legislation in 1986. It is hoped that the recommendation that place-of-safety orders – there are over 6,000 of them – will be confirmed by a court within a week of a single magistrate issuing one will also be enacted. For over a decade I have watched in despair as the personal social services have lacked the money necessary for full implementation of the 1975 Children Act, which I started first as private members' legislation and then was responsible for implementing as Minister of Health. The first two sections of the Act, which require all local authorities to provide an adoption service, have not been implemented after ten years; the guardianship provision, only in the tenth year. Nevertheless, the shift in attitudes from within, which produced in the Children Act the basic idea of putting the child's best interests first and foremost was an important and necessary change. Hitherto, the rights of the natural parent seemed to be given a higher priority than the rights of the child.

The hardest task facing any Government is how to create a structure whereby families are provided with more support and help if they look after sick, disabled or elderly relatives. The aim of the SDP's Carer's Charter is to make it easier for families to obtain more community support, as well as provide them with extra financial help. The value of such a Charter would be to provide a 'single door' access to community support. Local government social services would have to liaise with all caring agencies – the NHS, voluntary groups, the housing authorities, DHSS – to offer a package which guaranteed various items of support: an assured place in a residential home at specific periods, so that the carers can go away on holiday; a wider range of day-care centres; guaranteed minimum transport services; and a sitting service to relieve carers whose charges cannot be left alone.

The extra financial help would come through a carer's benefit. In the short term, this would mean extending the invalid-care allowance to married women. In the longer term, it would mean providing a carer's credit to be included in the SDP's Basic Benefit scheme.

Another policy initiative from which families would gain support is the SDP scheme for national community volunteers. We want such a scheme to allow young people to contribute to society, to be 'counted in', not, as so often at present, counted out. The scheme has been designed to overcome the joint crises of exclusion and care, and to fulfil a vision of an enabling state in which the statutory sector is buttressed by volunteers.

The scheme requires the active involvement of all our citizens, young and old, across the classes and drawing on different talents and skills. The aim is that by volunteering for a year at the age of eighteen or over (to avoid conflict with education or YTS), it will be possible to contribute to the community. It must not just attract those without a job, and there would be incentives for all to volunteer.

A responsible society is fundamentally sustained by attitudes, not by structures. If the attitudes of senior cabinet ministers and officials are sensitive to family needs and priorities, that is far more effective than any machinery of government changes. Creating a Minister for the Family tends to be the refuge for those who want to be seen to be doing something, and to commit themselves to nothing. There is no structure that can avoid the necessity of large government departments like education, DHSS, and environment having to co-ordinate their family policies.

The biggest rogue elephant in any serious approach to family policies is, however, the impact of the Chancellor of the Exchequer's Budget judgements. Subject to very little consultation beforehand, they can have dramatic and traumatic consequences. The machinery of government change that is urgently needed is for family impact statements in advance of all decision-making that can affect the family. The Cabinet Office should be obliged to provide such an independent statement on all policies, in the same way that the implications of all policies for civil service numbers and public expenditure are already provided.

It is to be hoped that many of the policies and attitudes described in this chapter would be reflected in any Government that the SDP/Liberal Alliance formed or influenced. It is hard to see such a combination of attitudes and policies coming from either a Conservative or Labour Government. Good government sees the relationship between an individual's rights and responsibilities as being the crucial element in making society itself more responsive and responsible.

12 Trust the People

Constitutional change holds the key to economic recovery, but first there has to be the political will to change the voting system. That political will can only come in two circumstances: if there is an outright SDP/Liberal Alliance victory, or if neither we nor the Conservative or Labour parties have an outright majority. The United Kingdom has had five minority Governments this century. From 1910 to 1915 a Liberal Government was sustained by the support of Labour and the Irish Nationalists. Three minority Labour Governments were formed in 1924, 1929 and February 1974. In April 1976 the Labour Government became a minority and remained so until May 1979.

It looks very likely that at the next election, or well before the end of the twentieth century, this situation will recur, and no one party will have an overall majority. What the creation of the SDP has done is to change the assumptions that will be made when such a situation occurs. With no past history it has, as a new party, found it easier to draw conclusions from the past and to define new criteria for action in the future. There will be no repeat of the attitudes that allowed the formation of the minority Governments of 1924, 1929 or 1974. The SDP/Liberal Alliance has made it clear that we have no intention of acquiescing, either by abstention or by voting for the formation of a minority Government that is not prepared to negotiate the text of the Queen's Speech to Parliament at the start of any period of government. A Queen's Speech that has not been negotiated is worthless. Even a promise in the speech to introduce legislation to provide for a referendum on proportional representation – unless underpinned by a detailed timetable and an agreed method of conducting the referendum and posing the questions – could easily be circumvented or delayed until, a few months later, another election was called, after votes had been bought or wooed, as happened in 1964 and 1974.

It is therefore known, and should be well understood before the next election, that no Queen's Speech will be accepted by us in the House of Commons unless it has first been negotiated, line by line, with the SDP/ Liberal Alliance leaders. Through a negotiated Queen's Speech we will ensure that any new Government will more accurately reflect the views of the majority of voters in the general election.

It is against that political reality that the Queen will exercise her prerogative as to whom to appoint as Prime Minister or decide whether to follow the precedent she set when she did not immediately appoint Sir Alec Douglas-Home as Prime Minister but asked him to go away and try to form a Government. Sir Alec Douglas-Home became Prime Minister only after he had assured himself that Rab Butler and other key figures would serve in his Government and that he would be able to govern without Ian Macleod and Enoch Powell. A new Prime Minister does not have to be appointed immediately. The Queen, as a result of consultation, can form a judgement as to who is most likely to be able to command a majority in the House of Commons and ask that person to try to form a Government. It is very much open to question in the circumstances of today whether the Queen would wish to appoint as Prime Minister a leader of a party that did not have a majority in the House of Commons and who had made it clear that he or she would not negotiate with any other party.

The 1977–8 Lib./Lab. pact has given some recent experience to draw on regarding inter-party agreements. A negotiated Queen's Speech and any accompanying agreements should be endorsed by the respective parliamentary parties, not just by the political leaders who have negotiated the text of the Speech and put their names to any accompanying agreement. It is too easy otherwise for back-bench Members of Parliament to disown agreements to which they have not been party. The lack of such an endorsement of the Lib./Lab. pact was a critical weakness in 1977 and 1978. At the very least, the Parliamentary Labour Party should have been asked to endorse the agreement with Liberal MPs that allowed the Labour Government to continue in office. Ideally, too, there should be an agreement that Parliament would not be dissolved for a period of time. An inter-party agreement, as distinct from a coalition, should aim for at least a two-year legislative programme, during which time there could be no election except in a well defined emergency or when the agreement had obviously been broken by one of the parties. While such an agreement could not be binding on the royal prerogative, it would place a moral duty on the Prime Minister of any Government that had a negotiated Queen's Speech accepted by the House of Commons to ensure a period of stable government and not to seek a tactical dissolution. It would also mean that the Queen, in deciding whether to grant the request for a dissolution, could take into account the terms of any agreement with the parties that had preceded Parliament's acceptance of such a Queen's Speech.

The reason for negotiating such an agreement is that the electorate will not want another election. Many voters will feel that the politicians in such circumstances have a duty to go further than negotiate an inter-party agreement, and that they should consider forming a stable coalition government with a negotiated programme that would best represent majority opinion. This would be in preference to an agreement simply to support a minority Government while declining to contribute members to such a Government. Forming a coalition is a very complex business, and without the readiness to forge a Government of national unity, it is hard for one party to force a coalition. A coalition could, however, become a particularly important priority in view of the seriousness of our nation's relative economic decline. If it looked likely that governing by inter-party agreement, as opposed to governing through a coalition, would mean postponing difficult or unpopular decisions necessary to the national interest, then politicians would have to accept the obligation to form a coalition.

The issue of which party the S D P/Liberal Alliance should talk to first is difficult to assess prior to an election campaign, when we will know more about what the other parties are saying. A good rule of thumb, however, would be to lean towards talking first to the party that had the largest number of votes rather than accepting that the party that still holds the reins of power and has the Prime Minister is automatically the party one should first talk to.

Slowly but perceptibly the British people are sensing that the coalition Governments of our European Community partners are successful. We have witnessed the economic recovery of all the countries within the Community. We have seen, for much of the post-war period, successful coalition Governments in the Scandinavian countries and in Austria and Switzerland. These coalitions are not unstable, nor are they weak. On the contrary, they are among the most stable democratic Governments in the modern world. Nor is it an accident that so many of these countries are among the most successful economically, the most successful in combating the effects of the recession. Italy, often derided in Britain for its many changes of government, cannot be that badly governed, as it has now surpassed our own standard of living. Newly democratic Spain has been well governed, initially by the centre-right, now by the centre-left, and looks set to surpass the UK's standard of living in the next decade.

It is in part because so many of these Governments are taking the trouble to preserve, instead of destroy, the mechanisms of social consensus that they are more successful economically than Britain. Their system of government encourages industrial and economic decision-making over ten- to twenty-year time-scales. Even Israel, with its too-pure system of proportional representation, has had an enviable record of national unity when forced to defend the state. The grand coalition of Labour and Likud from 1984 to 1986, though ideologically divided, was able to withdraw its army from deep into Lebanon. The coalition was able to tackle the highly inflationary situation, which meant unpopular constraints. The broader the coalition, the harder it is to reach agreement but the easier it is to implement the agreement. The narrower the coalition, the easier it is to reach agreement but the harder it is to implement the agreement.

The strength of a coalition Government is that it means open negotiation and open compromise. Negotiation at one level – between parties in government – encourages negotiation at other levels. Negotiations usually follow between the Government and the main social interests, whose consent is desirable, and in some cases necessary, if the rate of economic growth is to be increased. The central strength of proportional representation is that it fosters attitudes to the sharing of power that permeate government at every level. It would do this in the Westminster Parliament and in the corridors of Whitehall, in the council chambers of our cities, towns and parishes. It strengthens the long-term view as against short-term political expediency. It makes it harder for political ideology to dominate. It inculcates attitudes which spread out from politics into society, so that power in the economy and in industry also comes to be more widely shared.

It is interesting that the creators of wealth in our country are increasingly arguing for proportional representation. They know that pre-election consumer booms will not solve the underlying problems of our decline. They know Britain needs between fifteen and twenty years to recover, and that means a degree of political stability and commitment that has so far escaped us. Perhaps the most important change in public opinion is that a clear majority of the general public now agree with the proposition that it is vital to Britain's economic and social progress that proportional representation is introduced for elections to Parliament. Only a seventh of the population disagrees with that crucial linkage.

While proportional representation is a unique selling-point for the SDP/Liberal Alliance, there are, fortunately, Conservative, and a few Labour, MPs who also share our commitment, and it is important that this cross-party support is increased. The majority of Labour and Conservative MPs, when opposing proportional representation, campaign in unison. They often conspire together to preserve the status quo. Indeed, some Labour and Conservative politicians are quite blatant about it, arguing against change simply because it will make it more difficult for their party to win an election. Yet these politicians do not reflect the opinion of Labour and Conservative voters who are in favour of proportional representation by a margin of two to one.

Electoral reform is, and should become even more, a people's issue, not a politicians' issue. A new Reform Act is unlikely to come without the pressure of public opinion. It is reasonable to ask, therefore, how such pressure can be generated. It looks as if it could best be mobilized through a referendum. That is why the SDP will increasingly place the merits and the propriety of using a referendum for achieving electoral reform on the political agenda.

This is not a new suggestion. On 8 May 1911, as Leader of the Conservative Opposition, Balfour moved a new clause to the Liberal Government's Parliament Bill. That new clause stated:

A Bill which (a) affects the existence of the Crown or the Protestant succession thereto; or (b) establishes a National Parliament, or Assembly, or a National Council in Ireland, Scotland, England, or Wales, the legislative powers therein; or (c) affects the qualification for the exercise of the Parliamentary franchise or affects the right to vote at any Parliamentary election, or affects the distribution of Parliamentary seats; or (d) affects the powers of either House of Parliament or the relations of the two houses one to the other; shall not be presented to His Majesty nor receive the Royal Assent under the provisions of this act unless and until it has been submitted to a poll of the electors and approved at such a poll in accordance with the Schedule to this Act.

Balfour went on to argue, 'In the referendum lies our hope of getting the sort of constitutional security which every other country but our own enjoys.' The notion of the common sense of the people being the arbiter on great constitutional issues is very attractive.

A referendum was first accepted within the U K with the announcement on 24 March 1972 that a poll would be held in Northern Ireland. Interestingly, it was followed in Northern Ireland a year later by the introduction of proportional representation for the Northern Ireland Assembly. So in one part of the United Kingdom there already exists a different system of voting. The change was well understood by the voters and led to no technical difficulties in implementation.

As with all constitutional innovations, some people wish to go for total change and abandon the evolutionary approach. It has therefore been suggested by some that a referendum should be used extensively on a wide range of issues. A referendum is most frequently suggested to decide whether to reintroduce the death penalty, rather than leave this to a free vote by M Ps. Mrs Thatcher floated the idea of a referendum over trade-union reform. To widen the use of a referendum to policy questions means moving towards a plebiscitary democracy. That is a major consti-tutional change which is far better to evolve than embrace in a hurry. Yet M Ps like myself, who have always voted against the death penalty, are open to the accusation of being in favour of a referendum when it suits, as with the question of proportional representation, and against when one fears one's own position will be lost, as with the question of hanging. Parliament ought to be concerned when it finds itself, over a long period of time, at odds with public opinion. Perhaps it is the reluctance to let the common sense of the people be expressed which keeps public support for the death penalty so high. When an individual citizen, alone in a polling booth, has to face the responsibility for voting to license a decision to kill, many might rethink their opinion. They would have to face up to the instinctive repugnance most Home Secretaries have felt when faced with authorizing the death penalty. They would have to face the reality which M Ps have had to consider, that many a terrorist wants to be a martyr on the gallows. They would also have to face the fact that mistakes have been made and innocent men and women have been hanged. But for all that, the case for holding a referendum only on constitutional issues is still strong.

A referendum confined to constitutional questions can be justified as having a binding quality that is otherwise not possible, without a written constitution. It is also easier to combine the political parties, in a referendum campaign, on a major and politically divisive issue, than it is in the House of Commons. The experience of the European Community legislation which raised major constitutional questions showed that with the present polarized attitudes, and with stricter conventions on following the party whip, it is virtually impossible to hold a cross-party majority together long enough to support a Bill through the line-by-line voting on the floor of the House of Commons. It is easy to forget how nearly the European Community Bill was lost in the line-by-line struggle which, because it was constitutional legislation by convention, did not go to a committee of the House of Commons. In 1972 we Labour MPs who had voted in favour of entry accepted being told to follow the party whip and to vote against the Bill. This was on the dubious argument that only the votes of Government MPs should carry detailed legislation. In the case of the House of Lords reform of 1968–9, the Bill was lost by obstruction on the floor of the House of Commons, despite the Government having a large majority and there being all-party agreement.

A referendum can also be used, not just to provide, but also to inhibit constitutional change. The Scotland Act 1978 and Wales Act 1978 were amended by the critics of devolution so that they could only be implemented after a referendum in Scotland and in Wales, and only when an affirmative vote of at least 40 per cent of those entitled to vote had been obtained, and not simply a majority of those actually voting. The referendum that followed, as in the case of the referendum over membership in the European Community, was advisory to Parliament, but if less than 40 per cent voted, an order for the repeal of the relevant Acts would have had to be laid before Parliament. On 1 March 1979, the referendum was held. In Wales the proposals were decisively rejected; fewer than one in eight Welsh voters turned out in support. In Scotland, nearly 40 per cent of the voters stayed away, and the margin of the 'yes' vote was 3 per cent. The Scottish vote was described in the *Guardian* as 'a grudging, thin and meaningless consent', a significant and fair judgement from a newspaper that, while noting all the flaws, had described the Scotland Act as 'a potentially liberating force in British politics'. That referendum result meant that it was judged impossible to force through the Scotland Act. The Labour Government lost the support of the Scottish Nationalists and was thus defeated on a motion of no confidence, while the memories of the 'winter of discontent' were still fresh. The subsequent 1979 general election led to the election of Mrs Thatcher's first Government.

The result of the devolution referendum is cited by some advocates of proportional representation as a warning against calling a referendum to promote proportional representation. It is as if they fear the result. But if one cannot persuade a majority of the electorate, through a referendum, that proportional representation is a good thing, one has to ask whether it is wise to introduce such a major constitutional change. In circumstances in which there was no popular mandate, would such a change last? Constitutional change, even more than economic and social change, necessitates a degree of consensus that will ensure it lasts for at least a few decades, preferably longer. The legitimacy of forcing proportional representation through if one party has an overall parliamentary majority cannot be questioned; but the wisdom of doing so solely on the basis of having the support of a minority of the electorate, without consulting the people direct through a referendum, is very dubious. In Ireland, the biggest party, Fianna Fáil, has twice tried to get rid of proportional representation and bring in a majority system which would be in its own interests. The Constitution states that it can only be done by referendum, and the voters who have experienced proportional representation and like it have twice voted against changing the system, 52 per cent saying no to change on the first occasion and 61 per cent saying no to a change on the second occasion.

If no one party has an overall majority, the question of proportional representation will become one of the central questions in any negotiations over the shape and policies of a new Government. It is highly questionable whether one party to the negotiations has the right to force proportional representation onto the statute book. It could demand a Bill and a free vote, but that would be most unlikely to provide a genuine free vote, for the party view, and the vested interest in the *status quo* of many MPs, would be likely to predominate. It is impossible, however, to see any valid objection, in a situation where there was no overall majority, if the SDP/Liberal Alliance were to demand an advisory referendum on the question of proportional representation. Nor could there be any reasonable objection if the SDP/Liberal Alliance were to insist that the referendum be held within three months of voting for the Queen's Speech. A Speaker's conference, a Royal Commission – are all well-known delaying tactics. Delay, one is well aware, is in the interests of the party wanting to form a minority government and against proportional representation. That party will want to take power unfettered by any agreements, and to govern for a few months, just sufficient time to ensure that the Queen will accept a request for a dissolution. Then they can plan for an election as soon as they think they can win. That was the tactic in 1964 and again in 1974.

Some have argued that the question in any referendum should only be on the principle of proportional representation, not the detailed system of voting. Experience, however, indicates that the more specific the question, the harder it would be for the House of Commons to avoid enacting the necessary legislation. The normal practice of having such a constitutional Bill on the floor of the House of Commons would have to be followed, and those who were less than enthusiastic on the principle would concentrate on exposing the deficiencies of all the various methods of proportional representation. While they might not challenge the principle of the Bill endorsed by the referendum, they could well organize a vote against all methods of implementation. In effect, that would kill the Bill. The SDP/Liberal Alliance advocates the single transferable vote system which means grouping constituencies around definable community areas. There are strong arguments for putting that specific system to the test in the referendum. A vote merely for the principle in a referendum could well be circumvented by Parliament, and it is not fanciful to anticipate the critics voting down any of a variety of systems.

We know that after John Cleese made an SDP party political broadcast in December 1985, followed by a week's special effort to raise the public perception on proportional representation, it was possible to persuade even more than the 59 per cent which Gallup recorded in November as supporting proportional representation. This increased support offers some hope against the pessimists who believe that the 62 per cent level of support shown after the last general election, when the injustice was most clearly exposed, represented the highest possible plateau of support. Unlike previous mid-term polling on proportional representation, there has been no mid-term slump in support since 1983. It appears that the electorate is becoming more convinced of the need for proportional representation.

What is perhaps even more interesting is that Gallup showed, in November 1985, that if the SDP/Liberal Alliance campaigned to reform the voting system but only won enough seats to form a joint Government with another party, 49 per cent thought that the Alliance would be entitled to demand a referendum on proportional representation, and only 23 per cent thought that it would not be entitled to demand a referendum. When Gallup asked what should happen if the SDP/Liberal Alliance campaigned to reform the voting system and won enough seats to form a Government on their own, 52 per cent thought a referendum should still be held before bringing in proportional representation, with only 20 per cent thinking we should not hold a referendum. People appear to want a referendum to be held on this issue, whatever the political balance in the House of Commons after an election.

Good government requires not only executive and administrative ability but also, particularly against a background of relative economic decline, the ability to mobilize popular understanding for what will inevitably prove to be hard, uncomfortable policies. Lord Randolph Churchill's motto, echoed by his son, Winston Churchill, in the great debates on national defence in the 1930s, was 'Trust the people.' Trusting the people is the most likely way of first achieving, and then retaining, proportional representation.

Mobilizing consent is a political skill. To campaign for a referendum on proportional representation is to demonstrate confidence in the judgement of the British people. It has a fresh and infectious quality. Any political party that, in negotiations over the formation of a new Government, refused the request for a referendum would have some difficulty in explaining their refusal at the subsequent, and early second general election. It would be those who had refused who would be on the defensive. It would be they who would be seen to be fearful of the result. It would be they who were afraid to trust the people.

The longer this nation avoids facing the reality of its position, the longer it will remain divided and in decline. To recover our fortunes and regenerate our country, we must first become, once again, a united kingdom. Somewhere deep down we really have to build up our self-confidence, to restore the belief that people can fashion their own destinies, that government really should be by, for and of the people, that you can pull yourself up, that privates really do carry field marshals' batons in their knapsacks, that failures are not irreversible, that there is always a second chance.

We need to stop thinking politically in terms of class, left or right.

Instead we must create a society rich in the talent and diversity of individuals, where work is the means to leisure, where the arts and sport are not just the background, but essential elements for a varied, fuller and more peaceful life. Gradually, I think, people are beginning to see that the SDP/Liberal Alliance is engaged in something more than merely replacing one of the other parties – it aims to open up, decentralize and democratize our distorted, down-putting, opportunity-denying state.

Without constitutional reform, we will remain divided and will continue our relative economic decline. We will experience a further widening of the gap, with private affluence for the few and public squalor for the many. We will watch impotently as our industrial base shrinks and feel our prosperity withering and our self-confidence seeping away. It is a grim but realistic prospect. The alternative is to take the arguments for another great Reform Act, which would this time introduce proportional representation, directly to the people. We have to trust the people, in the belief that they will understand that this reform will unlock the energies, talents and essential decency of all those who want to see a united kingdom.

References

Introduction

1 H. Liebenstein, *General X-Efficiency Theory and Economic Development* (Oxford, Oxford University Press, 1978), p. 93.
2 Public Services Redesign Project, Hubert Humphrey Institute of Public Affairs, *An Equitable and Competitive Public Sector* (Minneapolis, University of Minnesota, 1984).

1 National Decline

1 Organization for Economic Co-operation and Development, *Main Economic Indicators* (Paris, OECD, various issues); OECD, *Economic Outlook*, July 1985.
2 United Nations Statistical Office, *Statistical Yearbook* (New York, UN, 1985).
3 United Nations Statistical Office, *Yearbook of National Accounts Statistics* (New York, UN, 1985).
4 ibid.
5 The 'go–stop' and 'stop–go' policies of successive Conservative and Labour Governments are documented in detail in M. Stewart, *The Jekyll and Hyde Years* (Oxford, Pergamon, 1978), ch. 1.

2 Bad Government

1 Norman Gash, *Sir Robert Peel* (London, Longman, 1972), p. 613.
2 John Walker, *The Queen Has Been Pleased* (London, Secker & Warburg, forthcoming).
3 Philip M. Williams, *Hugh Gaitskell* (London, Jonathan Cape, 1979), p. 612.
4 Arthur Schlesinger, *The Age of Roosevelt: Crisis of the Old Order* (Boston, MS, Houghton Mifflin, 1957), p. 129.
5 Hansard, 17 December 1852, col. 140.
6 *Financial Times*, 12 November 1985.

3 Better Government

1 John D. Fair, *British Inter-Party Conferences: A Study of the Procedure of Conciliation in British Politics 1867–1921* (Oxford, Clarendon Press, 1980).
2 ibid.

3 First Report of the SDP/Liberal Alliance Constitutional Commission, 1982.
4 Vernon Bogdanor, *What is Proportional Representation? A Guide to the Issues* (Oxford, Martin Robertson, 1984).

4 *National Security*

1 Alan Bullock, *Life and Times of Ernest Bevin* (London, Heinemann, 1960), p. 302.
2 Kenneth Harris, *Attlee* (London, Weidenfeld & Nicolson, 1982), p. 277.
3 Thirty-fourth Session of the Institut des Hautes Etudes de Défense Nationale (IHEDN), 14 September 1981.
4 Address to the IHEDN, 4 February 1978.
5 The French TV channel Antenne 2, *An Hour with the President of the Republic*, 19 June 1979.
6 SDP White Paper, *Defence and Disarmament – Peace and Security*, September 1985.

5 *Industrial Regeneration*

1 House of Lords, *Report from the Select Committee on Overseas Trade*, 238–I/II (London, HMSO, 1985).
2 Confederation of British Industry, *Change to Succeed* (London, CBI, March 1985); see also CBI, *Change to Succeed: The Nationwide Findings*, October 1985.
3 *The Government's Expenditure Plans 1986–87 to 1988–89*, Cmnd 9702–I/II (London, HMSO, 1986).
4 Memorandum from Terry Ward to the House of Commons Treasury and Civil Service Select Committee, November 1985.
5 *North Sea Report*, No. 152, December 1985, p. 3.
6 *Quality and Value for Money*, May 1985.
7 US Department of Commerce, May 1985.
8 Department of Transport report, *UK Merchant Ships Supply Forecast* (commissioned from the SEA group), 1985.

6 *Incomes Strategy*

1 HM Treasury, *Autumn Statement 1985* (London, HMSO, 1985), p. 11.
2 S. Brittan, 'Memo for Budget Weekend', *Financial Times*, 28 December 1985.
3 N. Foster *et al.*, 'Public and Private Sector Pay: a Partly Disaggregated Study', *NIESR Review*, February 1984, p. 22.
4 W. Brown, 'Facing Up to Incomes Policy', proceedings of the *Cambridge Journal of Economics* conference, June 1985, p. 9.
5 ibid., p. 10.
6 Foster, 'Public and Private Sector Pay', p. 24.
7 S. Hogg, 'Public Pay – a Productive Approach', *The Times*, 8 June 1985, p. 18.

8 ibid.

9 D. Brindle, 'Treasury Makes Pay Reform Offer', *Financial Times*, 8 November 1985, p. 18.

10 Megaw Report, *An Inquiry into Civil Service Pay* (London, HMSO, 1982), p. 47.

11 Brown, 'Facing Up to Incomes Policy', p. 11.

7 Industrial Partnership

1 J. Rawls, *A Theory of Justice* (Boston, MA, Harvard University Press, 1972).

2 Lord Beswick, *An Interim Report of the Review of Steel Closures*, Department of Industry, Department Paper 6093, 4 February 1975.

3 J. E. Meade, *Wage Fixing Revisited* (London, Institute of Economic Affairs, 1985).

4 M. Weitzman, *The Share Economy* (Boston, MA, Harvard University Press, 1984).

5 ibid., p. 53.

6 Meade, *Wage Fixing Revisited*, p. 42.

7 C. A. R. Crosland, *The Conservative Enemy* (London, Jonathan Cape, 1962).

8 Urban Regeneration

1 National Council of Building Producers, *Urban Regeneration for the 21st Century*, October 1985.

2 R. Hanson and J. Royce (eds.), *Perspectives on Urban Infrastructure*, Committee on National Urban Policy, September 1984.

3 R. Berger and R. Foster, *Public–Private Partnerships: The USA and UK Experiences*, Council for International Urban Liaison, November 1985.

9 Educational Equality

1 Robin Marris, *The Higher Education Crisis: A Sermon for Conservatives and Socialists*, Suntory–Toyota Lecture, 1985, pp. 24–9.

2 N. Evans, 'Adult Learning Entitlement/Pay as You Learn – Be Paid as You Learn?', SDP paper, March 1985, pp. 2–4.

3 HM Treasury, *Autumn Statement 1985* (London, HMSO, 1985), p. 22.

4 Advisory Board for the Research Councils, *Science and Public Expenditure, 25th April 1985: A Report to the Secretary of State for Education and Science*.

5 Sir Hans Kornberg, *An Address to the 147th British Association Annual Meeting*, Strathclyde University, 27 August 1985.

10 Health Care

1 N. Bosanquet, 'A Primary Care Fund', *Health Care UK*, 1986.

2 A. Maynard, 'Health and Personal Social Services' in P. Cockle (ed.), *Public Expenditure Policy* (London, Macmillan, 1985), pp. 138–9.

3 Organization for Economic Co-operation and Development, *Public Expenditure on Health*, Studies in Resource Allocation, No. 6 (Paris, OECD, 1984).

4 HM Treasury, *The Next Ten Years: Public Expenditure and Taxation into the 1990s*, Cmnd 9186 (London, HMSO, 1984).

5 N. Fowler, 'Announcement of NHS Growth Assumptions for the Next Ten Years', DHSS press release 83/118, 30 June 1983, subsequently confirmed by press release 84/26, 30 June 1984.

6 K. Andrews, 'Demographic Changes and Resources for the Elderly', *British Medical Journal*, Vol. 290, 1985, pp. 1023–4.

7 E. Grundy and T. Arie, 'Falling Provision of Residential Care for the Elderly', *British Medical Journal*, Vol. 184, 1984, pp. 799–802.

8 A. C. Enthoven, *Reflections on the Management of the NHS* (London, Nuffield Provincial Hospitals Trust, 1985).

11 Social Responsibility

1 Lord Scarman, *The Brixton Disorders* (London, HMSO, 1981), p. 4.

2 M. Plant, D. Peck and D. Samuel, *Alcohol, Drugs and School Leavers* (London, Tavistock, 1985).

3 Colin Brown, *Third Review of Racial Equality in Britain* (London, Policy Studies Institute, 1984).

4 *Reform of Social Security: A Programme for Action*, Cmnd 9691 (London, HMSO, 1985), Vol. 2, table 15(b), p. 47.

5 M. Anderson (ed.), *Sociology of the Family: Selected Readings*, 2nd edn (Harmondsworth, Penguin, 1980).

6 'Marriage is Good for You', *Economist*, 12 March 1983.

7 Hansard, 18 April 1973, col. 642.

Index

MORE ABOUT PENGUINS, PELICANS AND PUFFINS

For further information about books available from Penguins please write to Dept EP, Penguin Books Ltd, Harmondsworth, Middlesex UB7 ODA.

In the U.S.A.: For a complete list of books available from Penguins in the United States write to Dept DG, Penguin Books, 299 Murray Hill Parkway, East Rutherford, New Jersey 07073.

In Canada: For a complete list of books available from Penguins in Canada write to Penguin Books Canada Limited, 2801 John Street, Markham, Ontario L3R 1B4.

In Australia: For a complete list of books available from Penguins in Australia write to the Marketing Department, Penguin Books Australia Ltd, P.O. Box 257, Ringwood, Victoria 3134.

In New Zealand: For a complete list of books available from Penguins in New Zealand write to the Marketing Department, Penguin Books (N.Z.) Ltd, Private Bag, Takapuna, Auckland 9.

In India: For a complete list of books available from Penguins in India write to Penguin Overseas Ltd, 706 Eros Apartments, 56 Nehru Place, New Delhi 110019.